# Changing Voices

# Changing Voices
## The Modern Quoting Poem

Leonard Diepeveen

*Ann Arbor*

THE UNIVERSITY OF MICHIGAN PRESS

Copyright © by the University of Michigan 1993
All rights reserved
Published in the United States of America by
The University of Michigan Press
Manufactured in the United States of America

1996   1995   1994   1993     4   3   2   1

*A CIP catalogue record for this book is available from the British Library.*

Library of Congress Cataloging-in-Publication Data

Diepeveen, Leonard, 1959–
    Changing voices : the modern quoting poem / Leonard Diepeveen.
        p.    cm.
    Includes bibliographical references (p.      ) and index.
    ISBN 0-472-10369-5 (alk.)
      1. American poetry—20th century—History and criticism.
    2. Influence (Literary, artistic, etc.)   3. Quotation in literature.
    4. Intertextuality.   I. Title.
    PS323.5.D53   1993
    811'.509—dc20                                      93-9009
                                                          CIP

*For Susan Van Laar Diepeveen*

# Preface

*Changing Voices* looks at the consequences of those instances in Modern American poetry when a poet chooses not to allude to another text, but to quote it: to *exactly* duplicate a source, and in so doing to write those awkward and powerful texts that this book will classify as the Modern quoting poem. Quite by chance, the inevitable, involuntary consequences of quoting were parabolically demonstrated to me at a conference I attended several years ago at the University of Minnesota. The American writer Rosmarie Waldrop was there, reading from her *Differences for Four Hands,* a work that at several points quotes Lyn Hejinian's *Gesualdo,* a text of a very different sound. Waldrop prefaced her reading with a reading of *Gesualdo* and then went on to read her own work. Each time in *Differences for Four Hands* when Waldrop quoted Hejinian's text, a good third of the audience would shift slightly in its seat, sending a rustle of cotton through the auditorium. At the same time, one or two members of the audience would involuntarily grunt. The shifters and grunters reinforced in me a belief that quotations do get from its perceivers a different type of attention than do allusions, and that we do mark quotations off from the quoting text, sometimes in charmingly naive and involuntary ways.

However, this book began not with my certainty that I had discovered something everyone else had missed, but with my uneasiness that to insist on distinguishing allusions (a general term covering a variety of borrowings) from quotations (those *exact* borrowings from another text) was to introduce an awkward concept into a comfortable discussion. Criticism had refined our language so that we could now discuss in quite a sophisticated manner a general category, recently subsumed under such a term as *citation,* itself a reworking of such concepts as *borrowing, intertextuality,* and, of course, *allusion.* Such large categories, however, did not give readers a language to discuss the specific demands of quotations. What I discovered as I began this project was that quotation marks, italics, and other signals of an exact quotation have not counted as significant evidence in discussions of Modernism.

This book, then, begins with a simple premise: quotations are different from allusions. Initially, such a distinction demands a reconsidering of allusion. As the first chapter will show, allusion is a muddy term that handles a variety of types and styles of reference, for one can allude to more than just other texts. The *Oxford English Dictionary* defines allusion as a "covert, implied, or indirect reference." The indirection of the allusion, its implied status, I will argue, is its defining and most useful characteristic. Not for nothing can an allusion, with differing degrees of precision, refer to many things (not just texts), for inexactitude lies at its center. Quotation, on the other hand, is specific: the *exact* transferring of a text into another, new text. In this transfer quotations duplicate the content and texture of another work and consequently heighten the disruption that more general borrowings bring into a text. Determining that a borrowing has the exact status of quotation can, of course, degenerate into the concern of a desiccated footnote. However, the consequences of this exact duplication are essential, for in its exactness lies the quotation's power. The exactness of the quotation introduces into the quoting poem a disruption that radically changes the structure of the poem and how one can read it.

The distinction between quotation and allusion works well for most instances of intertextual borrowing, but the rigid distinction occasionally needs flexibility at some moments in quoting poems. The difference between quotation and allusion occurs along a sliding scale. As a necessary acknowledgment of those difficult points midway between pure quotation and allusion, quotation has occasionally a fluid definition in this book, for such borrowings as translations and citations of idiosyncratic but individual words can lean either toward allusion or toward quotation, depending on how they are structured in their new contexts.

This project points to a larger cultural phenomenon than just the quoting poem, for quotation's usefully intrusive texture and the problems it raises have a wide-ranging influence upon this century. Other media use quotation to explore the aesthetics of appropriation; indeed, appropriation of previously existing material may well be *the* aesthetic of this century. Not only does quotation extend to such prose writers as James Joyce and John Dos Passos, it reaches to other arts. In the years 1912–14 Picasso's and Braque's collages, homely compilations of rope, wallpaper, newspapers, and sand, set an aesthetic agenda followed by many artists in the years immediately after the war. Erik Satie and Igor Stravinsky quote folk tunes and such sounds of modernity as car horns, typewriters, and airplane propellors. Stravinsky and Satie are perhaps the most notable, but certainly not the only composers to experiment in this way. By the time one cites Charles Ives, Virgil Thomson, and Arnold Schönberg, one has a good sample of the major musical innovators of the early twentieth century.

In the visual arts the expanded roll call is equally impressive. Gris, Severini, Archipenko, Carrà, and Leger all made collages before 1920. Later movements sometimes in opposition to Modernist Cubism also use collage. Carra, Ernst, Schwitters, and Magritte, for example, moved collage into Futurism, Dada, and eventually into Surrealism. Artists such as Robert Rauschenberg, Sherrie Levine, Barbara Kruger, and Robert Longo have ensured that artistic appropriation of images forms a central controversy of contemporary visual art, and they have transformed the quoting artwork's effects sufficiently beyond Cubism to give it a Postmodern aura. Contemporary architecture ensures quoting a dominant presence in our culture. Philip Johnson's Chippendale pediment on the AT & T building shows not only the artistic functions of an intrusive, borrowed texture, it illustrates the potential for volatile public reaction. In some form, all these artists quoted; that is, they all inserted into their own artworks the unmediated physical presence of objects that had existed outside of the new artwork, and that had in them the presence of another creative personality (what some might call another voice).

However, although quoting is a big part of this century, my argument has a more limited scope because I argue that the technical aspect of quoting (its exactitude) is important. Discussing how the exactly duplicated texture of quotations functions demands specificity and does not easily translate from one medium to another. Keeping in mind that the technical things that happen in poetry cannot happen in painting, I have yet found it useful at isolated moments to talk about other arts. These moments function as asides, as a way of discussing the possibilities of quotation, and as a way of exploring the quoting mind-set. At all times, however, I direct the focus of this book to issues specific to a single art and genre: How is quotation transformed by, and how does it impinge upon, concerns specific to the making of a poem, such as lineation? Stanzaic form? Meter? What effect do these influences have upon the quoting poem and how we read it?

As part of the same wish to discuss with precision the technical aspects of quotation, I have limited the scope of this study even further, to *Modern* American poetry. A very different mind-set, indicated primarily through very different presuppositions about authorship, both accounts for Medieval quoting and separates it from Modernist concerns with quoting. Further, quoting really begins to assert itself as a technique in the twentieth century, despite some intriguing earlier moments such as Petrarch's canzone 70. I choose Modern American *poetry* for different reasons. Although the presence of quotations in prose writers like John Dos Passos and James Joyce indicates that quotations are important for twentieth-century fiction, poetry quotes in unique and problematic ways. As Mikhail Bakhtin points out, fiction (unlike poetry) begins with an assumption of multiple voices ("Discourse," 264). Quotations in fiction can thus be tied to much older and more binding discussions of characterization, narrative authority, and so forth. The quoting poem enters these sorts of discussions as a brash newcomer, setting the discussion on a quite new footing. For quoting poems, characterization and narrative are not the most useful paradigms. Rather, in quoting poems, a second voice appears in a seemingly alien environment, in what are most often lyric, nonnarrative poems. And often, when this second voice appears, neither it nor the first voice seems to occur as the result of character delineation. Rather, (as I show in chapter 4 especially), quoting adds some new ways of discussing ownership of a borrowed voice: stanzaic form, lineation, and metrics present complexities that are unavailable to fiction.

Obviously, many poets in this century quote. Some of the writers that I could have included in this study but chose not to are Charles Olson, Louis Zukofsky, William Burroughs, and Robert Lowell. Although in my conclusion I move in a direction that includes Williams, Ashbery, Rich, and the L=A=N=G=U=A=G=E writers, for the bulk of this study I concentrate on four poets: Eliot, Pound, Moore, and Cummings. I chose these four poets because in the years 1914–35 they begin quoting as an extensive poetic practice in this century. To varying degrees and in various ways, the quoting poets I primarily study have created poems that have defined and continue to define what is important to Modern poetry. For a variety of reasons William

Carlos Williams, the other major Modernist quoter, is separate from these four. At the time these quoting poems were making their mark, Williams was not writing quoting poems; his poetry was working in other areas of Modernism. But even then Williams's critical voice had some useful things to say about quotation and originality, arguments that I use in the third chapter. His publication of *Paterson* in 1946 is addressed separately, in the conclusion, not only because it happens twenty-five years later than the other major Modernist quoting poems, but also because it in many ways answers these poems, and in a fashion that is most useful to consider in the light of Postmodernism. With Williams the argument about quotation is much more overt than in the other quoting Moderns, and very clearly a response to Eliot and Pound. Thus, in both chapter 3 and the conclusion I examine his argumentative prose in some detail—his prose is his counterpoint to the less-detailed arguments of the other quoting Moderns, and *Paterson* is his counter-poem.

One of the challenges of this book is to acknowledge the obvious diversity of these four writers while holding together my insistence that their quoting is a shared characteristic. While this quartet was a prag-matic selection (i.e., these are the poets who at that time quote the most), I imply in the third chapter that the confluence of these four writers suggests that quoting is an American practice, coming partly from preoccupations with antecedents (Eliot and Pound) and with authenticity (Moore, Cummings, Eliot, and Pound). This is a book about *American* Modernist poetry. I also put these very different writers together because it is interesting to see how their differences are accen-tuated and hidden by quotation. Their quoting produces a welter of effects, for the act of inserting into a poem another voice has as many possible poetic ramifications as there are possible combinations of new and borrowed textures. There is more than one type of quoting poem, and these four writers are essential to understanding the range of the formal implications of quoting, a diversity that yet comes out of a single technique. Predictably, some of these poetic uses have dominated Mod-ernism and continue to dominate Postmodernism; others remain at the edges of one or both periods.

In putting these writers together I do not mean to suggest they are writers of equal talent or reputation. Eliot and Pound have been at the center of Modernism for years, while Moore is on the ascendant. Re-cent books on Moore have shown her to be much more complicated and Modern than has been critical wisdom up to this point. Yet her ascendancy shows Moore to present a type of Modernism different from that of Eliot and Pound, and challenges to the reputation of these two sets of writers come from very different types of readers. Cummings, by contrast, is in a state of neglect. While Moore's quoting is at least as interesting as that of Pound and Eliot, Cummings's approach is (as most professional readers seem to think of other aspects of his poetry) too monologic: a single, and at times facile, idea drives his quoting. As this text progresses (especially in my discussion of voice in chapter 4), it becomes clear that Cummings has limited range. Thus, while I am changing how we think of Cummings, I do not propose to change how we value him. Rather, Cummings is included because his limited range yet shows some of the possibilities of quotation that are not apparent in the other three writers.

This book suggests issues that ought to become part of reading these poems; it does not establish definitive readings of the poems it discusses. *Changing Voices* examines the quoting poem in its various manifestations, its distinction from alluding texts, and its contributions to some recurring discussions in Modernism: the issues of originality, impersonality, and poetic voice; the problems of obscurity and disjunctive structure; the role of metaphor; and the formation of literary canons. Quoting poems fit naturally into a discussion of these topics because it is hard to discuss them without using quoting poems as examples. One can hardly discuss heterogeneity without adducing *The Cantos* and its quotations. But more important to my purposes within this text, one can hardly discuss quotation without working with these topics. How can one analyze the quotations of *The Waste Land* without mentioning heterogeneity?

In examining these recurring topics in the light of quotation, I look at how quoting poems modify them. First, quotation can clarify these topics, as it does, for example, with disjunction. The causes and effects of disjunction, which can also be achieved using other means, become more clear when we examine the quoting poem—where disjunction *necessarily* appears. Second, quotation frequently exaggerates the effects of such issues as impersonality, for it creates a type of distance inaccessible to other poetic techniques. Finally, quotation makes other issues more problematic. For example, the borrowed status of quotation redefines and complicates discussions of poetic voice and originality. Since the definition of quotation that drives this book is based on a formal characteristic (the quotation's exactly duplicated texture), the beginning point of all these discussions will necessarily be formal—again, while my discussion of how quoting works in these poems is, I think, quite comprehensive, I do not intend to give comprehensive readings of these poems, readings that would extensively consider such issues as the politics of Modernism or Modernism's historical or philosophical context.

My first chapter argues that the exactly duplicated texture of a quotation separates it from allusion. Although allusion and quotation deal with similar concerns and exist on a single continuum, allusion changes the borrowed world; with quotations relationships are between borrower and borrowing, not within the borrowed text. The quoting poem's insistence upon this disruptive relationship creates a multiplicity of aesthetic effects and questions not accessible to alluding works.

Given this definition, three issues are then crucial: the structure of such poetry, the new meanings created by such poetry, and the voice created by this welter of borrowed voices. The second chapter examines the structure of this poetry and its effect on the reading process. It argues that the quoting poem introduces an unresolvable gap between quotation and new text, a gap that restructures how one reads poetry. The best model for reading quoting poems is not a form of linear development; rather, it is what Ezra Pound called "planes in relation." In the third chapter I use the prose of William Carlos Williams (particularly that of the 1930s, as he broods over the work of Ezra Pound), to raise the question of how quoting poems create new meanings. While Williams concentrated on how writers dangerously repeated a quotation's original terms when they quoted, the other quoting Moderns tended to explore how using the quotation as a formal object allows for quotation to take on new meanings, and to create at times a crude and difficult poetry. Finally, since I argue that texture is essential, I turn to the question of voice in the quoting poem. In the fourth chapter I discuss how this new meaning created by crudity raises a problem of poetic unity, a problem that is exacerbated and solved in the lyric and dramatic voices of the quoting poem. With its quoting poems Modernism begins a destabilization of the central voice much more complicated than we have suspected. My conclusion is a more speculative piece, a look at why those issues I have raised in the first four chapters might ensure that the quoting poem remains a useful option today.

Implicit, but surfacing at moments, is the question of why these writers quote. It remains implicit because the writers themselves never explicitly address why they quote rather than allude. However, one can begin such an address by briefly contrasting how the two major moments in the Western history of quotation differently deal with the relation between language and representation.

Quoting occurs in two large swatches in Western literary history. The second swatch is Modernism; the first is Medieval and Renaissance writing. Why these two points, and why is there a 250-year pause in quotation? The beginnings of an answer lie in the models of representation that Michel Foucault puts forward in *The Order of Things*. According to Foucault, preclassical writers founded their ideas of communication upon resemblances between objects and objects and between objects and words. For preclassical writers the universe was held together by likenesses that existed independent of the perceiving mind. Quotation was useful for preclassical writers because communication itself was a form of repetition; all communication occurred as a result of perceiving resemblances, or "commentary." When writers repeated things to establish a resemblance between them and their own text, they repeated the quotation's power. In the Renaissance, all the "insistent marks" of language "summoned up a secondary language—that of commentary, exegesis, erudition—in order to stir the language that lay dormant within them and to make it speak at last" (79). In this model of communication, commentary is a piling up of resemblances, and quotation is very good for accomplishing that. That "piling up" may account for the baggy form of earlier quoting: one could just keep on adding resemblances—addition of quoted material was useful for establishing resemblances, but any stopping point was arbitrary. Since there was little emphasis upon a text as a creation of a single ego, quotation did little to destroy the unity of the quoting text.

According to Foucault, after the Renaissance language takes on a new function. Classical sign theory defined a sign as a combination of signifier and signified. Consequently, as language in the classical era shifts to a signifier-signified relation, talking about that language changes from commentary (on earlier texts) to criticism: words no longer carry the truth, they interpret it (56). When writing turns to criticism, the function of resemblance disappears, along with most quotation. In this system quotation has little that is special about it; while classical writers do quote authoritative sources to buttress what they are arguing, particularly in poetry, such support can be as easily (and more neatly) controlled by paraphrase and allusion. Further, authority, and particularly the authority of the exact quotation, has much more force in preclassical writing and is consequently much more readily invoked there. Thus, in classical writing, quotation has no special status as an interpreter of truth. This system of representation is also not seriously challenged by the rise of romanticism, and quotation is further discouraged by some of the tenets of romanticism, particularly by the idea of the romantic poetic ego.

Yet the quoting poem does reappear in the wake of romanticism, not as a total repudiation of it and not as a return to preclassical theories of representation. As deconstruction has taught us, repetition is always repetition with a difference. Modernist and contemporary quotation is no exception. Despite its use of exact formal resemblance, quotation in a sense denies resemblance, and it certainly denies any preclassical formulations of resemblance. But contemporary writing still does quote because our contemporary world is a postromantic one, in which individual reactions and manipulations (formal things, "criticism" in Foucault's terminology) are often more important than the content of the work. Despite Modern disavowals of most connections with romanticism, this formalist emphasis that allows for quotation is an inheritance of the nineteenth century. Foucault glancingly argues that in the nineteenth century language attempts to become purely formal, a "pure language"; language becomes "detached from representation" and at times becomes "an act of writing that designates nothing other than itself" (89, 304). The quoting poem is the perfect, distanced medium in which these formal manipulations can happen. Thus, quotation happens in a postromantic age, an age that peculiarly combines a romantic sense of authorship, a search for a new poetic language, and a formalist poetic practice.

This formalist poetic practice surfaces in some more specific and technically manifested reasons for quoting, reasons that are more central to the writing of this book. My analyses of individual quoting poems show that the quoting poem fits in with and exploits such Modernist concerns as disjunction, crudity, and an impersonal (at times, even collective) poetic voice. Quoting further ensures that the poem remains concrete, and that the quoting poem avoids abstraction; for most quoting poets the quotation is a fact, not a symbol. As I suggest in my third chapter, poets quote because the quoting poem immediately addresses, in a Modernist manner, a recurring anxiety in American literature about antecedents and the creation of an authentic voice. Finally, my fourth chapter suggests that the quoting poem destabilizes the lyric voice, a destabilizing that Postmodern writers will exploit more fully.

In defining the quoting poem and redefining some central issues in Modernism, *Changing Voices* deals with a particular moment in Modernist history when quoting erupts. In doing so, I make a case for the originality of the Moderns and end with a speculative look at some aspects of quoting today. But those chronological moments do not drive this book; this is not a history of a style. This book's conceptual organization and its dependence on texture work out a more primary problem: establishing that the quoting poem exists as a style of writing. What drives this book, then, is how a quoting poem works: the variations that are available to writers, and how writers have used those variations.

# Acknowledgments

The greatest debt I have incurred in writing this book is a personal one. I owe it to my wife, Susan, whose camaraderie and love I attempt to imitate but can never hope to quote. My scholarly indebtedness and gratitude begin with the examiners for the dissertation from which this piece originally sprang. To Margaret Dickie, Arnold Stein, and George Hendrick I owe my thanks for redirection at an early stage of this piece. Emily Watts continues to be my model for a combined academic rigor and personal integrity. Also at an early stage of my writing, the Rosenbach Library and its curator at that time, Patricia Willis, provided excellent aid. Colleagues at Dalhousie University have given extensive readings and generous advice—I thank Victor Li, Anne Higgins, and Bruce Greenfield. A grant from the Dalhousie University Research Development Fund did much to oil the workings of this project, as did my editor at University of Michigan Press, Joyce Harrison, and her assistant, Robin Moir. Steven Gould Axelrod gave an extensive and useful reading of this manuscript. Special thanks are due to Reed Dasenbrock, whose timely encouragement and expert advice did much to make this book possible.

Grateful acknowledgment is given to those who hold copyright for the poetry and prose extracts quoted in this work: Carcanet Press Limited and Viking Penguin, a division of Penguin Books USA Inc., for "Self-Portrait in a Convex Mirror," copyright © 1974 by John Ashbery, from *Self-Portrait in a Convex Mirror* by John Ashbery. Steve Benson for permission to quote from "The Busses." Tina Darragh and Burning Deck Press for "ludicrous stick." Ron Silliman for "Blue" (*ABC*. Berkeley: Tuumba Press, 1983). Every effort was made to secure permission for the material by Adrienne Rich.

Grateful acknowledgment is given to MacGibbon & Kee for permission to quote from the *Complete Poems* of E. E. Cummings. "O It's Nice to Get Up In,the slipshod mucous kiss," "next to of course god america i," and the lines from "unnoticed woman from whose kind large flesh," "POEM, OR BEAUTY HURTS MR. VINAL," "why are these pipples taking their hets

Extracts from *Selected Poems of Marianne Moore* are reprinted with permission of Macmillan Publishing Company and Faber and Faber copyright 1935 by Marianne Moore, renewed 1963 by Marianne Moore and T. S. Eliot. Permission to quote from Marianne Moore's unpublished work has been granted by Marianne Craig Moore, Literary Executor for the Estate of Marianne Moore. All rights reserved. The following is used by permission of Viking Penguin, a division of Penguin Books USA Inc.: "Marianne Moore," edited by George Plimpton, introduced by Van Wyck Brooks, copyright © 1961 by *The Paris Review,* from *Writers at Work, Second Series* edited by George Plimpton, introduced by Van Wyck Brooks. The following is used by permission of Faber and Faber and Viking Penguin, a division of Penguin Books USA Inc.: "The Cantos," © copyright 1931 by Marianne Moore, "The Sacred Wood," © copyright 1921 by Marianne Moore, from *The Complete Prose of Marianne Moore* by Patricia C. Willis, editor.

Grateful acknowledgment is given to New Direction Publishing Corporation and Faber and Faber, Ltd. for permission to quote from the following copyrighted works of Ezra Pound.

*The Cantos* (Copyright © 1934, 1937, 1940, 1948, 1956, 1959, 1962, 1966, and 1968 by Ezra Pound)

*Gaudier-Brzeska* (Copyright © 1970 by Ezra Pound)

*Personae* (Copyright © 1926 by Ezra Pound)

*Selected Letters 1907–1941* (Copyright © 1950 by Ezra Pound)

*Selected Prose 1909–1965* (Copyright © 1960, 1962 by Ezra Pound, copyright © 1973 by the Estate of Ezra Pound)

*The Spirit of Romance* (Copyright © 1968 by Ezra Pound)

*Ezra Pound's Poetry and Prose: Contributions to Periodicals* (Copyright © 1991 by the Trustees of the Ezra Pound Literary Property Trust)

Grateful acknowledgment is given to New Direction Publishing Corporation for permission to quote from the following copyrighted works of William Carlos Williams.

*The Autobiography of William Carlos Williams*. Copyright © 1948, 1951 by William Carlos Williams.

*The Collected Poems of William Carlos Williams: Volume II, 1939–1962*. Copyright © 1944, 1953, copyright © 1962 by William Carlos Williams. Copyright © 1988 by William Eric Williams and Paul H. Williams.

*Imaginations*. Copyright © 1970 by Florence H. Williams.

*In the American Grain*. Copyright © 1925 by James Laughlin. Copyright © 1933 by William Carlos Williams.

# Contents

## CHAPTER I

# The Quoting Arts

I put all the things I like into
my pictures. The things—so much
the worse for them; they just
have to put up with it.
—Pablo Picasso

### "Take Some Scissors"

"A good stealer is *ipso facto* a good inventor," writes Marianne Moore in one of her notebooks (Moore Archive, 1250/1, 118). As do all good aphorisms, this phrase points in directions both predictable and surprising. It confirms our expectations, placing Moore in a line of poets who use gnomic theory to justify their idiosyncratic poetry; the statement has the right tone for a poet who wrote syllabic verse about pangolins, monkey-puzzle trees, and baseball. The equation between stealing and inventing also aptly describes Moore's poetic practice; for in stealing from sources as diverse as *New York Times* advertisements and *The Expositor's Bible*, *The Illustrated London News* and *The Epicure's Guide to France,* Moore has created one of the most idiosyncratic bodies of poetry in this century.

However, "inventive stealing" can take on a larger and more surprising function than satisfying complacencies about Moore's quirkiness. It points to an important aesthetic principle, one that other writers have found useful. For example, in his poem "To Make a Dadaist Poem" Tristan Tzara uses a more complex metaphor to argue for inventive stealing:

Take a newspaper.
Take some scissors.
Choose from this paper an article of the length you want to make
    your poem.
Cut out the article.
Next carefully cut out each of the words that make up this article and
    put them all in a bag.
Shake gently.
Next take out each cutting one after the other.
Copy conscientiously in the order in which they left the bag.
The poem will resemble you.
And there you are—an infinitely original author of charming
    sensibility, even though unappreciated by the vulgar herd.

(39)

Although Tzara's Dadaist humor—simultaneously undercutting and supporting the manifesto—resists intellectual analysis, the quoting poems of American Modernism show that Tzara's gnomic utterances are not oddball theory, but they point to the heart of many twentieth-century aesthetic systems. In the first, Modernist generation of quoting texts and poets alone (ca. 1914–35), specific applications of this appropriating aesthetic transformed poetic history, shaping poems as diverse as Moore's "An Octopus" and Pound's *Cantos*, Eliot's *The Waste Land* and Cummings's "next to of course god america i," poems at the center and at the periphery of American Modernism, poems that consequently have defined this part of Modernism for us. Yet the possibility for these differing directions proves both Tzara's and Moore's theory: stealing can be inventive in so many different ways that stealing virtually guarantees invention.

For all the creative diversity that spawned them and the textual strategies that separate them, these poems are of a single type, all copying recognizable verbal patterns from another text: these are *quoting poems*. Quoting poems incorporate phrases in the new poetic text that *precisely* duplicate the verbal patterns of the original source, stealing for the new poem the conceptual content *and the texture* of a previously existing text. Quoting poems do not transform to suit their purposes the words of the text from which they borrow; they duplicate the intrusive textural, material properties of another text.

The word *texture* is crucial for this study. In their stealing from other

2

texts, quoting poems do not *initially* receive the impetus for their energies from a paraphrasable, interchangeable conceptual content (such as plot, theme, or imagery) of that other text. While the conceptual content of quotations does form an integral part of the reading experience, it does not do so with the same primacy as it does for a more generalized allusion. In our reading experience of quoting poems the formal properties of the quotation precede and define their conceptual content, showing that the quotation is indeed unparaphrasable. *Texture* asserts the idiosyncratic rather than the interchangeable. *Texture* does not just define the sounds of a group of words, it has consequences. It shows how these sounds point to and are part of those words' individual, nonparaphrasable meanings. *Texture* also implies a quotation's history, its past, "original" use and this original use's earlier appropriations by culture.

This introduction of another texture into the newly created poem addresses all the aesthetic questions implicit in Tzara's methodology. Claims for originality, predictions of misunderstanding, prophecies that the quoting poem will resemble its compiler—readers can find all of these sometimes playful speculations embodied in quoting poems:

That freed her slaves on a Wednesday
Masnatas et servos, witness
Picus de Farinatis
and Don Elinus and Don Lipus
    sons of Farinato de' Farinati
"free of person, free of will
"free to buy, witness, sell, testate."
A marito subtraxit ipsam . . .
dictum Sordellum concubuisse:
"Winter and Summer I sing of her grace,
As the rose is fair, so fair is her face,
Both Summer and Winter I sing of her,
The snow makyth me to remember her."

(Pound, Cantos, 6.22–23)[1]

Although Pound incorporates phrases unchanged from their original context, through this babble of borrowed voices readers recognize a voice that they attribute to Ezra Pound, and to which they direct their frustrations with the text.[2] Neither does Pound's kleptomania stifle invention. In their new context the appropriated voices help to create a poetry less derivative than much poetry that contains no overt borrowing. Even today the disruption of this quoting poetry remains, along with its opacity. Jostling phrases such as "free of person, free of will / free to buy, witness, sell, testate" and "Winter and Summer I sing of her grace" more often block comprehension than aid it. (For earlier and new readers of Pound such experience is often called "shock value." *Disruption* implies the same kind, if not the same intensity, of thwarted expectations.) To return to Moore's phrase, stealing a texture makes Pound an inventor.

## Establishing a Continuum

Although critics industriously have identified the sources of many individual quotations, this criticism does not address a larger question: What is the role in a new text of an exactly duplicated, alien texture? Not only is most criticism of quoting texts concerned with individual quotations rather than this more systematic question, most criticism also orients itself to thematic and conceptual strategies, to identifying the place the borrowing has in the conceptual content of the original text and the new conceptual function it has in the borrowing text. What professional readers see and discuss are *borrowings, appropriations, intertextuality,* and *allusions.* In these discussions, the texture of the borrowed work functions primarily to point out parallel, contrasting, or subversive thematic strategies between borrowing and borrowed text. Such criticism does not distinguish quotations from allusions; instead, it handles quotation with categories most useful to allusion and treats quoting texts as if they present only the problems of an alluding text. Quotations do present these problems, but they also create some important new ones. Quotations' exact texture introduces a much more profound disruption, a disruption that creates new possibilities for aesthetic expression. Because the quoting poem creates new aesthetic possibilities with this nonassimilable textural evidence, quotation needs attention as a separate, recurring technique.[3]

I found my study upon the *difference* between quotation and allusion, a difference signaled by the formal signs of an alien texture. Obviously, such a foundation has methodological implications. Deconstruc-

4

tion's work on citation, repetition, and iterability presents a sophisticated approach to quotation that finds resonances in this book. Consider how this famous quotation from Derrida speaks to the project of *Changing Voices:*

> Every sign, linguistic or nonlinguistic, spoken or written (in the current sense of this opposition), in a small or large unit, can be *cited,* put between quotation marks; in so doing it can break with every given context, engendering an infinity of new contexts in a manner which is absolutely illimitable. This does not imply that the mark is valid outside of a context, but on the contrary that there are only contexts without any center or absolute anchoring [*ancrage*]. This citationality, this duplication or duplicity, this iterability of the mark is neither an accident nor an anomaly, it is that (normal/abnormal) without which a mark could not even have a function called "normal." What would a mark be that could not be cited? Or one whose origins would not get lost along the way? ("Signature," 12)

Derrida's claim has a largeness that many subsequent critics have found fruitful: repetition informs all of our writing; comprehension is possible only with iterability. If, as Culler argues, the implications of this passage are that every use of a word is a mentioning of it, that everything is citation (119–20n), then a book on borrowings has a large agenda before it—all communication. But forms of that book have already been written. The specificity of *Changing Voices,* its dealing with a *type* of citation, results in my working with ideas such as citation and repetition at a slant.

For example, take Derrida's claim that contexts have no center, that new contexts are illimitable. As Derrida claims in another context, "No meaning can be determined out of context, but no context permits saturation" ("Living On," 81). While not disagreeing with Derrida, I do redirect my approach to citation so that illimitable meaning is not the whole story of citation. I look not at how meanings are limitless, but at how writers attempt to control meaning. The forms of this control can be seen as the underlying subject of this book. As the quoting poem shows, the act of quoting is incredibly *directed:* any signal of a quotation redirects the reader's attention. A further critique of deconstruction's reading of the relation between citation and context can be found in an essay by Judith Still and Michael Worton, who argue that while quotation "does indeed generate centrifugality in reading . . . it also generates centripetality, focusing the reader's attention on textual functioning rather than on hermeneutics" (11), a critique that finds corroboration in Bakhtin, who argues that these two functions are inherent to all uses of language ("Discourse," 272).

Derrida's iterability argument also contains some presuppositions about priority (of mentioning over use) that I don't explore. What I do need is the sense that both are possible, and what happens when the most clear instance possible of mentioning—quotation—occurs. Because it is most often a quotation of a specific text rather than a "genre" quotation, does the quotation found in the quoting poem really have two "uses," and is it an instance of two "mentions"? The specificity of this sort of mention, signaled by the quoting poem's quotation marks, deconstruction does not address, and I need to *begin* with this specificity, not treat it as a special instance.

Since a concept such as *citation* is directed at all linguistic practices, citation rarely distinguishes between direct quotations and other ways in which language can be repeated. (Citation and iterability will have more resonance in my conclusion, where $L = A = N = G = U = A = G = E$ writing is discussed.) The most useful critic for my study of this form of intertextuality is Mikhail Bakhtin. Bakhtin, though firmly championing novelistic discourse, yet writes material that is applicable to the quoting poem. When Bakhtin grumbles about single-voiced poetry, he may in fact be using "poetry" as code for the monologic—he mentions "the majority of poetic genres" that use a "unity of the language system," and of "genres that are poetic in the narrow sense," in which "the natural dialogization of the word is not put to artistic use." Bakhtin's arguments about the dialogic and monologic, beginning as they do with *voice* rather than *text*, are useful for chapter 4, as is the concept of heteroglossia, which Bakhtin defines as "*another's speech in another's language*" ("Discourse," 264, 285, 324). In addition, his idea of the utterance as the basic unit of linguistic meaning, raises questions pertinent to this book ("Speech Genres," 71–73). Briefly, quotations function as sentences in a larger utterance, but they have the aura of an utterance still about them—the more they keep this aura, the more dramatic the voice of the poem seems.

Again, however, my very specific starting point may deflect some of Bakhtin's concerns. Bakhtin also does not look closely at poetic texts (using my definition now, not his), and while he does differentiate between forms of appropriation, he does not distinguish quotation from allusion. The primary way in which this study moves in directions differing from Bakhtin is that *on the basis of an exactly duplicated texture* it distinguishes quotations from allusions, and argues that this distinction allows for certain effects in quoting poems to become apparent. Throughout this book, however, I point out moments of convergence between this study and other, more general discussions of intertextuality.

The separate status of quotations can best be modeled by discussing quotation and allusion as two points along a continuum of textual appropriation. I stress a continuum rather than watertight compartments, for stealing words can range from exact copying, to mixing one's own words into the stolen, to borrowing not the words but their conceptual content. Intertextual borrowing can occupy a point anywhere along this line. Further, all borrowings, whether the pure allusion or the exact quotation, always have resonances from either extreme. Most allusions have some textural fringes which lead to effects which pure quotations more fully exploit; in their quoting, many writers exploit some of the effects more strictly developed by allusions. Quoting (and, by implication, allusion) is a mongrel technique. This study looks at the consequences for the text and for readers when borrowing leans toward the quoting rather than the alluding end of the continuum.

A comparison of points at opposite ends of the continuum shows that these ends are worlds apart. As these lines from *The Waste Land* reveal, allusions emphasize poetic strategies different from quoting strategies:

The nymphs are departed.
And their friends, the loitering heirs of City directors;
Departed, have left no addresses.
By the waters of Leman I sat down and wept . . .
Sweet Thames, run softly till I end my song,
Sweet Thames, run softly, for I speak not loud or long.
But at my back in a cold blast I hear
The rattle of the bones, and chuckle spread from ear to ear.

(67)

As he often does at the end of stanzas in this poem, here Eliot introduces a variety of literary sources. But in these lines of poetry, the allusion to Marvell ("But at my back") and the quotation from Spenser ("Sweet Thames"), although parts of the same continuum, begin from differing presuppositions and emphasize different effects.

The nontextual references in these lines uncover the differing effects of allusion and quotation, for nontextual references function in ways similar to textual allusions. As do textual allusions, these three lines refer to other "worlds," or systems of thinking about, structuring, and valuing reality.[4] In a paraphrased, shorthand way, these three lines bring into the poetry the values of these other worlds. The poetry in these first lines refers to social practices (leaving without addresses); early twentieth-century, "historical" London and its activities (loitering heirs and City directors); and pastoral tradition (nymphs). Set in a single context, the interaction among these three worlds directs irony at the new world Eliot's poem creates, an irony controlled by Eliot's repeating diction, syntactic unity, and unified topic. Thus, a poem can use the same principles to allude to an event, an object, or a text; to the Battle of Waterloo, the Holy Grail, or *Love's Labor's Lost*. Allusion is a very general term; because it has historically emphasized conceptual paraphrase, allusion can include both textual and nontextual references. This possibility for nontextual references is alien to quoting and points to the great distance between the presuppositions of the quoting and the alluding ends of the intertextual continuum.

As he does in the first three lines, in alluding to Marvell Eliot refers to a world outside of the poem; here, the world of Marvell's "To His Coy Mistress": "But at my back I always hear / Time's wingèd chariot hurrying near." The immediately noticeable difference is, of course, that this world alluded to is a textual world, a world that has the potential to be brought formally untransformed into the new text. Because this allusion moves from one text into another, it can bring into the poem many more of the alluded-to world's idiosyncratic structuring principles, in a way that the pastoral tradition and twentieth-century London cannot. The heirs of City directors are conceptually present, but one cannot touch, see, or directly hear them. Their actual physical presence in the text is, of course, impossible. In contrast, by textually alluding to the world of Marvell's poem, Eliot also brings in part of that world's texture, its material elements and stylistic presuppositions. This added ability is crucial to understanding any move to quotation, for textual allusions have usable characteristics that differ from those of nontextual references. Textual allusions ensure that the new poem's control of the reference has the possibility of an additional, textural struggle. Textual allusions allow Eliot to interact with the borrowed world on a more complex and intense level. He brings part of the borrowing's texture into the poem, and he interferes with or highlights the borrowing and its original function in a manner inaccessible to his nontextual allusions.

The poet's interference is crucial, for it ensures that allusions do not work with quotation's presuppositions. Thus, while *quotation* originally meant "to mark the number of," to simply refer to something, *allusion* has its Latin source in "to play with"—its form of reference suggests much more an interaction between borrower and source. In alluding to Marvell, Eliot plays a serious game; he *changes* the original wording, and these changes conceptually harness the borrowing's function in the new text. The changes establish control in a way similar to the "regular" poetry of the first three lines and dissimilar to quotations, which work through the illusion of a lack of control. The textual changes from Marvell, introducing the values that Eliot establishes throughout this poem, create an irony that advances principles introduced in the lines about the departed directors and nymphs. But Eliot creates this irony by using quite different materials. To the first line of his borrowing from Marvell Eliot adds "in a cold blast," an addition that accentuates the contrast between pleasure and onrushing death that Marvell creates in his poem. "Cold blast" makes certain not only that readers understand the purpose of the allusion, but the phrase also neatly ties in with some of the new poem's thematic concerns and image patterns, such as death and sterility. Eliot similarly replaces "Time's wingèd chariot" with the more ominous "rattle of the bones," a move that again (perhaps heavy-handedly) ensures that we see the heightened effect of Marvell's text in its new context. Again, the changes ensure a felicitous correspondence with other larger strategies of the new poem. The changes also create a clear parallel with the following "chuckle spread from ear to ear" and make that phrase anything but genial. Eliot's changes in the borrowings' diction ensure that the value systems of two different worlds in conjunction create irony.

While reading this allusion the reader (through the help of some textural evidence) ideally recognizes the inevitably disruptive intellectual pattern of a specific source, but the ironic strategy or voice in the new poem clearly attempts to override the center of the source's verbal patterns. The poet's controlling interference extends to the borrowed text's appearance. The allusion here (and allusions more generally) contains no visual dislocation. There are no quotation marks, no typography to set the borrowing off from the rest of the text. The allusion also has little sensuous dislocation. Eliot's textual changes ensure that the borrowing does not have a strikingly different style of language. Further, the allusion has no changes in meter that are governed solely by the verbal idiosyncracies of the borrowed text. Eliot keeps an iambic rhythm throughout these lines. The allusion's smooth appearance accentuates the fact that the minor textural disruption one does encounter serves conceptual ends. The original source's material texture primarily identifies the conceptual content of the appropriated source's world and is present only fleetingly and imprecisely, to point to a larger, more primary strategy.

This interference in the middle of the alluded text ensures that the poet controls the allusion's conceptual function. The changes in diction from Marvell's poem shift the focus to the intellectual content of "To His Coy Mistress," to what the poem "says." Eliot's new poem dominates by transforming the verbal idiosyncracies of the original source to fit more smoothly into the new poem's content and metrics. Without stifling the ability of the alluded material's conceptual content to reach to a text beyond its new setting, the new poem's voice controls the disruption of the borrowed material's texture. The change to a less disruptive texture also allows Eliot to shape the conceptual function of Marvell's phrase. He makes much more grim Marvell's original humor and sophistry. Eliot repeats when he alludes, but at the heart of his repetition is a change in which the poet's textural changes cause other changes to occur: not only do these borrowed texts now look and sound different, they also have a different meaning. With this sort of transformation conceptual content subsumes textural content. This hierarchy and its ability to give interfering poets conceptual and textural control of their borrowings is useful—with the exception of medieval and some forms of Renaissance writing, literature before this century used allusion as the dominant mode by which to appropriate texts.

More so than do quoting texts, alluding texts attempt to *assimilate* their borrowings; the poet does not present the allusion as a self-contained texture that refuses integration into the new text. This impulse to swallow the allusion shows the importance of unity for alluding poems, a unity that comes through strategies that recur in all alluding texts. For example, Eliot allows partial freedom to the diction and syntax of the alluded source, but the reins are always visible: "But at my back in a cold blast I hear / The rattle of the bones, and chuckle spread from ear to ear" (67). To control the poem by his own voice and poetic strategy, Eliot adds a syntactically completing line and varies the source's diction and syntax (adding the "cold blast," removing the superfluous "always"). Through textual changes the poet asserts his textural presence in the middle of another text, in this instance (and in much of Eliot's work) creating irony, but always proposing a unifying strategy at the moment of allusion.

The interfering strategies may get more complex, but they all illustrate the same process. Consider this example from *The Waste Land:* "I sat upon the shore / Fishing, with the arid plain behind me / Shall I at least set my lands in order?" (74). There are two quick allusions in these two lines, to Jesse L. Weston's *From Ritual to Romance* and to Isaiah 38:1. But Eliot minimizes the possible disruptions resulting from the conflation of two such dissimilar sources. Any disruption is first on a conceptual, not a textural level. Here, the diction follows one style. The language is uniformly complex and consistent with the voice of one speaker—no changing languages or shift into a highly ornate or Latinate style. Since "I" is repeated twice, the poet creates the illusion of a single voice and a single dramatic context. In addition, the line's metrical patterns do not shift from highly irregular to regular or vice versa. These textural strategies ensure that the lines do not exploit logical disunity as thoroughly as they could. Because of the repeating "I" and the lack of punctuation between the two allusions, readers forge a logical, paraphrasable connection between these two elements. A single identity speaks, and it speaks coherently. In Bakhtin's terms, allusions are monologic.

Since an allusion depends for its conceptual success on being recognized in this new context by readers, there may be some intellectual dislocation—the alert reader momentarily steps out of the world of the poem to another textual world. Prodding along his less-than-ideal readers with his appended notes to the poem, Eliot ensures that this dislocation occurs. But the mainly *intellectual* dislocation points out the allusion's conceptual importance, and the alluding text's strenuous attempt to assimilate it. With much of the texture of their sources scrubbed from them, allusions do not as violently resist their new function as do quotations. At their most extreme, allusions passively submit.

Quotations struggle to disrupt this hierarchy of the borrowed world in subjection to a new world. As the borrowed text slides along the continuum closer to pure quotation, readers hear more insistently the disruptive overtones of a second voice:

> By the waters of Leman I sat down and wept . . .
> Sweet Thames, run softly till I end my song,
> Sweet Thames, run softly, for I speak not loud or long.
> But at my back in a cold blast I hear
> The rattle of the bones, and chuckle spread from ear to ear.

(67)

In the simple clarity of its transformation from its source text, "By the waters of Leman" intensifies the issues seen in the poem's allusions. Again, with his changes in diction Eliot melodramatically asserts control over the center of borrowed text, the transformation acknowledging the value of conceptual paraphrase. But the original text leaves a strong residue: "By the rivers of Babylon, there we sat down, yea, we wept, when we remembered Zion" (Psalms 137:1). As a result of this more disruptive presence, "paraphrase of conceptual content" is too simplistic an analysis of this borrowed text. Tendencies seen in the Marvell allusion are heightened here. Too much of the source text's original texture is present, refusing assimilation into the new text. The presence of the original texture slides this text along the continuum, closer to pure quotation and its activities.

In the lines we have been using, readers find the quoting end of the continuum in Eliot's borrowing from Spenser's *Prothalamion,* with Eliot repeating the line and adding the phrase "for I speak not loud or long": "Sweet Thames, run softly till I end my song, / Sweet Thames, run softly, for I speak not loud or long." Eliot *quotes* the phrase "Sweet Thames, run softly till I end my song"; he gives his readers the exact, unmediated verbal texture of another text. The exactness guarantees a process simultaneously exaggerating and subverting what happens when one reads allusions, although some activities do not change. For example, the paraphrasable irony of the previous allusions is also present here. If they recognize the source of a quotation, readers go through the same conceptual activity as they do when reading an allusion, such as understanding the conceptual relation of the allusion's source to the new text.

But since Eliot does not interfere with the center of this quoted line, the quotation increases a textural disruption that complicates reading. More aggressively than does allusion, quotation bases irony and any uses of authority upon texture. Irony, authority, and other such perceptions of poetic stance come from readers' inferring a relationship between the alien texture of the quotation's world and the new or alluding lines of poetry in which Eliot's voice is more clearly present. Readers hear the original rhyme scheme, and they recognize Spenser's idiosyncratic use of "Sweet," "softly," and "song." These material elements of another world, bringing with them the texture of Spenser's poetic voice, introduce a formal elegance that juxtaposes a voice of an earlier era to what seems to be a voice of the modern era. This juxtaposition also happens a few lines earlier in *The Waste Land,* where Eliot quotes the same lines of Spenser:

> The river's tent is broken; the last fingers of leaf
> Clutch and sink into the wet bank. The wind
> Crosses the brown land, unheard. The nymphs are departed.
> Sweet Thames, run softly, till I end my song.
> The river bears no empty bottles, sandwich papers,
> Silk handkerchiefs, cardboard boxes, cigarette ends
> Or other testimony of summer nights. The nymphs are departed.
>
> (67)

Although the center of the borrowed text has a new function, this function is indicated by a relationship *between* borrowed text and new text, not *within* the borrowed text. Instead of discovering textural and conceptual control at the center of the borrowed text, readers of quotations look exclusively for this control in the structural oppositions of borrowed to new text. In *The Waste Land,* the opposition among conflicting physical textures strengthens the poem's irony and thematic framework. But the textural opposition makes such a framework depend much less upon a traditional notion of a single voice's controlling texture than upon the relation between quotation and new text. The unassimilable new poetic texture creates a disjunctive doubleness that structures *The Waste Land* and any quoting poem.[5]

This disjunction ensures that quotation has consequences for reading. When readers distinguish between quotations and allusions, in the complexity they find new modes of expression for poetry, new modes that a single response to both quotation and allusion could not discover. These complexities do not surface when critics treat passages that mix quotation and allusion as if the borrowings were parallel, as if to each borrowing the poet presents a uniform response. Such a move curtails the quoting poem's expressivity. For example, Grover Smith has the following reading of the passage I have just examined:

> The season is still winter, after the summer throngs have left the Thames, from which have long departed the fertility nymphs of Spenser's "Prothalamion." The attendance of nymphs at a marriage festival reflects disgrace on casual lovers by the Thames or "by the waters of Leman," the waters now of Lake Geneva, where Eliot, Byron-like, composed the poem, and of Babylon, where the exiled Hebrews sat down and wept. (83–84)

Writing a very different sort of text, thirty years after Smith's book, Calvin Bedient similarly homogenizes the text. According to Bedient the speaker of the poem "ironically compares himself to Spenser. . . . He mixes the lovely refrain from Spenser's song of the Brides . . . with the "brown" of his own spirit and age. . . . *He* can but speak, and not loud nor long" (109). A few pages later, Bedient writes of the speaker's looking "to Ezekiel, Shakespeare, Dante, Augustine, and the rest" (115). Certainly, the poem looks at these figures, but it does so in differing ways, ways that make problematic the whole idea of a speaker, ways that, in Bakhtin's terms, make this text much more dialogic than either Bedient or Smith suggest.

By contrast, readers find new forms of expression when they incorporate into their reading the observation that with the quotation from Spenser Eliot has done something new: he hasn't changed a borrowed text to suit his purposes. The quotation introduces an unannounced complexity into the poem, initially raising the question of *why* the borrowing hasn't been changed. Why does Eliot feel no need to transform Spenser? The question can be answered in several ways. First, at this point in the poem, Spenser's text, although coming out of a discussion of love like that of "To His Coy Mistress," has a clearer social agenda and a larger cultural function (signaled by readers' common perceptions of Spenser's general poetic project and by "Thames") that Marvell's text does not as clearly have. Eliot wants the whole of this effect. By virtue of its unchanged status Spenser's text also increases its status as a cultural artifact, a status that Eliot partially removes from

Marvell's text when he tampers with it. There are also some practical reasons for not changing Spenser. The quotation from Spenser is not well known; to change it would have less effect than the changing of Marvell's anthology piece would have. Eliot transforms Marvell with our knowledge of that text in mind; he keeps Spenser intact to ensure that by its sound we realize it comes from a specific source.

The quotation adds some further forms of expression, related to ownership of this borrowed voice. To read the quotation *as quotation* raises the following aesthetic problems: How can a voice unchanged from the sixteenth century carry twentieth-century irony? Does the irony function in precisely the same way that Marvell's text does, or does the quotation from Spenser have a nostalgia that the allusion from Marvell doesn't? If the poem's response to Spenser is nostalgic, does the musing voice of the poem quote these lines? How radical is the quotation's interruption? Eliot also could make much more extreme all of the above considerations by simply adding quotation marks to Spenser's text, removing ownership from the quotation, and to some extent denying responsibility for its effects.

In any case, such questions show that allusions and quotations create a poem of differing textures and allegiances. These differences are prag-matic in the fullest sense of the word, for a quotation is not so much an inherent entity as a functional entity: quotations are quotations only if they function as such. In *The Waste Land*, "London Bridge is falling down falling down falling down" is read as an exact quotation because of its popularity and individual readers' own cultural repertoire. Other quotations are recognized as such through notes that poets like Eliot and Moore append to their poems. Still other quotations function as such on faith, with the reader trusting the poet's use of quotation marks or italics as a reliable indicator of a quoted voice. Quotation marks or italics, coupled with a reader's not having the cultural repertoire to ascertain whether these enclosed words are indeed quotations, allow these enclosed words to function as quotations. Readers typically don't know whether Moore is actually quoting; they trust her. Quotation marks, even when not enclosing an actual quotation, always signal the appropriation of another voice or speech with which the author does not completely want to identify, as when someone apologizes for using a cliché by enclosing it in quotation marks (Hill, 142–43)—moving the language in the quotation from "use" to pure "mentioning."[6]

All quoting, then, exploits an alien texture, whether such texture be real or imagined. When a work of art quotes, the emphasis upon a "paraphrasable," nontextural world fades. The duplicatable formal properties of a world of texts become the first cause in the aesthetic equation, the elements from which readers take their cue on how to handle the quotation's conceptual properties.[7] Authors do not quote solely to echo the linguistic meaning of the quoted text—the quotation's material texture begins to assert itself. The less allusion and the more quotation readers encounter, the more the quoting poem appropriates and works with what some would call the *writing* of another text. The quotation goes beyond recording the purely intellectual content of a work (if that is ever possible) and calls attention to the quoted material's texture. As we shall see in chapter 4 and the conclusion, quoting has varying ideological agendas, but all such agendas result from quoting's formalist presupposition: disruption is based upon texture, upon certain formal characteristics of a work.[8]

This emphasis on texture has several results. As we have seen, quoting's emphasis on texture and de-emphasis of conceptual paraphrase increases the quotation's presence as indelibly alien, as an element opposing the borrowing text. The changing textures of the quoting poem easily create these oppositions because these textures so clearly lie on the poem's surface—one cannot easily read past them. Eliot's quoting of Baudelaire assaults the reader not just because of its content, but because it is spoken by a voice alien to what has preceded it, a voice of a different texture:

> "That corpse you planted last year in your garden,
> "Has it begun to sprout? Will it bloom this year?
> "Or has the sudden frost disturbed its bed?
> "O keep the Dog far hence, that's friend to men,
> "Or with his nails he'll dig it up again!
> "You! hypocrite lecteur!—mon semblable,—mon frère!"

> (63)

Readers notice the verbal patterns of this piece of text in complete opposition to the verbal patterns of the rest of *The Waste Land;* within the quotation itself one does not find Eliot's writing. The different language, the violence, and the simple fact that it is announced as a different voice (an announcement Eliot accentuates in his disruptive notes to the poem) contrast this section of poetry with the rest of the poem. Such textural conflict in quoting texts is both objective—the disruptions are verifiable—and culturally conditioned. Basically, heavy quoting is a new cultural phenomenon, and since readers have had more practice at smoothing over conceptual disruption, they still have difficulty creating a single textural framework that incorporates these new textures. That difficulty is precisely why quotation is so useful to the Modern poem, and why it is still useful today.

Quotations' separate textures signal that at the heart of the quotation is a lack of change: the look, sound, and meaning of the quoted text are in a profound way *identical* to their original use. Every aspect of these separate objects has previously participated in a different world, and this previous existence calls attention to and delimits quotations from the rest of the artwork. The conceptual disruption of quotations is as a result much stronger than that of allusions. Changing the texture of an allusion allows for changing its conceptual strategies to fit more smoothly into the new text. As the first cause upon which other oppositions depend, the quotation's exactly duplicated texture resists the new poem's attempts to subsume the quotation's conceptual content. Conceptual disruptions of theme, imagery, narrative, and logic intrude as a result of the quotation's textural disruptions. Quotation consequently intensifies the disjunction partially introduced by allusions and accentuates a very difficult reading process that emphasizes doubleness over a univocal structure. In service to features of the quoting poem's formal landscape, these disruptions shape the reading process, radically transforming the expressive capabilities of poetry. Bakhtin's assertion about the univocal assumptions of poetic genres is revealing; in poetic genres, "The word is sufficient unto itself and does not presume alien utterances beyond its own boundaries. Poetic style is by convention suspended from any mutual interaction with alien discourse, any allusion to alien discourse" ("Discourse," 285). To this idea of the poetic the quoting poem adds a new range of expressivity, causing quotation to be—bowing perhaps only to free verse—the most useful technical innovation of American Modernist poetry.

Through the simple act of introducing an alien texture, quotation intensifies problems introduced by allusion or creates distinctive ones, many of which touch on contemporary critical discussion. Quotation addresses the problem of influence, for quotations simultaneously affirm, antagonize, and feed off of their sources. By introducing the presence of another creative personality (no matter how mundane this personality is), quotation complicates and decenters the subject within the poem. Quotation shows that all intertextualities are not created equal, and that citation exists on multiple levels, with differing urgencies. Partially because of the disjunction it introduces (itself a complex critical discussion), quotation injects competing strategies into a single text, and often these strategies do not resolve as much as they subvert the quoting text.

Lurking behind these many concerns is a more basic problem, which forms the subject of this book. *How* can quotation speak on all these issues? More specifically, how can this unique example of intertextuality achieve diverse effects through the relationships among its physical texture, the physical texture of the quoting artwork, and the seam that welds the two together? To arrive at some answers, this study specifically considers how the poetic quotations of Eliot, Pound, Moore, and Cummings function, addressing as an underlying issue artistic quoting in general, and getting some sense of why quoting is so important to the art of this century.

### American Modernism's Quoting

In their quoting poems these American Modernist poets unpack the implications of the idea that one cannot paraphrase a texture, and that texture governs the conceptual content of the borrowed text: *how* one writes something is also *what* one writes. This awareness of texture gets coupled with an appreciation for disruption. Consequently, all quoting Modernists introduce to the reading process highly divergent effects, all of which are based upon the aesthetic disruption caused by an intrusive new texture. A good place to begin understanding the many changes quoting Modernism brings is in the writing of Marianne Moore, who initially seems quite close to the concerns of alluding poetry. Her quotations quietly slip into the rhetoric of her poetry:

> He runs, he flies, he swims, to get to
> his basilica—"the ruler of Rivers, Lakes, and Seas,
>     invisible or visible," with clouds to do
> as bid—and can be "long or short, and also coarse or fine at
>     pleasure."
>
> ("The Plumet Basilisk," 32)

Moore's quoting has a naive yet puzzling character. She repeatedly returns to what seems an uninsistent activity, the creation of an unobtrusive, casual presence. Moore brings to Modernist quoting a duplicitous simplicity that disarmingly questions the aesthetic presuppositions of previous literary borrowers. Late in her career (1956) Moore would ask, "Odd as it may seem that a few words of overwhelming urgency should be a mosaic of quotations, why paraphrase what for maximum impact should be quoted verbatim?" ("Idiosyncracy," 512). In this seemingly casual poetry the *exact* words are important, not just their paraphrasable baggage. Not only do the exact words fit, they are necessary. Quotations are le mot juste, not a practice into which one can slip at whim.

Quotations are urgent because Moore exploits their texture so heavily. Readers either do not know the sources of her quotations, or they do not know the specific function these quotations had in their original texts. Moore's notes to her poems ensure that the quotation's original function is unknown. Certainly, she typically names the source from which the quotation comes and the sentence in which the quotation appears. But given the obscurity of her sources, this identification does not clearly delineate for readers the quotation's place in its original world. The notes do not provide a determining context. For example, Moore quotes a now-(and then-) obscure source in "The Labours of Hercules":

> to persuade one of austere taste, proud in the possession of home
>     and a musician—
> that the piano is a free field for etching; that his "charming tadpole
>     notes"
> belong to the past when one had time to play them:
>
> (75)

Moore's note to this quotation reads: "'Charming tadpole notes.' *The London Spectator*" (129). Such an identification does not do much more than convince persuadable readers that this is indeed a quotation. The quotation's original function remains unknown because it is unimportant (although the fact that it is unknown is important); quotations do not have an authority of origin in her poetry. Moore does not quote to place herself in a prestigious literary tradition, to gain admittance to a select club. The quotation is crucial, but readers know only its texture and isolated conceptual content, and not any other of the claims that it theoretically could load upon the poem. As a result, the quotations in her poetry become cyphers of mysterious import, clearly asserting only their own alienness. The texture of Moore's quotations have a primarily negative function: at the center of these quotations, at least, one does not find the poet's voice. Quotations allow Moore to hide the identity and the texture of the new poem's voice:

> If "compression is the first grace of style,"
> you have it. Contractility is a virtue
> as modesty is a virtue.
> It is not the acquisition of any one thing
> that is able to adorn,
> or the incidental quality that occurs
> as a concomitant of something well said,
> that we value in style,
> but the principle that is hid:
> in the absence of feet, "a method of conclusions";
> "a knowledge of principles,"
> in the curious phenomenon of your occipital horn.
>
> ("To a Snail," 113)

Not only does the poem's rhetoric argue for contractility, so do its metaphors and its quoting. The occipital horn, a snail's primary sense organ, often also containing its eyes, doubles the quotation in that the snail can retract the horn into its shell. The quotations introduce a doubleness primarily acknowledging that a different type of text has become part of the poem, saying things the poet would rather not say. The desired aesthetic effect is not just certitude that the poet is *not* present in the quotations, but also a disruption upon perceiving an alien world's texture, a disruption that removes a unified aesthetic experience and hides the poem's persona.

E. E. Cummings's quotation eschews Moore's disinterested, ironic poetry in favor of a fierce poetry of direct social involvement. In his quoting, Cummings creates an inevitably passionate work far removed from most imagined centers of Modernism, work that finds few inheritors in contemporary writing. In his quoting poems, quotation, new poem, and authorial stance energetically struggle with each other and assert themselves unitedly against disinterested involvement:

"next to of course god america i
love you land of the pilgrims' and so forth oh
say can you see by the dawn's early my
country 'tis of centuries come and go
and are no more what of it we should worry
in every language even deafanddumb
thy sons acclaim your glorious name by gorry
by jingo by gee by gosh by gum
why talk of beauty what could be more beaut-
iful than these heroic happy dead
who rushed like lions to the roaring slaughter
they did not stop to think they died instead
then shall the voice of liberty be mute?"

He spoke. And drank rapidly a glass of water

(267)

The most angry of Modernist quoters, Cummings vents his spleen against a texture, the fact that many users of these quotations speak in clichés. In its quoting, this poem shows that the texture of one's speech indicates the depth of one's thought. The lack of alluding interference at the center of the borrowing signals that the speaker is not doing any thinking at all. Instead, the rapid linear enjambment, the cutoff phrases of incomplete thoughts, the constricting form, the absent punctuation, and the filler phrases ensure that the equation between texture and thought is violent, creating a fury that assaults the quotation's authority. Indeed, the quotation is an antiauthority. The voice behind the poem's satire enmeshes itself so unwaveringly in the satire that it lacks the self-deprecating irony that Moore uses and lacks the aesthetic distance and sophistication found in much of Modernism and Postmodernism.

As this chapter has already hinted, Eliot and Pound create yet other options for the quoting poem. For both poets, quoting also relates to a typical use of allusion, for quoting creates an authoritative canon of texts. But a shift has taken place, for in this quoted canon texture at times dominates more than does conceptual content. The direction of the borrowing's authority at times shifts to showing that the quoting poet can speak the "right" language, that he belongs to the right club.

Again, however, quoting has the potential to create differing aesthetic effects. Even though both Eliot and Pound emphasize textural authority, and both question what was the traditional canon, they create canons with very different presuppositions behind them, and with very differing aesthetic results. Although Pound's translation in canto I of Andreas Divus's version of Homer seems to point to a literary/social tradition equally comfortable to Eliot, Pound's concern with lost texts (as Philip Furia points out) leads him to Sigismundo Malatesta and John Adams. His recovery of these texts is sometimes frustratingly extensive, resulting in pages of quotation. Eliot's quotation is more fleeting, and rarely extends beyond the effortless display of knowledge indicated in single lines of text. Eliot also works with a much more standard version of the works constituting the literary canon. Yet the literary clubs that these poets create have some strange members. The works of the "great masters" exist side by side with other forms of writing, such as popular songs and nursery rhymes (Eliot), bills of lading and personal letters (Pound). Poetry begins to look and sound quite different—less clearly "literary," yet more learned and difficult, more what we today call *Modern*.

More important, almost any section of *The Waste Land* or *The Cantos* uses quoting's syntactic disruption to increase the fractured aesthetic experience found more subtly in the writing of Moore and Cummings, and to decrease paraphrasable or conceptual continuity between the quotation and new text. This disjunctive approach is more in line with the aesthetic experience of Picasso in his collage *Still Life with Chair Caning* and of Erik Satie in his ballet *Parade* and so takes in a larger part of Modernist history.

But a single discovery looms behind all this American Modernist quoting, a discovery exploited with differing intensities and to differing ends. *Changing Voices* will study how Modernist poets especially exploit the possibilities of a borrowed work, and how through that exploitation they created a moment in literary history whose results separated them from earlier poetry and fascinates and antagonizes contemporary writing. The key to my understanding of that highly diverse moment is texture, for in their quoting poems all four poets operate with the same presupposition: the quoted *texture* is important, and thus the quoting poem allows for possibilities unavailable to other forms of appropriation. Since those formal, textural aspects of another text are always slightly at odds with the borrowing text, this chapter has argued that the borrowed texture causes disruption to structure the possibilities of the quoting poem. The next chapter will attempt to describe the form of that disruption.

## CHAPTER 2

# The Structure of Quotations

The thing ["Marriage"] (I would hardly call it a poem) is no philosophic precipitate; nor does it veil anything personal in the way of triumphs, entrapments, or dangerous colloquies. It is a little anthology of statements that took my fancy—phrasings that I liked.

—Marianne Moore

## Gaps

Marianne Moore's critical pronouncements about her own work have the peculiar ability both to invite suspicion and to deflect it. "Marriage," one of her greatest and most ambitious works, Moore can "hardly call...a poem." In the face of this demurral, how can one begin to make large claims for this work? When Moore describes the poem as being composed of "phrasings that I liked," she makes her readers aware both of how playfully inadequate this description is, and how the phrase also refuses readers an entrance into finding more concrete structuring principles. Yet in this evasion Moore offers a sidelong description of her methodology: the poem is an anthology. An anthology is a collection of separate entities (originally a collection of flowers); separateness, with all its implications, is the key to understanding the structure of the quoting poem.

Because in their separateness quotations establish a *difference* from their surrounding text, a crucial rhythm appears in the reading process. In all quoting poems, even those as different as Moore's "New York" and Pound's *Cantos,* quotations introduce a two-stepped reading process into the quoting poem—the "regular" text's world bumps against the world of the quotation. Whether it is through the appearance of the changing languages, the quotation's placement on a line by itself, or the discrete introduction and closure of quotation marks or italics, each quotation visually coheres as a unit opposed to the rest of the text. These conceptual, textural, and visual delimiters ensure a slight stoppage and change in direction that disrupts the reading process:

> Ailas e que'm fau miey huelh
> Quar no vezon so qu'ieu vuelh.
> Our mulberry leaf, woman, TAN AOIDAN,
> "Nel ventre tuo, o nella mente mia,
> "Yes, Milady, precisely, if you wd.
> have anything made."
>
> "Faziamo tutte le due ...
> "No, not in the palm-room." The lady says it is
> Too cold in the palm-room.
>
> (*Cantos,* 29.144)

In recognizing the textural and consequently intellectual disjunction in these lines, readers give each quotation an additional type of attention—not just part of the linearity of the poem, this unit of words is a special unit within the poem, formed along principles different from and prior to the rest of the text.[1]

Certainly, this idea of separate groups within a text is not idiosyncratic to quoting poems. Wolfgang Iser argues that all reading processes relate groupings of text that are separated by "blanks" (120, 108–10). But quoting poems establish their separations in a curious and more antagonistic way. In most previous texts, gaps are signalled either by stanza breaks, changes in speakers (in dramatic poems), or other, less obtrusive ways, as in this stanza of Wordsworth's "Immortality Ode":

> There was a time when meadow, grove, and stream,
> The earth, and every common sight,
>      To me did seem
>           Apparell'd in celestial light,
> The glory and the freshness of a dream.
> It is not now as it has been of yore;—
>      Turn wheresoe'er I may,

By night or day,
The things which I have seen I now can see no more.

(271)

Creating meaning through gaps here is primarily a matter of exploiting the functions of regular syntax. Thus, one kind of gap appears after the second, third, and fifth lines; it creates a subject-predicate-subjective complement structure. In terms of punctuation, not only the periods but the dash interrupts the reading process while it points to a change in direction. Since this is poetry, line endings also function as gaps, here working most artificially and disjunctively in the second and third last lines, where the rhyme highlights the isolation introduced by the line ending. Except at times when there are stanza breaks, the groupings within texts are not accompanied by textural or logical disjunction to the degree that they are in many Modern texts. The poem does not startlingly force readers to acknowledge disruption. Whatever gaps there are smoothly help meaning to occur by breaking up meaning into manageable chunks. The gaps help create unified meaning.

All critics have noticed that in Modernist texts gaps function differently than this. They occur at unexpected places, without syntactic warning. They are disruptive. But these gaps, for all their disruption, create fewer disjunctions than do the gaps of quotations. Consider this highly disjunctive, but nonquoting section of *The Cantos:*

Palace in smoky light,
Troy but a heap of smouldering boundary stones,
ANAXIFORMINGES! Aurunculeia!
Hear me. Cadmus of the Golden Prows!
The silver mirrors catch the bright stones and flare,
Dawn, to our waking, drifts in the green cool light;
Dew-haze blurs, in the grass, pale ankles moving.
Beat, beat, whirr, thud, in soft turf
    under the apple trees,

(4.13)

The gaps are not alien to Pound's creative persona, for a single person seems both the creator and the speaker of these lines. True, with the final allusion to Whitman and the foreign languages this passage at times leans to quotation's borrowed texture, and so stretches the persona's limits.

But actual quotations exacerbate this disruption. A gap-concealing sequence breaks down much more explicitly in quoting poetry since readers do and must look at the quotation as an object by itself, created by principles alien and prior to the quoting poem, and subject to its own laws. Because quotations employ disjunction in ways inaccessible to nonquoting parts of the poem, poets use quotations to introduce disjunction at startling places within the poem. In *The Waste Land* the only startling disruptions *within* specific stanzas occur as a result of some form of quotation. As in most of Pound's *Cantos*, in *The Waste Land* almost all other major disruptions are announced by stanza breaks.

Thus, quotations are not disruptive just because of their alien texture; the *way* in which they appear is disruptive. Certainly, the quotation's gaps occur without earlier poetry's disjunction-concealing transitional markers and linear logic. Quotations often simply appear, syntactically unannounced but visually disruptive. But unlike nonquoting Modernist texts, quoting poems add one difference that comes as a result of these disjunctions. These disjunctions ensure that the quotation is not typically announced as the quotation of a character within the poem. There is very rarely a use of "he said," "she said," "according to" or any of those tags by which we critics announce our control of the quotations in our own discursive texts.

Certainly, at a few times quotations appear as part of a narrative situation in which such tags appear. But such uses are extremely rare. If the quotation is presented as part of a narrative situation, it is much more integrated than usual and is not emphasized as a disruptive object. Such moments appear in the work of Moore, but rarely:

> The decorous frock-coated Negro
> by the grotto
>
> answers the fearless sightseeing hobo
>     who asks the man she's with, what's this,
>     what's that, where's Martha
>     buried, "General Washington
>     there; his lady, here"; speaking
>     as if in a play—not seeing her;
>             ("Part of a Novel, Part of a Poem, Part of a Play," 20)

When the new poem addresses the quotation *as quotation,* as the textual product of someone else (although spoken by the speaker or a character in the new poem), the gaps become much less startling. The quotation here exists as a separate unit of thought, but the introduction of a speaking character's voice allows for the illusion of a single, controlling voice that exists *above* the quoted voice and that introduces and manages the quotation. A single narrative situation courteously bounds the quotation, and curiously makes it much less clear that this is the quotation of a *text.* Pound also uses narrative to hide the status of the quotation as text in the section of *The Cantos* quoted above : "'No, not in the palm-room.' The lady says it is / Too cold in the palm-room." (The mysteries seem unresolvable: Moore does not give a source for her quotation; in *A Companion to the Cantos of Ezra Pound* Carroll Terrell does not gloss these lines.) Such an integrated use of quotations moves the poem close to drama and narrative and is usually not the way quotations function within quoting poems.

More typically, the quotation does not speak from a narrative situation. Even supposing, as does Calvin Bedient in *He Do the Police in Different Voices,* that an individual quoting poem contains the voice of a single character who quotes or somehow controls the borrowings, this character is not constructed in such a way that she can be delineated through tags such as "she said," "according to," and so forth. Quotations are announced, but they are announced silently, through visual or less obtrusive aural cues. No *words* follow or precede to announce that these are borrowings. This silent shift to differing principles inevitably creates a blank space, a gap between quotation and new text, a gap that structures the reading of any quoting poem.

Since the text does not explicitly do it, readers themselves must acknowledge and find a use for the gap between the poem's different textures and conceptual strategies. They need to do so even in the case of Marianne Moore, whose work initially would seem least structured by overt gaps:

> The scentless nosegay
> is thus formed in the midst of the bouquet
> from bottles casks and corks for: sixty-four million red wines
> and twenty million white, which Bordeaux merchants
> and lawyers "have spent a great deal of
> trouble" to select, from what was and what was not

Bordeaux. A food-grape, however—"born
of nature and of art"—is true ground for the grape-holiday.
("Camellia Sabina," 28–29)

The gap's function is subtle. Given the obscurity of Moore's source, its nondistinctive language, and its unobtrusive fitting into the borrowing poem's syllabic patterning and syntactic structure, perhaps only the visual announcement indicates to readers that a passage has been quoted. But this silent visual gap allows for other confirmations of difference. Through seeing the quotation marks, readers know and read a second voice into the poem, and begin to attribute characteristics to it. Compare the sound of the quotations to the rest of the poem: "Have spent a great deal of trouble" and "born of nature and of art" have a slightly higher tone than the rest of the text. To sensitive contemporary ears, these phrases sound like bureaucratic prose that by its grandiloquence looks back to the nineteenth century. In fact, Moore tells us in her notes that the sources for these quotations are the *Encyclopedia Britannica* and the first volume of a work entitled *The Epicure's Guide to France* (124). The gap between quotation and new text, signaled by the quotation's sound and its quotation marks, is made more acute because readers tend to create a unified mass from the remaining, non-quoting texture of this poem. And the gap is silent: we don't know *why* Moore quotes certain phrases, why those particular statements "took her fancy." But all this silent and unaccountable difference gives the gaps a function—a quirkily disarming one, perhaps, but one that helps create the tone of Moore's poetry and deflect the poem from a too-comfortable status as an artifact of high art.

Other texts more explicitly—yet in radically differing ways—show that these silent gaps are not messy intrusions that must be read out of the text; they are integral to the text's meaning. For example, in Cummings's "MEMORABILIA" readers must use gaps to create a relationship among the satirized women, quoted text, and the poet silently yet clearly looming behind them:

believe

thou me cocodrillo—
mine eyes have seen
the glory of

the coming of
the Americans particularly the
brand of marriageable nymph which is
armed with large legs rancid
voices Baedekers Mothers and kodaks

(254)

The gap between quotation and new text, rather than simply opposing comprehension, allows meaning to occur that could not occur otherwise. The gap points to a meaningful relationship between quotation and surrounding text; the gap creates what Bakhtin calls an "utterance." The gap at the end of the second line eventually ensures that the crocodile's false tears are contrasted to the eyes of the quotation and their real, but satirized, experience. This satire is not made clear until the quotation ends, and the gap that follows it announces "the Americans" as a new completion for the quotation. This gap-structured meaning (which includes an awareness of two creative, sometimes competing personalities), with all of its usefulness in establishing irony, dominates the way people experience artworks that quote.

## "Planes in Relation"

However, no single principle encapsulates how these gaps might work; there is no Modernist theory of quotation. One arrives no closer to a clearly stated theory than in this chapter's protectively disarming epigraph from Marianne Moore. Yet the lack of a theory of quotation in Moore and others is not due to a lack of theorizing. Modernist writers enjoyed writing polemical theory, but with the possible exception of free verse, in their essays Modernist poets seem to be more interested in general principles than in the specific practices that might result from these principles. Thus, the rationale for quotation will be found tangentially in Modernist theorizing and will begin to suggest that quotation is a manifestation of several *tendencies* within several theoretical arguments.

One such tangential argument that relates to the gaps in the quoting poem is the argument over linear development in Modern poems. Traditional linear development, of course, was seen by many Modernists as inadequate for contemporary art, and thus the form by which Modern poetry ought to produce meaning was an urgent problem for Modernist polemicists. A year before the publication of *The Waste Land*, Eliot argued that the proper response to the needs of contemporary civilization was to "dislocate" language into meaning:

> Our civilization comprehends great variety and complexity, and this variety and complexity, playing upon a refined sensibility, must produce various and complex results. The poet must become more and more comprehensive, more allusive, more indirect, in order to force, to dislocate if necessary, language into his meaning. ("Metaphysical," 65)

Eliot's ideas were not produced in isolation; some version of Eliot's argument can be found throughout Modernist writing and throughout the years of high Modernism. In Pound's critical writing, explications of the ideogramic method emphasize a similarly awkward movement in poetry, one that does not seem to work with linearly structured logic. At the other end (1938) of the first generation of quoting poems, Pound retrospectively argued: "the ideogramic method consists of presenting one facet and then another until at some point one gets off the dead and desensitized surface of the reader's mind, onto a part that will register" (*Kulchur*, 51). On the basis of these sorts of statements, many critics have pointed out that the movement in much Modernist poetry (including all quoting poetry) is of a specific kind, outside of definitions that find movement only in linear narration.

The difficulty is in establishing what kind of movement it is. While reviewing Jean Cocteau's *Poesies* (1921), Pound contrasts narrative method to Cocteau's method of the city, leaving the reader no doubt as to which method Pound thinks more appropriate for the twentieth century:

> The life of a village is narrative; you have not been there three weeks before you know that in the revolution et cetera, and when M le Comte et cetera, and so forth. In a city the visual impressions succeed each other, overlap, overcross, they are "cinematographic," but they are not a simple linear sequence. They are often a flood of nouns without verbal relations. (110)

As Pound's statement shows, it is not that cinematographic (read "Modernist") art is static; indeed, the opposite is true. In the same manner by which Pound's phrases to describe the city are swiftly piled on top of each other, so the movement of cinematographic art is much swifter and more dazzling than that of village, narrative art. Pound's use of "flood" implies that the verbal relationships between impressions, so explicitly stated in the art of the village, must be inferred in the fast-moving art of the city. The relationships are present in the city, but their silence makes the movement bewildering in its speed—as *The Waste Land* was to show one year after this essay was published.

In 1930 Pound went on to argue that people no longer needed "to think in terms of monolinear logic, the sentence structure, subject, predicate, object, etc."; rather, "We are as capable or almost as capable as the biologist of thinking thoughts that join like spokes in a wheel-hub and that fuse in hyper-geometric amalgams" ("Epstein," 475). "Hyper-geometric amalgams" suggests a metaphor that only Pound could believe in, but throughout his career Pound did not argue that only his form of nonnarrative pyrotechnics was acceptable for Modern poetry. In his 1918 review of Marianne Moore, Pound had claimed that this oddly structured poetry (which at that point he was calling "logopoeia," "a dance of the intelligence among words and ideas" ["Marianne Moore," 424]) could be seen in poets as diverse as Moore, Eliot, Mina Loy, and Jules Laforgue, not just in the poets of "high," fragmented Modernism.[2]

Quoting poems clearly enunciate Modernism's sense of silent, swift movement. Modernist criticism, especially when read in light of quoting poems, describes a reading process in which the gaps (in an awkward, at times violent movement) present the world of the borrowing text, the world of the quoted text (including all its past uses), and some interaction between them. As does Donald Davie, Modernist theory asks readers to consider whether the relationship between fragments is a "poetic relationship" (227). Marjorie Perloff is a bit clearer on the form of this relationship. In her discussion of collage, Perloff argues that this art form "incorporates directly into the work an actual fragment of the referent, thus forcing the reader or viewer to consider the interplay between existing message or material and the new artistic composition that results from the graft" (*Futurist*, xviii).

In Modernist theory and in quoting poems this interplay is most accurately described as being that of "planes in relation." In *Gaudier-Brzeska* (1916) Pound uses this phrase to delineate how elements combine to form poetic structure:

One uses form as a musician uses sound. One does not imitate the wood dove, or at least one does not confine oneself to the imitation of wood-doves, one combines and arranges one's sound or one's forms into Bach fugues or into arrangements of colour, or into "planes in relation." (125)

"Planes in relation" suggests a nonmimetic art, an art that structures itself on self-contained sections separated by gaps, gaps that compel the different sections into relation with each other. "Planes in relation" further implies a movement whose values readers infer rather than explicitly find in the text. As seen in the quoting poem, the actual process is quite simple:

And in his waste house, detritus,
As it were the cast buttons of splendours,
The harbour of Martinique, drawn every house, and in detail.
Green shutters on half the houses,
Half the thing still unpainted.
                   " . . . sont
"l'in . . fan . . . terie KOH-
           lon-
           i-ale"
*voce tinnula*
"Ce sont les vieux Marsouins!"
He made it, feitz Marcebrus, the words and the music,
Uniform out for Peace Day

                                    (28.137–38)

The movement is a movement of planes because the various quotations and original text here necessarily function as discrete sections. The phrases "l'in . . fan . . . terie KOH- / lon- / i-ale" and "*voce tinnula*" must be read as separate chunks because they come from different languages and different contexts. *Voce tinnula,* originally from Catullus (Terrell 1:10), was used in canto 3 to lend resonance to the quoted biography of El Cid. Its previous uses both within and outside of *The Cantos* separate it here from the surrounding text. What it means for these separate phrases to move as "relations" is not clear, but it certainly implies a difference from linearity, a difference hinted at by silence. Perhaps "*voce tinnula*" functions as some sort of adjectival modifier of the phrase either preceding or following it; perhaps "l'infanterie" either is spoken by the person whose "waste house" is described earlier or it is a totally new direction in the poem. If Pound had clearly chosen to allude here, his interferences would begin to give such directions; at this quoting moment in the poem, however, the text does not explicitly define the relations between these discrete sections. They are simply "in relation"—no direction, no other characteristics of this movement are given.

To be sure, this process of discovering relationships among elements of a text can occur in all texts, for all texts have unstated interactions. But many Modernist texts are more jarring, and as such discourage lazy reading habits. As Reed Dasenbrock points out, readers must make connections between the gaps in Pound's poetry; given no syntactical and only traces of topical connections, readers must supply missing information (*Literary Vorticism,* 107). And quotations even further extend the sorts of information that one must provide, for in the quoting poem differing *textures* ensure that one can not partially obscure the gap by pretending all the planes in relation result from the same creative personality and operate by the same rules.

These unstated relations are integral both to the quoting poem and to Modernist theory. The concept of "relation" runs through all of Pound's Modernist theory; indeed, Reed Dasenbrock argues that Pound believes that the "essence of any situation is a relation" (*Literary Vorticism,* 108). In *Gaudier-Brzeska,* the book in which Pound initially presented the term "planes in relation," Pound also reprinted his Vorticist essay of 1914. Pound emphasizes energy, movement, and relation: "The image is not an idea. It is a radiant node or cluster; it is what I can, and must perforce, call a VORTEX, from which, and through which, and into which, ideas are constantly rushing" (92). In Fenollosa's theory, which Pound used as the basis for the ideogramic method, the created relation between two elements of the ideogram did not actually form part of the syntax, but sprang from it: "In this process of compounding, two things added together do not produce a third thing but suggest some fundamental relation between them" (*Instigations,* 364). This essay asserts the process that the quoting poem clearly demonstrates: the relation is inferred, added to the text by the reader.

Eliot's early essays also show that for both the poet and the reader poetic meaning only comes out of a relation of diverse elements. Eliot's platinum analogy in "Tradition and the Individual Talent" not only presents the supposedly impersonal poet, it discusses the creative pro-cess—how the mind "fuses" elements. Eliot argues that the poet "com-bine[s]" "a number of floating feelings ... to give us a new art emo-tion" (40, 41, 43). This process happens in all good poetry:

> When a poet's mind is perfectly equipped for its work, it is con-stantly amalgamating disparate experience; the ordinary man's expe-rience is chaotic, irregular, fragmentary. The latter falls in love, or reads Spinoza, and these two experiences have nothing to do with each other, or the noise of the typewriter or the smell of cooking; in the mind of the poet these experiences are always forming new wholes. ("Metaphysical," 64)

The importance of the events is not so much in the objects of percep-tion as in the relation between them, a point also argued by Fenollosa in his claim that "relations are more real and more important than the things which they relate" (*Instigations*, 377).[3]

In fact, all of quoting Modernism emphasizes relations. One early critic/painter, Amedée Ozenfant, argued that "eliminating all literal representation, the Picassos, the Braques, and the Archipenkos have shown again that which is essential in the works of a Claude Lorrain or a black man: *the optical relations of the MATERIAL*" (qtd. in Gam-well, 64). Gertrude Stein also noted the energy in the juxtaposition-induced relations of Cubist collage and trompe l'oeil, the realism in these objects "requir[ing] the rest of the picture to oppose itself to them" (*Picasso*, 23). In a letter to his dealer, Juan Gris wrote that if a prospective buyer of one of his collages "acquires the picture, he is free to replace the print [within the picture] by another one, even by his own portrait if he wishes. That can make it better or worse in the same way as the frame one picks out for a picture. It cannot harm the basic qualities of the picture" (qtd. in Wolfram, 19).[4]

This emphasis within quoting Modernism seems to mesh perfectly with the quoting poem, but it bumps awkwardly against ideas that appear to argue against movement, for Eliot's and Pound's critical writings can seem to bear out some version of static, instantaneous art. In describing Imagism, Pound defines an Image as "that which presents an intellectual and emotional complex in an instant of time" ("Few Don'ts," 200). Eliot argues in "Tradition and the Individual Talent" that the effect of canto 15 of the *Inferno*, "though *single as that of any work of art,* is obtained by considerable complexity of detail" (41, emphasis added). Further, the equation that Eliot presents in the objective correlative implies an instantaneous aesthetic moment ("Hamlet," 48), an instantaneousness he two years earlier (1917) had approvingly noted in reviewing Rimbaud: "The *Illuminations* attain their effect by an instant and simple impression, a unity all the more convincing because of the apparent incongruity of images" ("Borderline," 158).

These sorts of statements have led some critics (most notably Joseph Frank, with his idea of "spatial form") to argue that literary Modernism attempts some version of artistic instantaneousness: readers' dominant experience of some texts is not so much a process as it is a single moment that imposes a unity upon their reading experience. Critics have argued that since representation has historically been tied to temporal narrative, a nonlinearly structured work, based upon its own internal rules and uninterested in temporal representation, is therefore an instantaneous work.

How can my reading of quoting poems begin to reconcile these tendencies for both movement and instantaneousness in Modernist thought? I believe that movement described as some form of planes in relation dominates Modernist criticism, and that statements that seem to imply instantaneousness should be read against this backdrop. But even without this hierarchy, there are several reasons why statements about single impressions should be read suspiciously. First, such statements refer more to a formal unity than to a temporal or spatial unity. Second, such statements may not reflect what these poems actually achieve. In the same way in which these poets attempt a pure formalism and do not achieve it, these statements show quoting poets' *desire* for a formal unity in poems that, because of their disjunctions, strive against unity. The gaps in quoting poems separate the text into discrete elements that must be read separately. If in some way these works could be discussed as poems without any divisions (especially temporal or linear divisions), they must of necessity be unified. But Eliot doesn't *compress* language into meaning, he *dislocates* it. Finally, these poems may at times create an instantaneous *effect*. This effect occurs because at some level, in all quoting poems, silence is at the heart of the gap. When a poet in addition omits syntactic connections to underscore this silence, temporal and logical connections often also disappear. Thus, critics have not attempted to attach ideas of spatial form to Marianne Moore; they work on more syntactically disjunctive works:

I will show you fear in a handful of dust.
> *Frisch weht der Wind*
> *Der Heimat zu*
> *Mein Irisch Kind*
> *Wo weilest du?*

"You gave me hyacinths first a year ago;
"They called me the hyacinth girl."
—Yet when we came back, late, from the hyacinth garden,
Your arms full, and your hair wet, I could not
Speak, and my eyes failed, I was neither
Living nor dead, and I knew nothing,
Looking into the heart of light, the silence.
*Oed' und leer das Meer.*

(The Waste Land, 61–62)

More clearly than do the poems of Moore, this text ostensibly creates a spatial form because the missing syntax deprives us of narrative, temporal, and logical connectors. Syntax creates time. Because the silent gaps ensure that we do not know for certain which connection to use, it can seem that unstated connections don't exist.

But the silence does not imply spatial form, for these missing connectors must be inferred for the text to make sense. For the above text, here's how readers might complete that meaning: one could create a temporal relationship in which the quatrain from Wagner comes after a gap in time, but is spoken by the same speaker, the temporal space indicating a change in direction. One could create a logical relationship in which this Wagnerian question about crying is somehow answered by the hyacinth incident. Or, one could create a narrative relationship in which *"Oed' und leer das Meer"* is a distinct, omniscient comment on the situation that has just been presented. Quotation makes all this problem solving much more disconcerting, of course. So many of these problems could be cleared up if the role of the quoted text were more clearly presented, or if we could be more certain who was speaking the quotation.

All of these sorts of uncertain but inevitable reader-created completions give the text a fullness that restabilizes the text, and makes a temporal progression plausible. The reader-solved difficulties of quotations foreground reading as a strenuous process; in a review of Pound's *Poems 1918–21* Maxwell Bodenheim argued that Pound's "style demands a feverish mental agility on the part of his reader" (87). Instantaneous views of poetry do not take into account the reader's process as she stumbles through a difficult poem, attempting to understand structure, direction, and relationships among quotations. Reading Modern poetry, especially Modern quoting poetry, is a different process than earlier writing, but it is still a process, and the form of this process is important.[5]

As the preceding paragraph has begun to indicate, the relationships among textual elements in *The Cantos* and in any quoting poem are complex and are often so prominent that they dominate the structure of the quoting poem. Certainly, the amount and types of relation-structured reading in either quoting or nonquoting Modernist poems varies widely. At times it is so manageable as to be hardly noticeable:

> The apparition of these faces in the crowd;
> Petals on a wet, black bough.
>
> (Pound, Personae, 109)

The metaphor of "In a Station of the Metro" is a two-lined, two-termed equation. But the structure of this poem is not typical of Pound's poetry—its binary opposition is too neat. The same point might be made of most Modernist art, especially those works that quote, because their *many* unannounced differences from the borrowing work create a reverberating structural complexity that simple binary oppositions cannot contain. As Edward Foye points out, rather than being "systematic proto-structuralists interested in precise binary oppositions," Braque and Picasso were much more interested in the "free play" that arose from certain of their fixed concerns (58). In the quoting poem, quotations do not just oppose the new text in a single-directioned manner; they oppose it in terms of their supposed voice, original cultural function and status, ironic content, metrical form, and so on.

At the furthest extreme of this complexity readers can find Pound's *Cantos:*

> And then the phantom Rome,
>    marble narrow for seats
> "Si pulvis nullus" said Ovid,
> "Erit, nullum tamen excute."
> Then file and candles, e li mestiers ecoutes;

Scene for the battle only, but still scene,
Pennons and standards y cavals armatz

(7.24)

With Pound, the different languages, multiple voices, and unannounced changes in subject create complex interrelationships in which the interactions between amorousness, processions, and festivals only grudgingly outline a shadowy central purpose. This unclarity is muddled further because the relations are not all of the same sort. The beginning "And then" proposes a temporal progression from the material from Homer that has just preceded it. "Marble narrow for seats," as Carroll Terrell points out, alludes to Ovid's advice for successful seduction (1:29), to which the quotation that follows relates as a modulation. But this quotation begins a relationship different from that begun by the allusion that preceded it. The quotation is more clearly controlled by a central voice, someone who announces and manages the borrowed text: "said Ovid." The "Then" that follows the quotation reasserts the temporal relationship but modulates the text's subject to a religious procession that is situated in time by some words in Provençal that function as a quotation. The final quotation, from Bertrans de Born, modulates the text to a description of knights in springtime (Terrell 1:30). But its relationship to the borrowing text differs from those quotations that preceded it, for as an appositive it more smoothly fits into the poem's syntax, and it seems by that structure and its status as a foreign literary text to exist more clearly as an indicator of the speaker's cultural refinement. As this text shows, quotations complicate relations within the quoting poem by introducing a multiplicity of announced and unannounced terms on which to discuss relations among elements within the text: speakers, voices, temporal relations, reputations, canon formation, authority, and so forth.

Although they work toward ends differing from those of Pound's poetry, complex relations structure even Moore's poetry. In the passage quoted below, Moore's phrase "sophistication has, 'like an escalator,' 'cut the nerve of progress'" initially seems simple. After all, there is no syntactic disjunction. Unlike in Pound, the rhetorical argument is quite clear, and each quotation is a completed phrase. Yet although they fit smoothly into the syntactical progression of the poetry, the intrusive voices with which Moore sprinkles "People's Surroundings" create a complex structure of relations:

Here where the mind of this establishment has come to the
     conclusion
that it would be impossible to revolve about oneself too much,
sophistication has, "like an escalator," "cut the nerve of progress."
In these non-committal, personal-impersonal expressions of
     appearance,
the eye knows what to skip;
the physiognomy of conduct must not reveal the skeleton;
"a setting must not have the air of being one,"
yet with x-ray-like inquisitive intensity upon it, the surfaces go back;
                                                                              (80)

In contrast with the syntactic disunity that separates *The Canto*'s quota-
tions from the rest of the text, here syntactic unity indicates that the
contracted assumption in this poem is for a central poetic voice, and
disruption results when a new voice asserts itself. Further, the syntax
does not announce a new voice in the way that Pound announces Ovid
in the previous section. Yet even in Moore's poetry, when the quoted
phrases appear they have an alien stature, a stature that creates complex
relationships within the poem. The quotation marks announce a new
presence of dubious stature, while at the same time the smooth syntax
denies a new presence. Our noticing this relational incongruity struc-
tures our reading. Further, with phrases such as "in these non-commit-
tal, personal-impersonal expressions of appearance" and "'a setting
must not have the air of being one,'" the quoting text obliquely and
metaphorically refers to the quotations. Other phrases create more
problematic relations. With their explicit metaphors, how do the juxta-
posed phrases "like an escalator" and "cut the nerve of progress" relate
to the quoting text, to their original settings, and to each other? In
using these metaphors to relate to the new, quoting text, do readers
have to be nervous about violating whatever the original function of
these phrases might be?

These relationships also complicate the directions in which meanings
are produced. As Modernist criticism shows, relationships within the
Modern poem do not move smoothly forward; they point both forward
and backward. Eliot and Pound's relational language did not conceive
of the poem as solely a unidirectional, linear narrative. To use Eliot's
terms, the items within the aesthetic fusion (for example, within the
objective correlative) do not simply pile on top of each other in a

forward-moving, linear sequence. Pound's "hyper-geometric amal-
gams" suggests relations that could move both forward and backward.

The implications of this bidirectioned movement for the quoting
poem can be made quite clear. Wolfgang Iser argues that as we read
we divide a text into groups of related material, and that each textual
group either answers or negates the expectations of the previous textual
group, and creates expectations for the next (111–12). Quotations
heighten readers' awareness of this process by making problematic the
whole question of expectations. Quotations cause this reaction because
they have an unclear status. Although different quoting poems exploit
different uncertainties, all quoting poems create an unclear voice in
texts in which the relationships between moments of the poem are
silent, indicated by a gap. At the end of *The Waste Land* the phrase "*Le
Prince d'Aquitaine à la tour abolie*" is a quotation, and this change in
status from the surrounding text does not allow its relation with these
other elements to form part of a clear narrative. But this lack of a
narrative connection allows it to modify in a more open-ended way the
quotations immediately preceding and those following it. The quoted
phrases are so clearly separate from each other that some expectations
based on this separation *must* be created:

> I sat upon the shore
> Fishing, with the arid plain behind me
> Shall I at least set my lands in order?
> London Bridge is falling down falling down falling down
> *Poi s'ascose nel foco che gli affina*
> *Quando fiam uti chelidon*—O swallow swallow
> *Le Prince d'Aquitaine à la tour abolie*
> These fragments I have shored against my ruins
> Why then Ile fit you. Hieronymo's mad againe.
>
> (74–75)

The opening three lines about the Fisher King predispose readers to
accentuate motifs of regeneration and death when they reach "*Le Prince
d'Aquitaine à la tour abolie,*" thus creating a similar texture between
these two textual groupings. "*Le Prince*" reaches back to "London
Bridge," and makes more grandiloquent our reading of that phrase.
The two intervening lines, carrying a bulky load from their previous
contexts, are read in ways that best create a relationship with the lines

surrounding it. In their new context, these two lines from the *Purgato-rio* and the Philomela myth emphasize transgression, attempts at confession, and the failure of communication. The lines surrounding them, with their ruined monuments of civilization, seem to tie these flickers of missed connections to the fall of Western civilization and to hopes for regeneration or redemption.

Although the phrase *"Le Prince d'Aquitaine à la tour abolie"* can refer both backward and forward, it most clearly modifies those elements near it. All readers who attempt to create some meaning from this text decide where proximity no longer applies, and divide the poem into units. *"Le Prince d'Aquitaine à la tour abolie"* relates clearly to the following line, the image of ruin connecting the two. But its influence radically diminishes at "Why then Ile fit you," the changes in voice and topic presenting another of the poem's lurching beginnings. These two directions of relations allow quoting poetry to be considered in terms other than as an abstract narrative or as a propositional discourse, since both of these structures have difficulty functioning nonlinearly.

The relations in a quoting poem have complexities other than those created by direction. Since the gap is silent, readers need to base the relations they construct on some underlying principles, principles that account for the jarring interaction between quotation and new text. Readers must supply information to make the quoting text behave like a less disjunctive text—in effect, to give the text coherence. Therefore, in addition to noticing simply that a new world has been fused into the poem, readers attribute qualities to this new world; they attempt to discover its relevant stylistic and other values. This process is not random, for not all the values of the quotation initially seem equally useful in creating nondisjunctive meaning. Marianne Moore works with this discovery the most thoroughly. When "An Octopus" begins, it is clear that the "octopus" of the title is meant to create a metaphor for a glacier:

AN OCTOPUS
of ice. Deceptively reserved and flat,
it lies "in grandeur and in mass"
beneath a sea of shifting snow-dunes;
dots of cyclamen-red and maroon on its clearly defined pseudopodia
made of glass that will bend—a much needed invention—
comprising twenty-eight ice-fields from fifty to five hundred feet

thick,
of unimagined delicacy.

(96)

But as the poem continues, the quotations' most easily accessible qualities create confusion as to what the poem is about. They create confusion because the quotations increasingly seem to be redefining the poem's subject:

"Picking periwinkles from the cracks"
or killing prey with the concentric crushing rigour of the python,
it hovers forward "spider fashion
on its arms" misleadingly like lace;
its "ghostly pallor changing
to the green metallic tinge of an anemone-starred pool."
The fir-trees, in "the magnitude of their root systems,"
rise aloof from these manoeuvres "creepy to behold,"
austere specimens of our American royal families,
"each like the shadow of the one beside it.
The rock seems frail compared with their dark energy of life,"
its vermilion and onyx and manganese-blue interior expensiveness
left at the mercy of the weather;

(96)

Certainly, some qualities in these quotations, such as the sense of animation, are congenial to readers creating a nondisjunctive poem. But in the first few lines of this section of the poem, the quotations seem to be bending the octopus metaphor back upon itself, making it literal, and changing the poem's subject to that of an octopus. Moore adds to this confusion because in her notes to the poem she simply gives the titles of articles in which the quotations are found. No more specific context than that appears. The annotation "M. C. Carey: *London Graphic,* 25th August, 1923" does not clear up for readers which values of the "Picking periwinkle" phrase are most useful. (As it turns out, this article is indeed about octopi.) As Moore at times exploits quite thoroughly, this alien texture can at times be distracting.

Some other of the quotations' qualities are perhaps less confusing, but they certainly seem more explicitly tangential. "The magnitude of their root systems," Moore assures us, is from some work by John

42

Muir. The exact nature of the work is unimportant since the quotation seems to afford quite a smooth fit into the new poem. "Creepy to behold" creates a different slant on the problem. Although it initially referred to an octopus, here one could speculate on a variety of sources, including the National Parks brochure upon which much of this poem is based. What such a quotation does hint at is that its original subject matter is apparently not important.

So, in addition to their showing language's ability to be put to new uses, what are, for readers, the more useful values of these quotations? Here, as in any quoting poem, the most useful values relate to the rest of the poem by affirmation or negation (rather than by mere *difference*). In this poem Moore leans more toward affirmation than negation. One of the recurring values is the animated, animal-like activity that is found in both the quotations and the borrowing text. "Picking" and "spider fashion" affirm the values of Moore's original phrase "the concentric crushing rigour of the python." A spooky grandeur also is an underlying principle. Moore borrows phrases like "ghostly pallor," "creepy to behold," and "magnitude of their root systems" to affirm such qualities found in her own words like "hovers," and "rise aloof."

Such a close examination of the interrelations among the quotations of "An Octopus" changes how one reads this poem. For example, Bonnie Costello makes a similar point about how the poem hides its subject matter. Costello argues that confusion initially comes about because the subject of the poem is not named, and that the poem continues such deceptions: "We read 'an octopus of ice' and look for the resolution of terms, since an octopus is usually associated with fluid movement, ice with rigidity. Instead we are faced with another contrast in the opposite direction: the octopus seems 'reserved and flat,' stable, but lies 'beneath a sea of shifting snow dunes'" (82). More specifically addressing the possibilities of quotations, John Slatin argues that the quotations of "An Octopus" are "lenses" that slightly "distort" our vision as we read the poem, so that "in the course of the poem we see both the mountain and *the problem of seeing the mountain* from a number of different vantage points" (174). However, both critics stop short of the implications of the complex relations within the quoting poem. "An Octopus" has levels of confusion and distortion that can be addressed only when one examines the alienness of its quotations, and their complex relations to the new text. Quotations *inevitably* distort the subject matter of the new poem: they are in a new situation, and relate to the borrowing poem in ways idiosyncratic to their status as quotations. The confusion within the new text, then, comes from principles alien to the poem, and part of the aesthetic pleasure of reading this text comes from witnessing how the poet manipulates and relates all this material towards a single purpose.

If one is to use the texture of the quotation to full effect, most often a full awareness of the quotation's original context becomes more important than it usually is in Moore, and the quotation consequently complicates its relations with the quoting poem by being cited on one level as a cultural artifact. In such cases the source text often establishes values that affirm or negate those of the borrowing text. Such is the case when Cummings ends his poem "?" with a quotation and a cliché to poke fun at both popular celebrities and the disaffected attitude of the poem's speaker:

—Not
a bit of it,my dears merely the prime
minister of Siam in native

costume,who
emerging from a pissoir
enters abruptly Notre Dame (whereas
de gustibus non disputandum est
my lady is tired of That sort of thing

(243)

Here, knowledge of the quotation's original context is essential. It is equally essential—although used for quite different purposes—in *The Cantos*. Readers of *The Cantos* who know a lot about the Italian Renaissance can be much more complete in their uses of the Malatesta quotations than those whose knowledge is perfunctory. If one can grant the partial cooperation of the quoting text (something one cannot always do), the thoroughness and success of this discovery of values depends to a large part upon readers' cultural repertoire.

There are several other principles that complicate relations between quotation and borrowing text. Under the partial transformation of the new text the quotations sometimes partake in the traditional activities of allusions, especially satire, irony, and some cultural obeisance or granting of authority. Quotations raise problems of cultural authority so clearly and awkwardly because they do not have the overt imprint of the poet's voice upon them. But neither do they have their original function. The quotation can no longer function *exactly* as it did before. As Bakhtin argues for parody, to quote a text is to deny it its original status, and to turn its language into an image ("Prehistory," 43–45). As an image, the quotation *must* take on a new, complex function. But since neither the quoting poet nor the original author clearly takes responsibility for the quotation, a host of problems result. Is the quoting text and poet an equal of the quotation? A museum curator? A fawning courtier? Eliot's use of Verlaine's *Parsifal,* for example, raises these questions:

> O the moon shone bright on Mrs. Porter
> And on her daughter
> They wash their feet in soda water
> *Et O ces voix d'enfants, chantant dans la coupole!*
>
> Twit twit twit
> Jug jug jug jug jug jug jug
> So rudely forc'd
> Tereu

> (67–68)

The gaps between the quotation from Verlaine and the surrounding text complicate issues of authority in a way inaccessible to allusions. Verlaine's text has a history of cultural authority that the preceding bawdy song lacks, and Eliot wields this authority for his own purposes. But readers often sense several attitudes toward this and other "high art" texts Eliot borrows. One can simultaneously sense Eliot's reverence for the texture, for the sound of the foreign language; his demonstration to readers that he is aware of and is able effortlessly to use these texts; and perhaps his enjoyment both of the juxtaposition's startling humor and of being able to put this text to a use that Verlaine could not anticipate.

But the lack of syntactic connections dismantles any single-mindedness in Eliot's attitude and removes it to an irrecoverable distance. In this passage the gap between the quotation and surrounding text implies that the quotation is being used as an authority to satirize contemporary society. We at times unsafely assume that an unannounced gap between a borrowing text and a quotation from the canon necessarily implies respect toward the quotation and irony toward the world of the poem. Here, it is unclear how much Verlaine is implicated by the world of Mrs. Porter and her daughter. Because of such treatment of its quotations, *The Waste Land*'s cultural obeisance is always slightly askew, slightly ambiguous. In contrast to the poet's interference at the center of an allusion, a move that tends to make the cultural obeisance more clear, one of the characteristics of the Modern quoting poem is that it treats direct admiration for sources somewhat suspiciously. In the quoting poem's use of the quotation's authority, gaps subvert authority and complicate both the original function and the quoting poet's presence.

Other uses of relations are similarly complex. For example, among many other uses Moore juxtaposes the banal origin and ordinary function of the quotation in its original text with its aesthetic function in the new text:

> What stood
> Erect in you has withered. A
> little "palm-tree of turned wood"
> Informs your once spontaneous core in its
> Immutable production.
>
> ("Pedantic Literalist," 54)

Moore's notes to the poem tell us that the origin of the quoted text is Richard Baxter's *The Saints' Everlasting Rest* (128), a textual world more likely to direct readers to extracting paraphrasable meaning than to focusing upon what we often think of as aesthetic values. But traditionally aesthetic functions are inescapable once Moore through quotation marks designates these borrowed words as "poetry." The inauspicious phrase "palm-tree of turned wood" can be seen to have a nice balance of repeated frontal stops (the middle *t*'s and the beginning and ending *p* and *d*), a balance accentuated by the two complex nouns that are separated by a preposition. The phrase also takes on the status of metaphor; it follows the language of the borrowing text as it continues to apply to a human being the language of vegetable growth and animation. As Moore has pointed out in her poem "Poetry," this shifting function can help to erase the distinction between prose and poetry.

This banal/aesthetic contrasting relation also characterizes much of E. E. Cummings's poetic project. But Cummings typically has the banal quotation in its new, aesthetic context (the quoting poem) satirize the world, including the artistic presuppositions, of its old context:

> (Case in point
>
> if we are to believe these gently O sweetly
> melancholy trillers amid the thrillers
> these crepuscular violinists among my and your
> skyscrapers—Helen & Cleopatra were Just Too Lovely,
> The Snail's On The Thorn enter Morn and God's
> In His andsoforth
>
> do you get me?)
> ("POEM, OR BEAUTY HURTS MR. VINAL," 228)

The world of Browning's "The Snail's On The Thorn" seems stupidly naive in this new context—the original values don't fit. Through his use of capitalization, the "andsoforth," and the closing question, Cummings perhaps pedantically ensures that readers are aware of this misfit.

Never the most subtle of poets, Cummings yet shows in his quoting poems some idiosyncratic possibilities that the peculiar structure of quotations brings into a text. As it has for Moore, Eliot, and Pound, these possibilities within Cummings's quoting poems result from a single source: the gap that the quotation brings into the new text. In discussing the gaps of the quoting poem and the effect of this structure on the reading process, this chapter has used a recurring argument within Modernism to claim that the relations within the quoting poem are complex in a way peculiar to that genre. The next chapter again reworks some recurring issues in Modernist theory, showing how the quoting poem uses the activity just described to probe what it means for a borrowed voice to create new meanings, and how these new meanings are inevitably part of an aesthetics of crudity and difficulty.

CHAPTER 3

# The Shock of the Exact

> Let me indulge in the American
> habit of quotation
> —Ezra Pound to William Carlos Williams

## Making It New

Although with the ascendancy of New Criticism two quoting poems—
*The Cantos* and *The Waste Land*—had for several decades a hold on the
literary landscape that is hard to overstate, quoting poems in general
also met with repeated forms of resistance. Among these poems' first
readers, Harriet Monroe found *The Cantos* to be merely "clever"
("Pound," 214); for Louis Untermeyer, initially *The Waste Land* was
"cryptic in intention and . . . dismal in effect" (152); in a 1922 symposium
on Moore that might at best be described as mixed, Marion Strobel
grumbled about "the contortions of Miss Moore's well-developed
mind" (qtd. in Monroe, "Symposium"); and E. E. Kellett, writing of
the quoting in Cummings's *is 5*, groused, "As for its text, we are in the
position of the Ethiopian eunuch, except that the Philip rarely appears.
It quotes, but we know neither that it is quoting, nor whom it is
quoting from" (74).

While in a survey of criticism these sorts of attacks on the quoting
poems' obscurity are the most apparent (and take on issues that I
address in the second half of this chapter and in my discussion of
dramatic voice in the fourth chapter), a few critics began to probe an
issue that is more necessary as a first step to understanding the function-
ing of the quoting poem. Originality, a central term in all Modernist
poetics, presses most tellingly upon the quoting poem, for the first

49

quality of a quotation is not its difficulty, but the fact that it is a borrowing. Its words have existed before, sometimes centuries before, sometimes achieving great cultural resonance. Readers either know or construct a history for the poem's quotations; even in Moore's poetry, where at the most one might be able to assign a generic source for the quotation, quotations are never completely unknown artifacts. Quotation marks ensure that readers are aware of two struggling forces: the quotation's previous existence and something of the quoting poet's hold over the quotation. But the gaps in the more disjunctive quoting poems don't give readers a clear sense of the poet's allegiances to the quotations, and readers' ambivalences about the originality of the quoting poem is an ambivalence about these allegiances, about the poet's choice of and attitude towards the quotations; in short, an ambivalence about how the quoting poem's gaps function.

Certainly by the early 1920s questions of the originality of American poetry had been raised often, and along some clearly defined lines. Most notably, Ralph Waldo Emerson, raising the question recurringly in his essays, sets up a blunt opposition, the terms of which Modernism inherited, and which were redirected as a result of the quoting poem. In his *Journal,* Emerson states tersely, "I hate quotation. Tell me what you know" (110). The oppositions are clear: shared, old knowledge versus personal, new knowledge. No wonder some initial readers, particularly those who had a commitment to an indigenous, American art, balked at the quoting poem.[1]

The discussion of originality thus begins with concepts that seem easily resolvable. For example, in his appreciative 1922 review of *The Waste Land,* Edmund Wilson claims that the poem "confirms the opinion that we had begun gradually to cherish, that Mr Eliot, with all his limitations, is one of our only authentic poets." But Wilson's review also raises some ambivalences: though the poem is "simply one triumph after another," it lacks "structural unity," and readers can validly object that "there can be no room for original quality" in a poem that has so many references, allusions, and quotations (139, 142, 143). The poem's quotations, with the jarring relations they enact, contribute to structural disintegration. More important, the borrowings can so dominate that the borrowing voice is muffled; there is no sense of an *interaction* between old and new text that redefines the old texts. If something might sum up several influential reactions to the originality of quoting poets, it might be Gertrude Stein's pronouncement about Hemingway:

"he looks like a modern and he smells of the museums" (*Autobiography*, 204).

That, of course, is a damning quip, given how obsessed most Moderns were with originality and the new. Writers and artists associated with avant-garde movements culminating in Dada and Futurism become obsessed both with originality and with what attitude one should have to one's antecedents in order to achieve this originality. Marcel Duchamp painted a mustache on a copy of the *Mona Lisa*. Guillaume Apollinaire wrote in his analysis of Cubist painting that "you cannot carry around on your back the corpse of your father" (10). A writer like William Carlos Williams, applauding the conclusions this distrust of predecessors reached in the 1913 Armory Show in New York, naturally would distrust Eliot's and Pound's quoting poetry.

Predictably, Modernist quoters did not think they were carrying their fathers on their backs, and they were not convinced that originality and borrowings ought to oppose each other. In the first place, originality was a complicated concept for the quoting Moderns; it resonates most strongly in the work of Eliot and Pound, who use documents loaded with historical and cultural resonance, and who consequently form the focus for the first half of this chapter. As do many contemporary quoters, Ezra Pound thought it was impossible for a text to be absolutely new. In an October 1908 letter to Williams, Pound attacks unthinking uses of tradition and then presents a four-item list to instruct Williams in the "ultimate attainments of poesy." Included in one of the four items is this terse phrase: "Utter originality is of course out of the question" (6). Yet during the next twenty-five years all poets who began their careers of quoting thought they were creating a new form of poetry, and often attacked other contemporary writers for adding nothing to poetry that had not already been done. Employing a curious juxtaposition, in this same letter to Williams Pound both defended his own quoting and attacked derivative poetry:

> Why write what I can translate out of Renaissance Latin or crib from the sainted dead?
>     Here are a list of facts on which I and 90,000,000 other poets have spieled endlessly:
> 1.  Spring is a pleasant season. The flowers, etc. etc. sprout, bloom, etc. etc.
> 2.  Young man's fancy. Lightly, heavily, gaily, etc. etc.

3. Love, a delightsome tickling. Indefinable etc.
   A) By day, etc. etc. etc. B) By night, etc. etc. etc.
4. Trees, hills etc. are by a provident nature arranged diversely, in diverse places.
5. Winds, clouds, rains, etc. flop thru and over 'em.

(4)

With this insistence upon both the impossibility of utter originality and the necessity for the new, Pound assured Harriet Monroe that Eliot was the only American who had "actually trained himself *and* modernized himself *on his own*" (*Letters,* 40). For Pound, "trained" pointed to Eliot's awareness of and some subservience to tradition; "modernized" pointed to the new, with the italicized "on his own" certifying that this modernizing was personally authentic and original. Thus, a few years later Pound could write to Eliot that the quoting *Waste Land* was a triumph: "Complimenti, you bitch. I am wracked by the seven jealousies" (*Letters,* 169).

Pound's seeming to believe that a thing can be new without being original shows a complex attitude to originality, but a complexity that isn't formally worked out in his own writing. While never a systematizer, Pound is not alone in his ad hoc approach to originality—something that, taken with his many quips about newness, perhaps suggests the term's resonance rather than its unimportance. It is not surprising, then, that with this unsystematic approach the public arguments for and against the originality of the quoting poem deflect off each other rather than resolve anything. But these arguments' obliquity to each other is itself instructive, and suggests that the reasons for the obliquity might be found in considering what definitions of originality writers on both sides of the argument used, and what originality might look like in each case.

The most systematic critic of Eliot's and Pound's quoting poems is William Carlos Williams, primarily because his interaction with these writers always centered around ideas central to their quoting and originality. Williams, twenty-five years after the first outburst of quoting poems, would present *Paterson* as his poetic reply to these poems and their quoting. His first quotation in the body of the poem a quotation of himself, Williams in his epigraph presented his quoting poem as "a reply to Greek and Latin with the bare hands." While his often splenetic reactions to Eliot's quoting are the most cited, most of Williams's systematic excursions are both quite different from these outbursts and remarkably similar. They are different in that Williams reserves his virulence for Eliot, who epitomized the most irritating trend in Modern letters. But Williams's single-directioned attack on Eliot also typifies a trend in Williams's critical writing, for Williams treated many writers as illustrations of individual paradigms, with all the useful simplification that might entail. When Williams writes about Poe, for example, he does not give a very balanced reading of that writer, but he does present an excellent discourse on what originality might mean in an American context. Williams's discussions on quoting and originality can be found in three sites, each centered around an individual: his essay on Poe in *In the American Grain* (1925); various essays on and letters to Ezra Pound, written primarily during the 1930s; and a lengthy pedagogic "Open Letter" to Kay Boyle, written in 1931.[2]

As a prelude, consider Williams's more spectacular reactions, his reactions to Eliot. A few years before the publication of *The Waste Land*, Williams, frustrated over the setback he imagined the publication of "Prufrock" gave to his concerns for a new American poetry, argued that these new looking poems actually smelled musty:

> But our prize poems are especially to be damned not because of superficial bad workmanship, but because they are rehash, repetition—just as Eliot's more exquisite work is rehash, repetition in another way of Verlaine, Baudelaire, Maeterlinck—conscious or unconscious—just as there were Pound's early paraphrases from Yeats and his constant later cribbing from the Renaissance, Provence and the modern French: Men content with the connotations of their masters.
>
> It is convenient to have fixed standards of comparison: All antiquity! And there is always some everlasting Polonius of Kensington forever to rate highly his eternal Eliot. It is because Eliot is a subtle conformist. It tickles the palate of this archbishop of procurers to a lecherous antiquity to hold up Prufrock as a New World type. Prufrock, the nibbler at sophistication, endemic in every capital, the not quite (because he refuses to turn his back), is "the soul of the modern land," the United States! (*Kora*, 24)

For pre-*Paterson* Williams, at least, the Modernist tradition beginning in the allusive "Prufrock" and peaking in the quoting poem was a swindle: just old wine in new wineskins. The publication of *The Waste Land* exacerbated these issues. Williams called the poem "the great catastrophe to our letters . . . which gave the poem back to the academics" (*Autobiography*, 146).

Williams's virulence is puzzling, but the issue he addresses has a more sophisticated rationale than what appears here. The paradigm behind his distrust of Eliot is clarified in Williams's discussions of the "local." Consider the enigmatic parenthetical claim that Prufrock "refuses to turn his back": it is a metaphor that Williams was to use in another place, and with reference to another figure from American literature. In constructing his myth of America in *In the American Grain*, Williams sees Poe as his hero:

> The difficulty is in holding the mind down to the point of seeing the *beginning* difference between Poe and the rest. One cannot expect to see as wide a gap between him and the others as exists between the Greek and the Chinese. It is only in the conception of a *possibility* that he is most distinguished. His greatness is that he turned his back and faced inland, to originality, with the identical gesture of a Boone.
>
> And for *that* reason he is unrecognized. Americans have never recognized themselves. How can they? It is impossible until someone invent the ORIGINAL terms. As long as we are content to be called by somebody else's terms, we are incapable of being anything but our own dupes. (226)

In using the less-than-expected example of Poe (why not Whitman? Emerson?), Williams goes through many of the rhetorical moves that characterize his argument about originality: for Americans, originality is found in the land and away from Europe; this originality isn't necessarily expressed as a content, but as a gesture; the writer who performs this gesture is unrecognized, unrecognized because America doesn't have its own terms, but continues to use the terms of another culture.

The term holding all these assertions together is the local. In his lengthy letter to Kay Boyle Williams would claim that "everything we know is a local virtue" (*Letters*, 130). Obviously, the local is a place and a time—for Williams, it was the modern United States, of which he claimed to T. C. Wilson that "no region on earth has a tradition more vital to modern letters" (*Letters*, 141). Eliot's problem was that he believed that poetry "increases in virtue as it is removed from contact with a vulgar world" (qtd. in Mariani, 334). In contrast, to Boyle Williams made his stance as clear as it ever was throughout his life: "Either I build here or there will be no building as far as I am concerned" (132–33).

This local, however, is not presented as an individual's choosing of what is the relevant data, but more as an objective reporting:

> To be democratic, local (in the sense of being attached with integrity to actual experience) Stein, or any other artist, must for subtlety ascend to a plane of almost abstract design to keep alive. . . . Yet what actually impinges on the senses must be rendered as it appears, by use of which, only, and under which, untouched, the significance has to be disclosed. It is one of the major problems of the artist. ("Work of Stein," 351–52)

Williams would call for the epic poem as "newspaper," which would have "facts, facts, facts, tearing into us to blast away our stinking flesh of news. Bullets" (qtd. in Weaver, 120). For Williams, writing about Pound's *Cantos,* this objectivity, this move "away from the word as a symbol toward the word as reality" ("Excerpts," 107) was central to contemporary writing. While Eliot (for reasons presented later in this chapter and in chapter 4) clearly did not meet this criterion, and while Williams never claims that Pound adequately uses the local, Williams does argue that in Pound's writing "the word has been used in its plain sense to represent a thing—remaining thus loose in its context—not gummy—(when at its best)—an objective unit in the design—but alive" ("Excerpts," 111). In the work of a truer artist than Pound, such objectivity, when grounded in the local, would lead beyond the local to a universal understanding. In his searching for an artist who could do this, Williams found the photographer Walker Evans, for whose work Williams would claim, "It is the particularization of the universal that is important" ("Sermon," 283). Poe also did it, for Poe, "being thoroughly local in origin, has some chance of being universal in application" (*American Grain,* 222). Williams would argue that the poet must "write particularly, as a physician works, upon a patient, upon the thing before him, in the particular to discover the universal. John Dewey had said (I discovered it quite by chance), 'The local is the only universal, upon that all art builds'" (*Autobiography,* 391).

The last move that Williams makes in his argument for the local and for originality is an awkward one, being tied up with Williams's discussions of a new line, but it is essential to understanding his objections to many quoting poems. In the quotation from Poe used at the beginning of this chapter, Williams called for someone to "invent the ORIGINAL terms. As long as we are content to be called by somebody else's terms, we are incapable of being anything but our own dupes." The "terms" for Williams are a process, the process by which the local (especially speech) gets transformed into art. "Terms" implies that the local is not just a work made up of local materials, for then Hawthorne would be the great American author, not Poe: "Whereas Hawthorne, in his tales, by doing what everyone else in France, England, Germany was doing *for his own milieu*, is no more than copying their *method* with another setting; does not ORIGINATE; has not a *beginning* literature at heart that must establish its own rules, own framework,—Poe has realized by adopting a more elevated mien" (*American Grain*, 226, 229). Poe's work shows that these terms come from more than subject matter: "By avoiding, of necessity, the fat country itself for its expression; to originate a style that does spring from the local conditions, not of trees and mountains, but of the 'soul'—here starved, stricken by loss of liberty, ready to die—he is *forced in certain directions for his subjects*" (*American Grain*, 227).

As Williams was to argue in connection with Gertrude Stein, the right terms are both moral and technical ("1 Pound Stein," 163), and they have to do with the sound of the American language, and how that sound might be measured in a new prosody. Much more frequently than he argues that the writer finds the universalizing local in subject matter, Williams argues that the writer finds the local in speech. To make speech local, the necessary prerequisite is to argue that there isn't a single form of the English language, but to insist, as Williams often did, that different English-speaking localities have different languages. A writer's words have to be near at hand; two years before the publication of *Paterson* book 1 Williams would argue that "when a man makes a poem, makes it mind you, he takes words as he finds them interrelated about him and composes them—without distortion which would mar their exact significances—into an intense expression of his perceptions and ardors that they may constitute a revelation in the speech that he uses" ("Author's Introduction," 54). Thus, Williams would write to Boyle: "A minimum of present new knowledge seems to be this: there can no longer be serious work in poetry written in 'poetic' diction. It is a contortion of speech to conform to a rigidity of line. It is in the newness of a live speech that the new line exists undiscovered. To go back is to deny the first opportunity for invention which exists. Speech is the fountain of the line into which the pollutions of a poetic manner and inverted phrasing should never again be permitted to drain" (*Letters*, 134).

The right terms allow one, then, not just to use new things, but to use the old with a fresh purpose, as did Poe, who "was willing to go down and wrestle with its [America's] conditions, using every tool France, England, Greece could give him—but to use them to original purpose" (*American Grain*, 225–26). Williams thought Pound came half way. According to Williams Pound also attempted to relate the present to the past in his quoting poem: "As to the Greek quotations— knowing no Greek—I presume they mean something, probably something pertinent to the text—and that the author knows what they mean. . . . But in all salient places—Pound has clarified his out-land insertions with reasonable consistency. They are no particular matter save that they say, There were other times like ours—at the back of it all" ("Excerpts," 106). Williams consequently could argue that the language of Pound's *Cantos* lives, as he did to James Laughlin: "It lives; even such unpromising cataloguing as his *Cantos* of the Chinese kings, princes and other rulers do live and become affecting under his treatment. It is the language and the language only that makes this true" (*Letters*, 191). But yet for Williams the work of Pound falls short: "So far I believe that Pound's line in his *Cantos*—there is something *like* what we shall achieve. Pound in his mould, a medieval inspiration, patterned on a substitution of medieval simulacra for a possible, not yet extant modern and living material, has made a pre-composition for us. Something which when later (perhaps) packed and realized in living, breathing stuff will (in its changed form) be the thing" (*Letters*, 135 [to Kay Boyle]).

Thus, as implied in the suggestion that Pound's work might present a *future* model, quotation has its dangers. To Kay Boyle, Williams would grumble that Pound was teaching the modern language "classic dancing" (132); in a review of Pound, he would argue that Pound's poetry "is patterned *still* after classic meters and so does often deform the natural order—though little and to a modified degree only (nor is his practice without advantages as a method). Pound does very definitely intend a modern speech—but wishes to save the excellences (well-worked-out forms) of the old, so leans to it overmuch" ("Excerpts," 107). Pound's difficulties are magnified in the work of Eliot, most spectacularly in his quoting poem, which would exacerbate things since it would copy both sound and sense: "The forced timing of verse after antique patterns wearies us even more and seduces thought even more disastrously—as in Eliot's work. But a new time that catches thought as it lags and swings it up into the attention will be read, will be read (by those interested)" (*Letters,* 136). To Jean Starr Untermeyer, Williams would write: "Men like Eliot and Pound and many lesser examples have run away from the elementary necessity for differentiating the two prosodies [British, and an as-yet-to-be-found American prosody]. They never got to know the problem. They avoided it" (270). In a special issue of the *Briarcliff Quarterly* dedicated to the work of Williams, Williams argued that Pound "left the States under the assumption that it was mind that fertilizes mind, that the mere environment is just putty" ("Australian," 205). For Williams this was a dangerous belief, ultimately leading writers like Pound and Eliot to be "translators," and dangerous ones at that:

> The forms of the past, no matter how cultivated, will inevitably carry over from the past much of the social, political and economic complexion of the past. And I insist that those who cling basically to those forms wish in their hearts for political, social and economic autocracy. They think in terms of the direct descent of great minds, they do not think in terms of genius arising from great movements of the people—or the degeneracy of the people, as known in the past. ("Australian," 207)

Because of these political consequences that were often the result of quoting old forms, Williams did not trust Eliot's relationship with Marvell to have the sense of liberation found in Duchamp's reworking of the *Mona Lisa,* for Eliot was not changing the terms to fit Modern America.

Why do quoting poets and Williams come to different conclusions about the possibilities for originality in the quoting poem? Perhaps more pressing, since both quoting poets and Williams believed that modern times demanded modern forms, and that it was possible to transform preexisting materials, why did Williams talk right past Eliot and Pound, and why weren't Eliot and Pound always listening? After all, there are points of contact that suggest this might have been a fruitful discussion. Both sides of the discussion believe in transformation; they both believe in the concrete; they both believe that art must become universal. But they begin with such different terms; to make Williams's *objections* to Pound and Eliot clear I have to start with Williams's peroration in his argument for the value of the local in art. According to Williams, that these expatriate quoters didn't transform their quotations is their key problem, and it is displayed most specifically in their quotations. (Williams begins his discussion of proper American work with ideas of the local, not transformation, the reasons for which I will discuss later). Behind this inital assertion lurk Williams's reasons: they didn't invent new terms, they weren't rooted in a specific place and time (Eliot), or, at least, the right place and time. For Williams, who did not object to quoting per se, Eliot and Pound fall into this trap: because they repeat the terms of the quotation's world, they tend to repeat the quotation's original function.

But Eliot and Pound begin their discussions of transformation with an idea of and preference for the universal rather than the particular and local. While Williams did grumble about these writers' refusal to use the American local, neither he nor Pound discussed the relationships between these opposing coupled terms: local/transformation and universal/transformation. Thus, although these terms form the basic split between them and Williams, as they are structured here these are not the terms that drove the historical argument between Pound and Williams. They argued about whether or not transformation existed in these poems; they argued about the value of the local versus the universal; but they did not argue about how their differing positions on the latter functioned as their premises for their argument about the possibility of transformation. As a result, they talked past each other.

Pound's emphasis on the universal implies that the disparate objects (often both historically and culturally disparate) of the quoting poem must relate to each other; they must be translatable. Eliot and Pound moved to a formal concept like *pattern* as the central term to support their arguments about translatability and originality. For these quoting Moderns, users of old texts for a new and epic purpose, the central term is pattern, not local. *Local* does not as easily believe that details are translatable, while a belief in pattern leads to a view of history as synchronous, and of the quotation also participating in the artwork's autonomy.

Because Eliot and Pound begin with an assumption of a universal pattern that gives meaning to widely dispersed local details (and not first with the sense of the particulars of a locality), their view of history takes on some idiosyncratic characteristics. My earlier quarrel with Joseph Frank leads me naturally to posit for these quoting Moderns a view of history something like planes in relation, thus paralleling the move that Frank makes from his conclusions about spatial form to a synchronous view of history (59–60). The best version I have discovered is in Dasenbrock's *Literary Vorticism,* which argues that Pound, Eliot, and Joyce imposed a pattern on history: for these writers, history "is a pattern, not a line" (144; see also his *Imitating the Italians*). For these writers the past in a narrative, chronological sense is not interesting; what is interesting is the past as pattern, a pattern that transcends the local, a pattern that is sometimes thought of as always having been out there, at other times thought of as having been just imposed by the quoting poet. Eliot claims that such a resituating of the past allows for originality since it "makes a writer most acutely conscious of his place in time, of his own contemporaneity" ("Tradition," 38).

This patterning of tradition creates a formalist, atemporal version of originality. As Rosalind Krauss argues in a discussion of Picasso, Modernism's extensive use of the past "allows for the rewriting of succession (diachrony) as system (synchrony), thereby producing the ahistorical object" (92–93). "System" (or patterned) art argues that the dominant relations in the quoting artwork are not ones of temporality. According to Pound and Eliot, by asserting the patterned character of art, quoting artists removed the mustiness from earlier writing and claimed their own originality (by discovering the pattern and putting it in a new context) while they were most deeply steeped in the past. If one can expunge the sense of pastness from the past (by removing it and one's own writing from claims for the local), one can skirt Williams's objections. Relations can now take on new, different forms, generally based on formal or rhetorical characteristics.[3]

Quoting poets cannot, of course, remove the past entirely; there is primacy in this patterning of history. But by knowing how to create patterns of urgent use for the twentieth century, some quoting poets claimed to achieve originality. Eliot could argue that "the most individual parts of [a poet's] work may be those in which the dead poets, his ancestors, assert their immortality most vigorously" ("Tradition," 38). Approvingly quoting T. S. Eliot, Marianne Moore commented that the "master-quality" of *The Cantos* was its "concentrating the past on the present" ("Cantos," 272); Pound at one point argues that "works of art beget works of art" ("Status Rerum," 125). The converse is equally true: contemporary art allows us to see with new eyes the art of the past. Picasso points out that

> to me there is no past or future in art. If a work of art cannot live always in the present it must not be considered at all. The art of the Greeks, of the Egyptians, of the great painters who lived in other times, is not an art of the past; perhaps it is more alive today than it ever was. (qtd. in Barr, 270–71)[4]

Several identifying features of patterned art encourage *quoting* as a form of expressing the new. First, if the past and the present are part of a single pattern, it is only a small step to include them both in the same work of art, for patterning removes some awkward differences between quoting and quoted text. Second, as J. Hillis Miller points out, the notion of a collective personality that this sense of a pattern implies is also a rationale for quotation. Eliot, for example, expanded the boundaries of his self to encompass all history (177). Finally, Modernist writers' rethinking of history and their consequent emphasis upon the autonomy of the art object allows for two things. It allows both for the quotation to have some autonomy from its previous uses and for the quoting work by itself to create its own rules for producing meaning, rules to some degree independent of the quotation's original uses.

This emphasis upon the artwork's autonomy and the poet's discovering of a pattern leads to anachronistic originality: the borrowed object can be put to radically new uses. For many quoting Moderns the idea of anachronistic originality became an energizing force. Picasso's African masks were put to uses alien to their original ceremonial functions. Satie's airplane propellors and typewriters choreographed a ballet. Cummings's quotations, taken out of their original patriotic or mercantile contexts, subvert their original contexts. The radicality of some of these changes suggested a similar metaphor for two quoting writers. Eliot would argue that "immature poets imitate; mature poets steal"

("Massinger," 125), and Marianne Moore would assert that a "good stealer is *ipso facto* a good inventor" (Moore Archive, 1250/1, 118).

As the metaphor of theft might suggest, such anachronistic borrowing was not always well received, and, as the reaction to the 1984 Museum of Modern Art exhibit "Primitivism in Twentieth-Century Art: Affinity of the Tribal and the Modern" demonstrates, it continues to be a problem in assessing Modernism. Pound encountered such a reaction to the following lines from his "Homage to Sextus Propertius":

> My vote coming from the temple of Phoebus in Lycia, at Patara,
> And in the mean time my songs will travel,
> And the devirginated young ladies will enjoy them when they have
>    got over their strangeness,
>                        * * *
> My orchards do not lie level and wide
>                as the forest of Phaecia,
>                the luxurious and Ionian,
> Nor are my caverns stuffed stiff with a Marcian vintage,
> My cellar does not date from Numa Pompilius,
> Nor bristle with wine jars,
> Nor is it equipped with a frigidaire patent;
>
>                                          (208–9)

"Devirginated young ladies" and "frigidaire patent": these sorts of transformations drove academic critics wild, and for reasons opposing those of Williams. They criticized Pound not because he was repeating Propertius, but because he was using him in a way Propertius could never have intended. In discussing the last few lines of the above quotation, W. G. Hale of the University of Chicago offered the following criticism:

> Mr. Pound seems to have taken *liquor* as spirituous. He must then have thought of age as appropriate, and so have interpreted *Marcius* as referring to the legendary King Ancus Marcius; after which it was easy to add another legendary King, Numa Pompilius. The result is three lines, all wrong, and the last two pure padding. (157)

The triumph of the high Modern quoting poem ensured that Hale's "all wrong" was to disappear until fairly recently, when it has reappeared, but with a different sort of moral force than Hale used.

Williams's objections to anachronism are perhaps closer to Postmodernism than they are to W. G. Hale. For Williams, anachronism doesn't violate the integrity of the past; it violates the integrity of the local. This objection ties together Williams's strenuous assertions both for transformation and for "facts." Williams wants facts so much because he doesn't want anachronism and things being translated too easily. Watching Williams closely, one might sense some difficulties in his theorizing at this point. Williams had called for the poem as fact, and he also calls for things (facts) to be put to new uses, a move that must mean they are no longer the same facts that they once were. In my reading of Williams, I have found a two-step analysis to be most useful. On the one hand, Williams does believe that there are things in the poem that might be called facts—these particularly show up in his earlier work, and tend to be accurate descriptions of objects, and the accurate transcription of American speech rhythms. As his career moves closer to *Paterson,* his poetry more often shows things from the American scene that are put to new uses (the newspaper accounts in *Paterson,* for example). By their proper transformation these things also become facts, or, at least, metaphorical pointings to the facts. This is crucial for understanding the quoting poem and its claims to originality: if things are put to a new purpose they de facto are not quotations anymore. *Transformation,* however, is a term that applies primarily to material from outside being transferred to the local. The local itself is not transformed. In defining his terms and his theory Williams never calls his quotations in *Paterson* "quotations"; they are always "prose" or "facts." Williams thus has a sense that one local is better for a poet than are some others; Pound and Eliot don't believe this. For Williams, Eliot's problem, and Pound's at times, was that in his denigrating the local in favor of the universal he did not accomplish this transformation. He simply quoted.[5]

Modernist quoters (including writers like Moore and Cummings, who did not work with historically weighty documents in the way that Eliot and Pound did) found "transformation," free of every commitment but the commitment to universality, to be the most useful category to apply to their poems, especially when quotation marks presented the borrowed phrases as precise duplications. According to Eliot, only totally new uses for the quotation produce good art:

One of the surest of tests [of a poet's quality] is the way in which a poet borrows. Immature poets imitate; mature poets steal; bad poets deface what they take, and good poets make it into something better, or at least something different. The good poet welds his theft into a whole of feeling which is unique, utterly different from that from which it was torn; the bad poet throws it into something which has no cohesion. ("Massinger," 125)[6]

Here, "imitate" is opposed to "steal." Imitation results in works that have "no cohesion," while stealing results in works that are "unique, utterly different" from their sources. These new and alive works are never quite the same again. Pound's phrase "make it new," a dictum repeated throughout *The Cantos,* acquires resonance—the antecedent for "it" is not necessarily poetry as a craft, but Pound's version of the past poetic/political tradition. Even for the quoting poem, the sine qua non is difference, originality, but by a very different route, and with very different consequences than those proposed by Williams.

### Creating a Canon

What does this originality look like? To believers in radical transformation, writers for whom the local is not a primary issue, the materials that comprise this originality may seem like a secondary issue. Yet this is where I need to begin, for the choice of materials, in interaction with the quoting poem, reveals something: at times a recurring texture (Moore and Cummings), at times an ideology that might be slightly separate from a texture (Pound and Eliot), and at times a content and texture inextricably linked (Cummings).

Originality develops on several levels, in ways that specifically develop the idiosyncratic differences among these quoting poets. As this century has discovered for photography, duplication need not stymie originality. At the most primary level, for both the quoting poet and the photographer, selection of subject matter leads to originality.[7] Selection leads to originality on two levels: first, selection puts the borrowing into a new context and causes it to engage in new interactions. I will examine the form of those interactions later in this chapter. Second, for each poet the selections and the uses to which they are put are quite predictable, but predictable because of habitual moves in the quoting poet's transforming control, not because the quotation repeats its original function.

Each quoting writer repeatedly returns to an idiosyncratic canon of sources, consequently shaping in similar ways the interactions between quotations and new text. Thus, Pound characteristically borrows from literature, historical sources, and those texts concerned with ethics. He avoids syntactic connections and puts these sources together in surprising configurations to give us his version of urgent news in the past and present. Eliot culls his quotations from a more mainstream literature than does Pound. Since we have a history of reading these sources, the more recognizable *cultural authority* of these quotations (I am not implying that the individual sources themselves are always more recognizable) makes their interaction with the borrowing text seemingly easier to recognize than such interactions are in Pound. Cummings uses instantly recognizable sources from popular culture. The strong lyric voice he employs consistently overrides the disruptive tendencies and redirects the earlier functions of the borrowed texts. Moore turns to journalism and to other kinds of texts for which (in her poetry) recognition of the original context is usually unimportant. She constructs a poetry with an alien quality at its center, a quality that makes strong assertions of ego seem out of place. In allowing recurring interactions, each canon forms part of an author's originality; Dante and the uses to which he is put are as foreign to Moore as an opaque insistence upon feature articles is to Eliot.

As part of the quoting poem's originality, those recurring interactions with borrowed texts establish the cultural status of those borrowings. As Reed Dasenbrock (and before him, Williams) points out for Ezra Pound, choosing a section of the past to write about confers importance on it (*Literary Vorticism*, 106). The use of the past in the present implies some usefulness in and dependence upon the past. This dependence does not necessarily have to be respectful, but it often is. Quoting an elite tradition often puffs up the quoter, showing him to be part of a select club that knows the argot of educated poetry. Eliot's quoting at times has this tone, while it simultaneously resurrects texts to show their relevance in defining his modern wasteland.

Less exclusively literary in his quoting, Pound is also more obviously up front about the political importance of his quoted texts. Philip Furia points out in *Pound's Cantos Declassified* that canon formation is essential for Pound's quoting of documents. Pound attempts to erase the blackout of history—texts that have been suppressed for the dangerous truths they contain. As Furia also argues, Pound is interested in textual transmission, how important texts have almost been lost but for some translation, which in turn has almost been lost. Consider, for example, the first canto, which uses Anglo-Saxon rhythms as it translates a translation of a passage from the *Odyssey,* a passage that Homer in turn borrowed from an earlier story. When Pound somewhat pedantically identifies for readers his borrowing, he shows that his establishing a canon of sources is not slavish imitation of masters, it is a salvage operation:

> Lie quiet Divus. I mean, that is Andreas Divus,
> In officina Wecheli, 1538, out of Homer.

(5)

Not primarily concerned with their relation to past literary history, Moore and Cummings do not fit as neatly into the concerns just analyzed as do Pound and Eliot. Their selection of a canon and its structure in their poetry takes on different, but equally original forms. Although it happens also with Eliot's quoting of dance-hall songs and Pound's use of documents, Moore and Cummings *exclusively* use their canons of quotations to expand the subject matter of poetry, not to promote individual texts: Moore expanded poetry to include what she in "Poetry" called "business documents and school books" (*Selected Poems,* 52); Cummings, to include popular culture. In effect, Cummings's directed satire, aimed at the quotations' contemporary speakers, creates a relationship between quotation and borrowing text that argues that these quotations are important enough to attract abuse; while Moore's poetry, by including feature articles and advertisements, undermines usual concepts of what are fit materials for poetic expression.

Indeed, Moore's poetry uses a quotation to argue that it is not valid "to discriminate against 'business documents and // school books'; all these phenomena are important" (52). The idiosyncrasy of her canon formation, directed at opening the larger literary canon to new classes of expression, contrasts to Pound's desire that certain individual texts achieve dogmatic importance. Not a poet to hector readers to man the barricades, Moore's involvement with the world is highly personal. In an interview with Donald Hall, Moore asserts, "If you are charmed by an author, I think it's a very strange and invalid imagination that doesn't long to share it. Somebody else should read it, don't you think?" (260). Moore shares with readers individual moments of texts, and in so doing makes a point about the status of all texts.

In addition, Moore's canon formation causes a self-expression different from that of the other poets. Because Moore primarily uses quotations contemporaneous with the poem she is creating (or, at least, the temporal differences from the quoting text are not important), because she doesn't heavily depend on contrasting the quotation's original rhetorical function with its function in its new setting, and because these quotations only marginally attempt to impinge on the social world of the reader, Moore's poems, much more than those of Cummings, Pound, and Eliot, only tangentially relate to the reader's political world.[8]

Directing her canon formation to a class of documents, eschewing other political results of her poetry, and hiding her transformations of the quotation, Moore is the most cavalier about her own originality in her poetry. For example, she calls her poem "Marriage" "a little anthology of statements that took my fancy" ("Foreword," xv). As does her previous statement about being "charmed" by an author, this phrase has overtones of a highly personal reaction, and it creates substantial interpretive difficulties. For the author of a collection of essays disarmingly titled *Predilections,* is "fancy" an aesthetic principle? Conceptual? Is it based upon personal reminiscence? The quotation's idiosyncratic appeal? "Marriage" itself seems to give no clear answers:

> he has prophesied correctly—
> the industrious waterfall,
> "the speedy stream
> which violently bears all before it,
> at one time silent as the air
> and now as powerful as the wind."
> "Treading chasms
> on the uncertain footing of a spear,"
> forgetting that there is in woman
> a quality of mind
> which as an instinctive manifestation
> is unsafe,
> he goes on speaking
> in a formal customary strain,

of "past states, the present state,
seals, promises,
the evil one suffered,
the good one enjoys,
hell, heaven,
everything convenient
to promote one's joy."

(86)

As a concept that seems to give a single reason for the choice of individual quotations, "fancy" does not have stability throughout this passage. In this section of "Marriage," the last quotation seems to have been chosen for its rhetorical balance of contrasts and repetitions, and its climactic list structure. Its rhetorical flourishes also show this quotation's transparent conceptual usefulness. By contrast, the waterfall quotation, like that of the spear, seems useful for its ability to interact with the quoting text to create a metaphor. But there is little more to be said for these two quotations—they seem to exploit neither rhythm nor other sound patterns. None of these quotations (to my mind) seize the imagination as memorable lines of poetry in which all of these sorts of functions fuse, but such an aesthetic does not seem to guide this poem. In contrast to some of Pound's more homely quotations, Moore's quotations have no past literary or political history for which they might be chosen. Moore could have chosen them for any number of reasons, and the reasons are opaque. Small wonder that Moore so easily created and maintained the public impression of her poetics as a poetics of restraint.

Any canon of sources creates new meanings by using the poet's and the reader's cultural repertoire. Pound needs to give the appearance of knowing the Malatesta documents fairly well in order to use them, although his use of esoteric texts, surrounded in *The Cantos* by very unclear contexts, may make his actual knowledge untestable for the ordinary reader. At times, the poet's cultural repertoire also extends to the reader, for at times quotation marks are secondary indicators of quotation. Eliot does not have to surround "London bridge is falling down falling down falling down" with quotation marks in order for readers to recognize a quotation; most Western readers' cultural repertoires take care of that. This easy availability of popular culture allows Cummings to make his satiric enjambment between quotation and borrowing text more violent, for he can quote without separating quotations from the new text with quotation marks or any other distinguishing punctuation:

"next to of course god america i
love you land of the pilgrims' and so forth oh
say can you see by the dawn's early my

(267)

In this poem readers implicitly are to realize that phrases are abruptly cut off, and to recognize what words should usually complete those phrases. With the canned phrase "and so forth," Cummings also refers to the banal place of the quotation in the readers' sensibility.

Adequate cultural repertoire implies that the reader be very clear as to how the quotation is being transformed in its new setting, and how extensively that transformation deviates from the quotation's original use. But such cultural knowledge can be intimidating, for a quotation functions *as quotation* in a reader's cultural repertoire only if the reader recognizes the borrowed material as an exact duplication. Allusions require a much less definitive knowledge to function as part of one's cultural repertoire—it takes less knowledge to recognize a resemblance than it does to recognize a duplication. As a consequence, in the quoting poem most recognitions are more tenuous than those accorded to quotations from popular culture, and are not as dependent upon a community of readers' general cultural awareness as we might suppose. Other than "London Bridge," is there any quotation from *The Waste Land* that is immediately recognizable as an exact quotation from most readers' (including honest educated readers') canon of sources? Even for the most educated of readers, "London Bridge" will have a more instant accessibility than does Kyd's *Spanish Tragedy*. And so at times readers double-check for the presence of quotation marks to ensure that their own cultural repertoire is up to snuff.

The checking often extends to the poem's notes. Eliot's notes ostensibly help readers to discover the quotations' functions and to add the quotations to their own cultural repertoire. However, Eliot's magnanimity is not uncomplicated. In the first place, it was not an instinctive generosity. Apparently bowing to the mechanics of publishing, which demanded a work longer than the 433 lines of the poem, Eliot appended the notes that have become so much a part of the poem's complete text.

But it is the tenuousness of readers' cultural response that is perhaps the primary reading activity to which the *The Waste Land*'s notes speak (notes that do not, by the way, gloss "London Bridge"): the notes implicitly recognize readers' cultural limitations and make clear to readers the club to which Eliot does, and to which the reader might not belong. Much of the difficulty of the poem is in discovering the attitudes of this club, and what requirements there are for membership. The notes ambiguously aid this process. For example, "that Shakespeherian Rag" goes undocumented, while the more literary "*Poi s'ascose nel foco che gli affina*" receives the following annotation:

> V. *Purgatorio*, XXVI, 148.
> "'Ara vos prec per aquella valor
> 'que vos guida al som de l'escalina,
> 'sovenha vos a temps de ma dolor.'
> Poi s'ascose nel foco che gli affina."
>
> (80)

This help is help only if readers couple this note with a working knowledge of Italian and *The Divine Comedy*.

These varied interactions that result from a canon of sources can have overtones of the misreading Harold Bloom describes in *The Anxiety of Influence,* for the new poet's idiosyncratic perception of the quotation's original function partially shapes its changed function in the new poem. But for the purposes of this book it is more useful to describe the structure of such misreadings as they are presented at specific moments in the quoting poem. In all these varied uses of canon formation, the quoter presents himself obviously as manipulator, presents a consistent interaction with a consistent *kind* of text. By a variety of means, the quotation's new cultural value becomes clear. Through the poet's interaction with the quotation, readers see—often for the first time—the quoted material as alive (Pound), as part of an important tradition (Pound and Eliot), as poetry (Moore), as commentary on contemporary culture (Pound, Eliot, and Cummings). Cummings's and Moore's poems show that the importance conferred upon the quotation does not have to be in line with its original use. Cummings causes his readers to see his quotations from advertising and patriotic songs in a much less naive light than they are seen in their original contexts; Moore wants readers to see her quotations as textured parts of a work of art rather than as the sterile givers of information that they are in their usual contexts. Quotations are a way—sometimes simultaneously—to give and not to give respect to the quoted source; the quoting poem flouts and flaunts poetic tradition.

## New Metaphors

As the quoting poet's selection of quoted material indicates, quotation guarantees that the splicing of two radically differing objects results in new meanings. This process has a larger status in Modernist theory than just the quoting poem. Most notably, Sergei Eisenstein discussed this interaction between juxtaposed objects as montage, a term that had wide currency in popular discussions of Modernism:

> *two film pieces of any kind, placed together, inevitably combine into a new concept, a new quality, arising out of that juxtaposition.*
> This is not in the least a circumstance peculiar to the cinema, but is a phenomenon invariably met with in all cases where we have to deal with juxtaposition of two facts, two phenomena, two objects. We are accustomed to make, almost automatically, a definite and obvious deductive generalization when any separate objects are placed before us side by side. (4)

Because of the separation between the quoting text and the quotation, the quoting poem creates an obvious test of this principle. First, it will be clear to those who recognize the quotation whether its juxtaposition with the borrowing text has resulted in "a new concept, a new quality." While other sorts of juxtaposed elements do not have a previous function to supply a contrast, the quoting poem highlights both the earlier function and any attempt to change that function. Second, their different origins ensure that the quotation and the borrowing text exist as two separate objects that have been placed together; the quoting poem is a heterogeneous object.

Understanding the consequences of this heterogeneity clarifies how montage functions in the quoting poem. Heterogeneity is a concept central to most definitions of Modernism, but one that acquires some peculiar functions in the quoting poem. Heterogeneity is now more radical and less resolvable, since it is the product of two competing personalities: the quoting poet, and the author of the quotation. In discussing his experience of Stravinsky's *Sacre du Printemps,* Eliot acknowledged the structural heterogeneity of this work of borrowed cultural artifacts and approvingly commented on some of heterogeneity's poetic—and, by implication, social—uses:

> In everything in the Sacre du Printemps, except in the music, one missed the sense of the present. Whether Strawinsky's music be permanent or ephemeral I do not know; but it did seem to transform the rhythm of the steppes into the scream of the motor horn, the rattle of machinery, the grind of wheels, the beating of iron and steel, the roar of the underground railway, and the other barbaric cries of modern life; and to transform these despairing noises into music. ("London Letter," October 1921, 453)

The different *origins* of the sounds create meaning. The structural heterogeneity implied by Eliot's list is essential to giving the "sense of the present," and "to transform these despairing noises into music." Eliot uses the same principles in his reading of *Ulysses.* According to Eliot, Joyce's "manipulating a continuous parallel between contemporaneity and antiquity [gives] a shape and a significance to the immense panorama of futility and anarchy which is contemporary history." This "mythical" method, which creates "order and form" and makes "the modern world possible for art," creates new meanings out of disparate but conjoined elements ("Ulysses," 177, 178).

Like Eisenstein, Eliot and other quoters create works that demonstrate that heterogeneity is not a description of chaos; its structure can create meaning. In proposing how this meaning is produced, Modernist quoters describe a structure that takes on the function of metaphor. In his review of Stravinsky, Eliot describes the sense of the present created by this heterogeneity in metaphoric language, while the structure of the music doubles Eliot's metaphoric description of it: the list of particular sounds are the "barbaric cries of modern life," which in turn are transformed into music. The music has a metaphoric structure. Eliot develops a similar theory of metaphor in the objective correlative. Eliot argues that for readers the "dominant tone" of a work of art comes about because "a number of floating feelings, having an affinity to this emotion by no means superficially evident, [have] combined with it to give us a new art emotion" ("Tradition," 43). Eliot's formulation is not limited to one moment in Modernism. A decade or more earlier, just as Modernism was beginning to be conscious of itself, Pound argued that metaphor arises from the "swift perception of relations," and, grandly concurring with Aristotle, he saw metaphor as "the hall-mark of genius" (*Spirit,* 158). Pound's later use of the ideogram also involves metaphoric techniques because it brings together items that had been previously separated, and from this uniting establishes an "identity-in-difference" (Schwartz, 86).

If metaphor is defined as the meaning produced by the fusing of heterogeneous elements, the metaphorical implications of Modernist art become even more clear in Eliot's essay on the metaphysical poets, where Eliot argues that much poetry has "a degree of heterogeneity of material compelled into unity by the operation of the poet's mind" ("Metaphysical," 61). The good poet creates metaphors:

> When a poet's mind is perfectly equipped for its work, it is constantly amalgamating disparate experience; the ordinary man's experience is chaotic, irregular, fragmentary. The latter falls in love, or reads Spinoza, and these two experiences have nothing to do with each other, or with the noise of the typewriter or the smell of cooking; in the mind of the poet these experiences are always forming new wholes. ("Metaphysical," 64)

In its creation by artists and use by audiences, Modernist art—and, in uniquely important ways, Modernist quoting art—is an art of structurally expressed, disjunctive metaphor.[9]

From the seventh canto, Pound's description of Henry James furnishes a good example of how this theory works in the quoting poem:

> And the great domed head, *con gli occhi onesti e tardi*
> Moves before me, phantom with weighted motion,
> *Grave incessu,* drinking the tone of things,
> And the old voice lifts itself
>     weaving an endless sentence.
>
>                                                             (24)

The quotations, compiled from Dante and Virgil, and describing Sordello, Horace, Homer, Ovid, and Venus (Terrell 1:31), inevitably function differently here than in their original settings, since the objects of their original description (Homer and others) are only equivocally present in this new text. The original context has been cut away, and a new replaces it. The epic quality of the original settings transforms and is transformed by this new setting. The quotations in this new context also refer to Henry James and give him, somewhat ironically, some of the attributes that the quotations in their original texts gave to their original referents. James is reconceptualized in strange terms, for readers recognize that these terms more typically modify other objects. The quotations create metaphoric parallels. As does Dante's Sordello, James has "eyes honest and slow"; he moves with "solemn movement." These quotations now exist in a new context in which the functions of the quotations have modulated so that they join in characterizing this person who is "drinking the tone of things," and who is capable of "weaving an endless sentence." The quotations' interactions with their surrounding text have changed to irony and aggressive definition of a modern writer's place in the canon: James as the last continuator of the Homer-Ovid-Flaubert-etc. tradition.

As this example from Pound shows, the metaphor in the quoting poem has a tension between language's abstract and concrete properties. The new context ensures that the quotations modify Henry James while the quotations' concrete properties resist this new function and point back to their original functions. On the one hand, the quoting poem's metaphors are abstract: general, overarching qualities tie the compared element to the comparing text. In reading the metaphor we still must include the abstract element (those qualities that can create a single tradition from Homer, Ovid, Flaubert, and James) in order for the metaphor to make sense. But metaphors are also concrete: specific details of the metaphor refuse to allow the abstraction a comfortable existence. The Italian has an earlier function that the text insistently points to by virtue of the fact that the Italian is a quotation. This quotation does not just refer to James, and it does not just compare James to Sordello and Flaubert; it creates a James-Sordello-Flaubert construct. The concrete qualities of this quoted text refuse to allow readers simply to substitute for the quotations a phrase comparing James to these writers. Metaphors generally, including the metaphor structures of the quoting poem, require people to communicate in terms of the physical world. If the poem were to have no such reliance upon concreteness, it could as easily allude to these other texts, and make the abstract connections much more explicit.

Such a preference for concreteness makes sense, for the unresolvable concrete qualities of the metaphor give the metaphor (and the quoting poem) its uniqueness as a construct. In "A Few Don'ts by an Imagiste," an early essay Pound thought important enough to reprint in 1918 (after his Vorticist phase), Pound exhorted poets to "go in fear of abstractions" because abstractions make for "mediocre verse": "Don't use such an expression as 'dim lands of *peace*.' It dulls the image. It mixes an abstraction with the concrete. It comes from the writer's not realizing that the natural object is always the *adequate* symbol" (201). As does metaphor, quotation inevitably functions as the "natural object," bringing concreteness to the text. Pound's use of the ideogram similarly deemphasizes abstraction, although it does allow abstraction a role. As Sanford Schwartz points out, by presenting concepts through pictures, the ideogram ties the abstract concept to the concrete particulars that are its expression (87). In the construction of this sort of poetic meaning, the concrete particulars never disappear.

More than any other Modernist technique, quotations supply this metaphoric concreteness. A telling test of quotation's concreteness and its resultant ability to create metaphors occurs in Moore's poetry, Moore being the least sensuous in her quoting. It is initially difficult to see the concrete element in Moore's quotation of Henry James that concludes her "New York":

> it is not that "if the fur is not finer than such as one sees others wear,
> one would rather be without it"—
> that estimated in raw meat and berries, we could feed the universe;
> it is not the atmosphere of ingenuity,
> the otter, the beaver, the puma skins
> without shooting-irons or dogs;
> it is not the plunder,
> but "accessibility to experience."
>
> (77)

Certainly, the final quotation's denotations contain nothing but abstractions. But as in all of Moore's poetry, these lines curiously waver between the concrete and the abstract, a wavering that in this case moves right into the middle of the quotation.

On one level the quotation's abstraction is the antithesis of the concrete list before it, just as it syntactically opposes the list. But the "it is" construction used throughout the poem, and implied in the closing phrase, is used in the rest of the poem to introduce specific, concrete elements of a definition/metaphor (the "it" being the abstraction never defined in the poem): "It is a far cry from the 'queen full of jewels'" (77). (Moore uses this structure to integrate quotations in other poems also, such as in "When I Buy Pictures" and "To a Snail.") The rest of the poem thus has a clearly metaphoric element, now partially shared by the quotation, which, as an abstraction, is yet a concrete instance of what is being defined. The poem, searching for the apt metaphor among items as diverse as fine fur, raw meat, and berries, an "atmosphere of ingenuity," otters, beavers, plunder, and "accessibility to experience," asserts that it has found this metaphor most satisfactorily in the last line.

As do all of Moore's quotations, this last line comes from a textual world with a very different function than the world of the borrowing poem, and thus the quotation has some degree of metaphoric stretching to undergo to fit into the world of the new poem. What makes this metaphoric stretching more odd, and more inherently concrete, is that Moore is not very interested in the original rhetorical context of the quotations she uses. The new context almost completely subjugates the quotation's original meaning, leaving just the quotation's alien texture to point to an earlier function. Although throughout her career she gives notes to her poems, in "A Note on the Notes" in *The Complete Poems* Moore does not see these notes as anything more than acknowledgments of borrowing, and she urges her readers "to take probity on faith and disregard the notes" if they impede the reading (262). As several critics have pointed out, other than for understanding the composition process the notes are not very helpful (Borroff, 110; Costello, 6). But as Bonnie Costello goes on to argue, this lack of extratextual allusion results in the quotation's surface texture being all-important. Moore attempts to capture the style rather than the intentions of her source's world (185).

Quotations always supply metaphorlike, concrete specifics, even when the unifying abstraction behind them is most clear, as it is in Cummings's poetry:

> according
> to such supposedly indigenous

throstles Art is O World O Life
a formula:example,Turn Your Shirttails Into
Drawers and If It Isn't An Eastman It Isn't A
Kodak therefore my friends let
us now sing each and all fortissimo A-
mer
i
ca,I
love,
You.

        ("POEM, OR BEAUTY HURTS MR. VINAL," 228–29)

The concrete details of the phrase, the capitalization, and the sense that Cummings uses this quotation for its idiosyncratic textural properties as an advertisement rather than for its specific rhetorical content—all these give the quotation specificity. The poem's use of "example" makes it perhaps too clear that the following quotations are concrete illustrations of an abstraction, but the poem is consistent in overtly establishing a relationship between concrete details and the abstract principles that guided their selection.

The concrete elements just described in both poems occur as the accidents of particular texts, but they also hint that there is something *inherently* concrete and sensuous about quotations. As they do in the poem just quoted, quotations must always first recreate the physical voice of another physical text before they can use its abstract content. Either the quotation marks or readers' knowledge of the quotation *as* quotation ensure this primacy, even when nothing of the quotation is known. Even when the quotation functions as part of readers' cultural repertoire, readers' knowledge of the quotation as quotation inevitably occurs as a result of the quotation's sensuous properties (diction, language, meter) rather than its conceptual content. This knowledge of the quotation *as* quotation separates the quotation from the quoting text and further highlights its sensuous properties. Delimited by various means, quotations are objects within the poem—they have a separate existence apart from the poem's rhetoric, and just as the poem as an art object emphasizes its sensuous properties, so does the quotation.

This level of concreteness is not always the same—Pound uses techniques that draw much more attention to the quotation's concrete properties than does Moore in her poetry:

These fragments you have shelved (shored).
"Slut!" "Bitch!" Truth and Calliope
Slanging each other sous les lauriers:
*That* Alessandro was negroid. And Malatesta
Sigismund:
> *Frater tamquam*
> *Et compater carissime: tergo*
> > *. . . hanni de*
> > *. . dicis*
> > *. . . entia*

Equivalent to:
> Giohanni of the Medici,
> Florence.
Letter received, and in the matter of our Messire Gianozio,

(8.28)

Pound's interest in concreteness at times radically demands the quotation's exact transcription. Here, the quotation acknowledges that a wax seal partially obscures the quoted text (Terrell 1:37). This quoting poem shows that the quotation's concreteness increases as disjunction increases, as the quotation uses differences of voice, diction, metrics, or imagery to separate itself as an object from the new text. Concrete elements separate the robust description of Truth and Calliope from the official prose of the Malatesta quotation. These concrete elements force any metaphor structure to acknowledge, and not to write over them.

So far, however, I have dealt with only one pole of the opposition: for all its concreteness, the quotation's world also introduces an exactly duplicated conceptual or abstract element. Eisenstein argues for montage that we make "a definite and obvious deductive *generalization* when any separate objects are placed before us side by side" (4, emphasis added). For Eliot, ideally concreteness and abstraction exist in a tense balance. Using ideas that find more systematic expression in his thesis on Bradley, Eliot argued that experiences that were simultaneously "sensuous and intellectual" had the most value: "certainly many men will admit that their keenest ideas have come to them with the quality of a sense-perception; and that their keenest sensuous experience has been 'as if the body thought'" ("Sceptical Patrician," 362).

Such generalization especially structures reading processes that attempt to unify the quoting poem. Full exploitations of the quotation's abstract properties always demand that the quoting poem concurrently exploit the quotation's assimilability into the new poem. In Cummings's poetry and in some of *The Waste Land* the abstraction can be quite clear, as the quotation easily accepts and affirms the abstractions imposed by the quoting poem's world.

The presence or lack of syntactic integration complicates usage of the quotation's abstractions. In a poem without a linear rhetorical structure, the clearer the poem's abstract background relates to the quotations, the more the poem's quotations are able to function as symbols. Symbols, while they may participate in propositional and narrative discourse, do not have these qualities within themselves. This principle explains why the quotations at the end of *The Waste Land* have symbolic overtones. To some degree, these quotations do not so much create a proposition as they represent a concept, such as "ruin" or "failure to communicate." The same is true of the recently quoted poem by Cummings: the quotations are symbolic of the easy answers that consumerism presents. By contrast, the less the quotation syntactically opposes its new surroundings (the more smoothly it fits into the poem's texture and rhetoric), the less likely there is either complete free play or a symbolic function (with symbolism's ensuing concreteness in service of abstraction), and the more likely the quotation aids in establishing just the quoting poem's rhetoric.

Of course, these distinctions can't be completely clean—within a quotation there always is some concreteness. However, the smoothly integrated quotation can aid strongly in establishing a rhetorical grid, as Moore's poetry shows most clearly:

"Taller by the length of
    a conversation of five hundred years than all
        the others," there was one, whose tales
            of what could never have been actual—
were better than the haggish, uncompanionable drawl

of certitude; his by-
    play was more terrible in its effectiveness
        than the fiercest frontal attack.

The staff, the bag, the feigned inconsequence
of manner, best bespeak that weapon, self-protectiveness.
("In This Age of Hard Trying," 50)

Since the quotation doesn't introduce a noticeable disjunction of meter, syntax, or diction, and since the rest of the poem takes up the possible disjunction of image (the quotation's topic) and ties it to the rhetorical strategy of the poem, the quoting poem's rhetorical structure overruns the quotation. In the case of this poem, the overrunning is quite complete. Because the poem establishes a new world that comfortably encloses the quotation's world, the quotation's imagery fits in with the poem, as does its rhetoric. No knowledge of the source exists to allow properties outside of the snippet just quoted to interfere with the new world of the poem. Indeed, only the original voice (signaled by the quotation marks, the peculiar content of the metaphor *within* the quotation, and a few qualities of the diction) resists the world of the new poem. As a result, in these lines the metaphoric structure and concrete resistance of this quoting poem is small, with little stretching required to fit the quoting poem's world over the quotation.

Why are poets interested in the quoting poem's metaphor structure? For the same reason that Pound was (mistakenly) excited about the ideogram: he believed that the ideogram combined pictures of objects in order to make an abstraction. Pound argued that Chinese writing put together the pictures for rose, iron rust, cherry, and flamingo to make the concept "red." The virtues for poetry are clear: "Fenollosa was telling how and why a language written in this way simply HAD TO STAY POETIC; simply couldn't help being and staying poetic in a way that a column of English type might not very well stay poetic" (*ABC,* 22). Those writers who quote ensure that they stay in contact with concrete objects. As do metaphors, quotations allow poets to avoid overworked or hackneyed language often found in abstractions (witness Pound's excoriating "dim lands of peace"), and to create a new poetic language.

## Crude and Difficult Poetry

Pound disliked overworked language and dead metaphors because they could not create new meanings. Most positive critics of quoting Modernism, following Pound, usually noted how the act of quoting enlivens the quotation and gives it a new, original quality. Thus, for all his ambivalences, Edmund Wilson argues that in *The Waste Land* Eliot is a poet who "has brought a new personal rhythm into the language and who has lent even to the words of his great predecessors a new music and a new meaning" (144). Similarly, Maxwell Bodenheim posits that "the Cantos represent the nervous attempt of a poet to probe and mould the residue left by the books and tales that he has absorbed, and to alter it to an independent creative effect" (91).

From the preceding chapter we should suspect this analysis of how quotations relate to the borrowing text. Although these critics are right to discuss a transforming interaction, their emphasis on the powerful, transforming poet is slightly skewed. These early critics have an overwhelming confidence in the unity and single impression of the new artifact: the original source leaves no messy contamination in the new poem; there is no awkward doubleness. At this level, Williams was right; such confidence in leaving the quotation's past behind is naive. Quotations dramatically illustrate that the new meanings which result from the quotation's juxtaposition are *much* more complicated than that. The newness is a combination of old and new elements. Herman Meyer in *The Poetics of Quotation in the European Novel* more accurately describes the texture that results from quotation as "a unique tension between assimilation and dissimilation" (6). And Bonnie Costello points out how, as applied to Moore's quotation, such tension makes the poetic project much more sophisticated, and meaning much less static than a simple unidirectional transformation allows. Quotations interact with elements both inside and outside of the poem (163).

As does the quoting poem's idiosyncratic use of concrete and abstract properties, the form of this interaction finds expression in metaphor theory. Among the various theories of metaphor, therefore, the one that best addresses the "tension between assimilation and dissimilation" is the idea that a metaphor occurs when two elements usually thought unlike are yoked together, such as in the statement "the professor clawed my paper." The opposing elements of the metaphor undergo what James Ross calls "semantic contagion" (32): the elements of one field of meaning (cats) force themselves upon another (higher education). Hearers and creators of the metaphor wrench meaning from this forcing. Thus, metaphors are not merely decorations that could easily be replaced by a more exact paraphrase (likewise, quotations are not merely decorations which could be replaced by allusions). As John Searle points out, metaphors are not paraphrasable, for without using the metaphor we will not duplicate the "semantic content" that the hearer comprehended in the original utterance (123). Modernist quoting exploits this notion of metaphor as an unparaphrasable comparison that fuses an uncomfortable unity between two different worlds. Quotations insist that semantic content be *precisely* duplicated, not paraphrased. In the quoting poem the sense of difference never can be read past or erased, as it can be in a dead metaphor. On a grand scale and in just as disconcerting a manner, quotations repeat metaphoric structure.

When the quoting poem, with its metaphor structure, creates a poetry that is both crude and unsettling, it does not do so as a divergent moment in Modernist history. Awkwardness is neither accidental nor inconsequential; Modernist quoters saw it as essential for art in this century. According to Françoise Gilot and Carlton Lake, Picasso reminisced in the following way about the beginning of collage:

> If a piece of newspaper can become a bottle, that gives us something to think about in connection with both newspapers and bottles, too. This displaced object has entered a universe for which it was not made and where it retains, in a measure, its strangeness. And this strangeness was what we wanted to make people think about because we were quite aware that our world was becoming very strange and not exactly reassuring. (77)

Eliot even more stridently insisted upon this point. His highly erudite verse makes him somewhat defensive, and he defends not "strangeness," but "difficulty":

> We can only say that it appears likely that poets in our civilization, as it exists at present, must be *difficult*. Our civilization comprehends great variety and complexity, and this variety and complexity, playing upon a refined sensibility, must produce various and complex results. The poet must become more and more comprehensive, more allusive, more indirect, in order to force, to dislocate if necessary, language into his meaning. ("Metaphysical," 65)

Eliot's confidence may rankle a bit here. He employs a strident repetition of "must," a word that appears in each sentence, and he ends with terminology that increasingly suggests a violent structure: "comprehensive," "allusive," "indirect," "force," "dislocate." However, as many readers have discovered (although with less of Eliot's insistence upon their necessity), difficulty and awkwardness do go together in Modern writing.

In the quoting poem specifically, difficulty comes about not because of obscure sources (although some sources may well be obscure), but because the poem insists upon duplicating concrete elements of another text. Such leaning towards the particular often pushes to the background abstract structures such as rhetoric and symbolism. As a result, a good part of the quoting poem can remain unaccounted for or opaque, especially when readers encounter a poem that is neither clearly symbolic nor clearly rhetorical:

After him and his day
Were the cake-eaters, the consumers of icing,
That read all day per diletto
And left the night work to the servants;
Ferrara, paradiso dei sarti, "feste stomagose."

"Is it likely Divine Apollo,
That I should have stolen your cattle?
A child of my age, a mere infant,
        And besides, I have been here all night in my crib."
"Albert made me, Tura painted my wall,
And Julia the Countess sold to a tannery . . ."

(Pound, *Cantos*, 24.114)

The disjunction and the shortness of the quotations obfuscate any rhetorical effect. When Pound uses quotations for rhetorical effect, his disjunctive structure demands a lengthy quotation in order for the argument within the quotation to be clear. (He does not employ the clear alignment of the quoting with the nonquoting elements of the text, as Moore does.) As for symbolism, readers need some general schema to which both parts of this text can subscribe. The structure of these lines should indicate a clearer relationship between the quotation from the Homeric Hymn and Niccolò d'Este, who has been the subject of much of this canto. But one cannot easily find it, and on these levels the purpose for the quotation from the Homeric Hymn remains obscure.

Eliot has also articulated the structure of this difficulty, this dislocation. Eliot points out that the force of any argument against a poetry of contrasting elements lies "in the failure of the conjunction, the fact that often the ideas are yoked but not united" ("Metaphysical," 60). Difficulty can fail; it fails when the stretching between two elements is so great that it disallows a connection. The possible lack of a system to yoke materials also informs much quoting poetry. At times, the values of the conflicts between two worlds are just not clear. As Eliot points out, sometimes the affinity between different worlds is "by no means superficially evident" ("Tradition," 43). In the quoting poem the affinity can be hard to find for several reasons: either the reader is trying to find the wrong structures in the worlds of the quotation or quoting poem (i.e., the reader is not ideal), or the quoting poetry hides the relevant structures, or the structures do not exist. In any of these cases, the poetry is sending out incomplete or ambiguous clues for reconciling the world of the quotation to the world of the new poem. As with an orthodox metaphor, quoting poet and reader must share a "system of principles" to communicate (Searle, 113).

Despite Eliot's warning, quoting poetry (including his own) inherently flirts with such difficulties. In the quoting poem, "dislocating language into meaning" is tricky business. It is difficult to make exact the relation between quotation and quoting text, given the quotation's individual texture. The new strategy of the text and the original strategy of the quotation can never mesh perfectly, and consequently, perfectly stable, univocal meanings are hard to come by.

Certainly, alluding texts also create an uneasy relationship between their own strategies and those of their borrowings. Wolfgang Iser argues that allusions provide a contrastive background to their borrowing text. The new context, in turn, acquires its meaning through interacting with the background functions of the allusion. With the old context functioning in this way, allusions do not merely repeat old functions—they are "depragmatized," made unfamiliar, and take on new functions (79–80, 93).

But new texts easily appropriate allusions because the gaps are not sharp; the world alluded to has open borders. Quotations introduce new complexities and stronger disjunctions into the struggle between old and new contexts. The quotation's exactness brings with it more of the quoted text's original world than do allusions from the same text. The result is that the quotation's original function asserts itself more strongly than does that of allusions. Because quotations bring in their own exactness much more strongly than do allusions, the depragmatization into new meanings seems more dramatic, the delineation from the new text more sharp, and the metaphors much more awkward.[10]

For example, quoted and quoting text in *The Cantos* often have principles that weakly connect with each other. This is true even of the Malatesta cantos, which show little disjunction of subject matter. The strongest rhetorical relationship critics have found are the "subject rhymes": the poem addresses a topic, an address that doesn't so much make a rhetorical point as impose a pattern, both on history and on the poem. Subject rhymes have the benefit of stretching across many cantos, and so create the "constituting metaphor" that Edwin Fussell describes in *Lucifer in Harness*. But subject rhymes do not argue. As Christine Froula points out, the subject rhyme allows Pound to affirm the idea of belief without committing himself to any single one of these images as capturing "reality." Pound more often wanted an abstract image than an argument (24). Therefore, sometimes the abstract principle in a quoting poem's metaphoric structure is not so much a rhetorical statement as it is a topic, a principle of organization, or the recurring clash of discordant voices and textures—these alternate possibilities seem to be true of much of *The Cantos* and other poems that allow their controlling principles to be directed by a very sensuous medium.[11]

However, such readings must ignore much of the sensuous specificity of the poem. One cannot comfortably stretch this topic into a logical proposition that writes over or accounts for the concrete elements of the poem. Emphasizing the sensuousness of the medium complicates Pound's poetry. Because he might consequently compromise the quotation's sensuous integrity by ignoring certain of its idiosyncrasies, Pound refuses to clarify the relationship between quoting and quoted text. *All* the elements of the quotation jostle for attention—sometimes confusingly, as when Pound presents parts of words or quotes at length while reciting building lists and legal documents.

But especially in the earlier Cantos, which use many different short quotations, difficulty arises because Pound's own creativity cannot subsume all of this specificity. At times, such as when Pound adds Ameri-

can colloquialisms to Malatesta's bureaucratic prose, the addition causes
a new, disruptive concreteness that the poem's controlling world can
hardly keep in line:

And tell the *Maestro di pentore*
That there can be no question of
His painting the walls for the moment,
As the mortar is not yet dry
And it wd. be merely work chucked away
   (*buttato via*)

(8.28)

If reading is to be a process in which widely disparate elements become
metaphors as they combine into a single paraphrasable meaning,
Pound's poetry is inherently difficult:

Formando di disio nuova persona
One man is dead, and another has rotted his end off
Et quant au troisième
Il est tombé dans le
De sa femme, on ne le reverra
Pas, oth fugol ouitbaer:
"Observed that the paint was
Three quarters of an inch thick and concluded,
As they were being rammed through, the age of that
Cruiser." "Referred to no longer as
The goddamned Porta-goose, but as
England's oldest ally."

(27.129)

The many changes in topic, diction, and images subvert a reader's
ability to establish metaphoric structures. As soon as one world appears
it is replaced by another; the image of individual men creating and
dying is replaced by two subject-less images of prewar politics. The
relation between the two sorts of images has resonance, but it is hard
to determine its pitch. Pound works here with some equation between
desire and war, but the quotations' specificity creates problems in deter-
mining what that point may be. After all, Pound seems to have a very
different attitude to the writer of the *Wanderer* ("oth fugol ouitbaer")

than he does to the prewar politician ("Referred to no longer as / The goddamned Porta-goose"), but the differences do not have a clear principle of contrasts that would allow the two quotations in conjunction to construct a third point.

A wider scope, less attuned to the text's concrete particulars, might make it possible for readers to perceive an argument. The controlling world in this canto might be said to be all of history, but the vagueness is not helpful. On another level, language itself might establish the qualities of a single world, but once more the swiftness and radicality of the changes do not allow a single world to set itself up as dominant. Perhaps the structure means to establish the equality of linguistic experience, but again the vagueness is not helpful. Metrical or image patterns might establish metaphoric relationships, but they too slip away as soon as they appear.

The gaps are easy to see, but it is difficult to determine their functions. Images appear briefly and just bump against each other, ensuring only the most ghostly of abstractions in the metaphoric structure. Consequently, the most recurring consistency in *The Cantos* is this fading in and out, a relation perhaps between presence and the lack of it. In this setting, Pound emphasizes the sensuousness and individuality of each quotation or image, since he creates so little else that a reader can surely grasp. Understanding the exact form of this experience is important, for in Pound's work it is not first of all Derrida's endlessly receding context that subverts stable meanings; rather, it is an aggressive sensuousness that both encourages awkwardness and subverts determinacy.

Quotations and topics are usually longer and recur more frequently in the middle and late cantos than they do in the early cantos and at many of the beginnings of cantos. But although they clearly set up a world with clear abstract and concrete properties, lengthy quotations also present problems for metaphoric structures. Metaphors occur only when readers realize a gap from one system of codes to another has been rapidly crossed. Lengthy quotations emphasize the middle texture of the quoted piece rather than its edges. The lengthy quotation exists more like itself than like a part of a poem; however, its being *quoted* in the poem ensures that its texture and concreteness dominate.

Consider, for example, the Adams cantos. As Philip Furia points out, Pound in these cantos is attempting to bring these documents into public consciousness (87–102). The length of the individual quotations matches Pound's obsession to restore these documents. In these lengthier quotations, Pound cannot help but have the quotation's rhetorical content strongly assert itself, limiting the possible interactions Pound may construct between the quotation and the poem. The interactions are fewer, and the aggressive individuality of the lengthy quotation controls their qualities. The length of the quotation allows the specific texture of that quotation to establish a presence that cannot be dominated by the rest of the poem or easily function as part of a metaphor. The metaphor structure disappears, and the quotation's texture and dogma triumph.

Even when, as in the poetry of Marianne Moore, quotations are on several levels snugly ensconced within the poem, readers cannot completely erase the sorts of difficulties which Pound's poetry raises. Like metaphors, recognized quotations are always disconcerting, introducing an uneven texture into the reading experience:

> Principally throat, sophistication is as it al-
>
> ways has been—at the antipodes from the init-
>    ial great truths. "Part of it was crawling, part of it
> was about to crawl, the rest
>    was torpid in its lair." In the short-legged, fit-
> ful advance, the gurgling and all the minutiae—we have the classic
>
> multitude of feet. To what purpose! Truth is no Apollo
>    Belvedere, no formal thing. The wave may go over it if it likes.
> Know that it will be there when it says,
>    "I shall be there when the wave has gone by."
>                                    ("In the Days of Prismatic Colour," 62–63)

The last line does not introduce a radically different world of language, for the lack of disjunction and the introduction of the quotation as the voice of a character smooths over much of the contrasting worlds. But the last line yet introduces a linguistic struggle, for its personal quality introduces a new type of language into the poem—this line contains the poem's first personal pronoun. More typical, and showing more clearly the wrenching effect quotations can have on poetic language, is the passage's first quotation. The shift from abstract, Latinate language, to the more active verbs and the concrete, Anglo-Saxon of the quotation ("about," "rest," "lair," "crawl,"), a shift signaled at the most basic level by word length, causes the quotation to introduce a different type of language into the poem. The jostling of these different languages forms more of the poem's aesthetic texture at this point than does the linguistic unity established by the poem's first twenty lines.

Finding a relation between quotation and quoting poem that removes all difficulties is less true to the functioning of the poem than is acknowledging its uneven texture. For example, attempts to unify the metaphors of *The Cantos* around some thematic concern, as does Daniel Pearlman's *The Barb of Time,* nudge themselves past the obvious disunities of the poem, and miss much of the aesthetic experience of reading. By now, critics have uncovered and elucidated most of the sources for *The Waste Land;* the poem's substantial remaining obscurities lie in how to relate these sources to the rest of the text. In this quoting poem, most difficulties come about because of obscure relations between quoted and quoting text, not because of the obscurity of the sources.

Dependent upon the extreme concreteness of recalcitrant, unparaphrasable metaphor structures, these obscure relations were integral to Modernism. Whereas John Crowe Ransom would complain that readers "cannot pass, in 'The Waste Land,' without a convulsion of the mind from 'O O O O that Shakespeherian Rag,' to 'Shantih shantih shantih'" (177), for many Modernists the deliberately clunky structure of the quoting artwork exemplified a new aesthetic of crudity, an aesthetic that is at the center of many discussions of Modernism. Several critics have pointed out how Modern art attempted to remove the "fine" from fine art (for example, Janis and Blesh, 10–11; Daix, *Cubists,* 14–29). The removal certainly reaches its apex in Dada, with its found objects and its undertones of nihilism. To be sure, crudity is relative. A work such as Marcel Duchamp's urinal entitled "Fountain" still retains some shock value, but its whimsy is more easily perceived these days than it was at the time. From our present perspective, Cubist collage seems similarly tamer, merely whimsical and "interesting." But what now seems incongruous and playful once startled and outraged viewers. The irregularly cut pieces of newspaper, placed on the "once-sacred" canvas oil painting deliberately shocked viewers through its incorporation of folk-art materials into "serious art" (Janis and Blesh, 3).

In its original function Cubist collage protested the slickness and technical facility of "official" art, which Cubist artists thought had degenerated to the merely decorative. One of the ways artists protested was through using materials at the time considered antiartistic, such as newspapers and oilcloth. However, whether or not these materials were inherently ugly, Cubist artists appropriated them in a manner that prevented the artwork from acquiring any smoothness or virtuosity. The artwork was inherently crude. Picasso, Braque, and Gris not only stated at some time their dislike of oil paint's "slickness" (Seitz, 22), they followed through in practice, at times mixing sand or ashes into their paint to disallow the possibility of virtuosity (Kahnweiler, 88).

Pierre Daix argues that this desire for crudity changes the way artworks signify. The signifier now reveals itself in awkward and imperfect elements (*Picasso*, 148). The structural implications of this crudity are simple, and their perception is not limited to the original audience. The crude artwork inherently has contradictions; it revels in them and refuses to allow readers to ignore them. In a collage's use of ugly materials, the different textures refuse to cohere. Bits of newspaper are awkwardly cut out, not forming accurate squares, but being close enough to the form to point at it insistently. As E. H. Gombrich points out, by bringing in real objects in a distorted, disunified context, the quoting artist prevents representation: "If illusion is due to the interaction of clues and the absence of contradictory evidence, the only way to fight its transforming influence is to make the clues contradict each other and to prevent a coherent image of reality from destroying the pattern in the plane" (281).[12]

As it was for painting, quoting poetry's attack on the pretty was an attack on outmoded forms, on clichés. The poets discussed in this study saw themselves in rebellion against the metrically smooth and the pretty in art, and they revolted by being deliberately awkward. Moore expressed her dissatisfaction by opening up the canon to include what had been previously thought of as clunky, utilitarian prose, and she subverted expectations of metrical regularity by writing syllabic verse. In "POEM, OR BEAUTY HURTS MR. VINAL," Cummings stages his attack by satirizing Harold Vinal, who, during the year that saw the publication of *The Waste Land*, published *White April*, a collection of poems that had the distinction of being published in the *Yale Younger Poets* series. Cummings's poem alludes to Vinal's "Earth Lover" (Lewis Miller, 349–50, 354). Vinal dedicated his book "To Mother," and, in a section of the book called "Sonnets for Weeping," ends "Earth Lover" with the following lines:

Alas, how short a state does beauty keep,
Then let me clasp it wildly to my heart

And hurt myself until I am a part
Of all its rapture, then turn back to sleep,
Remembering through all the dusty years
What sudden wonder brought me close to tears.

(22)

I include this bland sentimentality not as a lesson in how estimations of quality change, but for how it works as an object of Cummings's critique. Cummings's poem argues along lines congenial to Williams, claiming that Vinal's work, in its allusion to previous literary history, uses old forms untransformed. At its center, Cummings's poem argues that Vinal's clichés have lost their ability to communicate:

i would

suggest that certain ideas gestures
rhymes,like Gillette Razor Blades
having been used and reused
to the mystical moment of dullness emphatically are
Not To Be Resharpened.

(228)

For Cummings, the offenders are "these gently O sweetly / melancholy trillers" who write things like "Helen & Cleopatra were Just Too Lovely, / The Snail's On The Thorn enter Morn," and so on (228). As the capitalization indicates, Browning's work has been consumed by the public and has lost its ability to create new thought. Eliot and Pound similarly dislike the pretty and the regular, and their prose (perhaps because they were more concerned than Cummings or Moore with their own place in the canon) pointedly attacked the dull use of worn-out linguistic forms.

Although Moore and Cummings attack traditional pretty language most noticeably and do so by the very content of their quotations, one should also notice the unobtrusive radicality of the quoting poem's assault on language, for it extends beyond subject matter to the very means by which poetry is constructed. As did collage artists, quoting poets (especially Eliot and Pound) achieved these metaphors by ensuring that to their readers their work would seem crude and nonvirtuosic. The *fact* of quoting makes Moore's poetry difficult; quotations restrict virtuosity. Just as the quotation's exactness often creates an awkward-fitting metaphor, so does the texture of the quoted language inevitably clash with the quoting text, the two systems in conflict creating an art that achieves its power through this crudity. These poets created ideo-gramic, structural metaphors that present entire worlds in conflict, not just resolvable conflicts within the poem's single world or voice. The irregular and jostling meters, the nonmellifluous shift from one pattern of speech to another—all these are decisions of a revolution in language, decisions to create a crude syntax. As Eliot has demonstrated, one can be crude and awkward while quoting Dante. Pound even goes beyond this effect by introducing an American yawp into his Renaissance sources, a move which not only causes the quotation to rebel against the rest of the text, but causes it to convulse within itself.

The introduction of crudity was not per se an assault on beauty; it was an assault on the easy and predictable (pretty) ways in which other artists constructed beauty. In this context, quoting artists, attacked by Williams for being derivative, vigorously denounced uses of previous voices. As Pound notes, the unthinking, easy use of the past is a trap:

> Don't allow "influence" to mean merely that you mop up the particular decorative vocabulary of some one or two poets whom you happen to admire. A Turkish war correspondent was recently caught red-handed babbling in his dispatches of "dove-grey" hills, or else it was "pearl-pale," I can not remember. ("Few Don'ts," 202)

The mellifluous, traditional forms and rhythms are too easy. But the structural effects required to avoid this banal prettiness are more important than subject matter. The structure of the language shows no thought behind it, and canned phrases can easily be substituted for each other. Language *in its structure* must create new metaphors.

This view of language radically changes what one might think of as "new" speech. Pound defended archaism in poetry by attacking the favoring of an American "natural language" over other poetic languages: "The common word is not the same thing as *mot juste,* not by a long way. And it is possible to write in a stilted and bookish dialect without using clichés" (*Gaudier-Brzeska,* 115). The common word or natural expression can create as many clichés as did the old forms. Pound collapses the distinction between "bookish dialects" and natural speech. Not just so-called natural speech, but *all* dictions—including the crude, imperfectly fitting diction of the quoting poem—can be the exact word. Although they at times function as ready-mades, ideally quotations do not become canned phrases in the quoting poem. Quotations avoid this unthinking use of language both because they are startling (just by virtue of their being *quotations*) and because they have never before been put to their present uses.

Thus, the originality of quoting poetry responds doubly to Williams. On one level, Williams was right: certain qualities of specific quoting poems take on old connotations. Quotations use a previous voice and take on some of its qualities, including such technical aspects as its meter. The quoting artist does not fulfill the romantic ideal, creating a completely new world with each new work of art. But, as Williams himself (working with materials quite different from those of other quoting poets) was later to discover in *Paterson,* the quoting poem achieves originality precisely through *managing* this duplication. Quotations create new metaphors through the disruptive way in which the old language of quotations awkwardly jostles against the quoting text. Awkwardness, here discussed as an aesthetic virtue, is discussed in the next chapter as raising aesthetic problems. The peculiar awkwardness of the quoting poem creates problems for poetic unity, problems that poets dramatize in the quoting poem's voice.

## CHAPTER 4

# Poetic Voice in the Quoting Poem

Omnis intellectus est omniformis

[Every intellect is capable of assuming every shape]
—Marsilio Ficino and Ezra Pound

## Poetic Unity

Crudity fractures unity; in the welter of borrowed voices that is the quoting poem, crudity fractures unity in idiosyncratic ways, for quotations inevitably fight poetic unity. Just because quotations do fight and raise a distracting rumpus, they always partially succeed, creating opportunities for unique forms of management of this disturbance. Certainly, in this Postmodern age it may seem naive to use unflinchingly the concept of unity, but Modern quoting poems demand that one consider unity as an attempted aesthetic structure. Although quoting poets self-consciously attempted to break with traditional poetry (or, at least with their constructions of recent literary history), they still shared some of its traditional concerns, concerns that these poets addressed in the instructions they left for their readers and in the poems themselves. Unity is one of these concerns.

As we have seen in discussing the quoting poem's structures of relations, Eliot's statements favor unity as a reader's first principle of aesthetic evaluation. At the time *The Waste Land* was being written and published, Eliot was publicly arguing that poetry is a "fusion of elements," the uniting of several disparate elements; he similarly argued that "a degree of heterogeneity of material compelled into unity by the operation of the poet's mind is omnipresent in poetry" ("Tradition,"

42, 43; "Metaphysical," 61). With this emphasis on unity, Eliot was not being deceptive when in 1923 he wrote to L. A. G. Strong that "*The Waste Land* is intended to form a whole" (qtd. in Langbaum, 96). Other quoting poets employ a similar aesthetic. Admitting that some sections of *The Cantos* were presented "perhaps too enigmatically and abbreviatedly," in 1922 Pound wrote to Felix Schelling that "I hope, heaven help me, to bring them into some sort of design and architecture later" (*Letters,* 180). The strong thematic unity throughout Moore's poetry and the formal coherence of Cummings's oeuvre suggest an even more all-encompassing unity as a first principle.

But especially in highly disjunctive poems, the most traditional form of unity, that of a single speaker arguing or narrating a coherent set of propositions, is not operative. The aesthetic problem for these poets and their first readers, then, was to discover how quotations, how this crude heterogeneity of different structural codes, voices, and original thematic functions, could produce a unified reading of a poem—a unified reading that also was true to life in the twentieth century, to Eliot's "barbaric cries of modern life," to Pound's art of the city, the "flood of nouns without verbal relations." To move beyond traditional notions of rhetorical unity, readers need to direct energies away from the poem's rhetoric and toward how the poem works, toward how the quotations are managed.

In order to address the question of quotation as the Moderns use it, perhaps the most useful concept under which to discuss this management is *voice*. There are other models by which one could discuss this management, of course. A term such as *writing* offers a critique of the primacy of speech, and it also presents a useful way into discussing how poems interact with other texts. But voice is useful for this discussion of the quoting poem not only because that is the paradigm the Moderns use. Voice also allows me to construct a personality for the quotation, for the quoting poem is often a struggle of personalities. Voice gives me a better model for distinguishing between quotations and allusions. The peculiar context that voice can evoke, a context that (among other things) assumes the stability of the individual subject, is also useful, particularly as it undergoes stress in the fractured unity of the quoting poem.

Voice implies an arranging principle. Linda Wagner rightly observes that voice enables other traditional unifying elements of poetry (theme, imagery, etc.) to assume coherence. Once readers establish a poem's voice, other elements, including lineation, repetition, and diction, necessarily take on the shape they have in a particular poem (97–98). By describing the poetic voice, readers find the strategy that governs a poem's unity. Voice also has some important resonances for quotation. A particular voice is established by the texture of a work, the same texture that is crucial for the quotation's functioning. Further, the signs of a quotation (quotation marks, italics, etc.) add an urgency towards finding a voice, for they suggest a human source, an earlier voice. The act of enclosing the quotation in quotation marks indicates that, unless one can establish that the phrases of the quotation were initially assembled by chance, the quotation functions as a group of words initially spoken by someone other than the speaker of the poem. This voice can have the calm sonority of the *Encyclopedia Britannica* or the brassy sound of Madison Avenue, but it is always a voice; it always implies a speaker with detectable characteristics.

The function of voice in *The Waste Land, The Cantos,* and the longer Moore poems such as "An Octopus" has consequently become a central critical problem because readers need a unifying system that can tie together the quotations and the disparity they introduce into their poems. A primary reason that finding unity based on a single voice has been unsuccessful is that readers' attempts to create a single voice are often naive, based more on wishes than on acknowledging that quoting poems work differently from nonquoting poems. Despite textual evidence to the contrary, readers strain to imagine and thus "create" (reading teachers might call this "vocalize") a single, chordal voice telling us the poem. This section from *The Cantos* shows how the process establishes itself:

Et omniformis," Psellos, "omnis
"Intellectus est." God's fire. Gemisto:
"Never with this religion
"Will you make men of the greeks.
"But build wall across Peloponesus
"And organize, and . . .
                damn these Eyetalian barbarians."
And Novvy's ship went down in the tempest
Or at least they chucked the books overboard.

                              (23.107)

Because we know a single author fashioned this poem, we often attempt to construct an overriding single voice for this section and for all *The Cantos,* a voice that here *quotes* Psellos, Gemisto, and that slips back to its own sound with the narrative about Malatesta Novello. All of the poetry, including the quotations, *somehow* is Pound's voice. This identification becomes firmer the more it seems that autobiography impinges on the writing, as it seems to do, for example, with the Pisan cantos. And reading tastes are generally still conservative: the main reason the Pisan cantos are the most attractive of Pound's cantos is that this voice is so clear and unambiguous. But this insisting upon a voice is both circular and subjective (there is a voice because I sense a voice, and I sense a voice because it is there), and does not answer the question what Pound's voice sounds like—or how it is constructed.

On a similar plane, but with diminishing naïveté, readers create a voice from what is not quotation. In Moore's poetry, for example, nothing could be more typical than to imagine as the authentic voice of the poem those phrases that are not quotations:

> Prince Rupert's drop, paper muslin ghost,
>     White torch—"with power to say unkind
> Things with kindness, and the most
>     Irritating things in the midst of love and
>         Tears," you invite destruction.
>
> ("Pedantic Literalist," 54)

This nonquoted voice, then, is easily imagined as speaking the quotations. The quotations thus are not the poem's "pure" voice, but the poem's voice quoting a text. The language used here to describe this process betrays the major presupposition behind many reading experiences: there *must* be a single voice, a single subject, speaking the poem.

Highly disjunctive poems and poems that quote heavily illustrate the presuppositions behind our reading process more dramatically. For example, in what seems to be an attempt to wrest control back from the disruptive quotation, Pound at the end of his first canto dramatically steps back from his quoting:

> And he strong with the blood, said then: "Odysseus
> "Shalt return through spiteful Neptune, over dark seas,
> "Lose all companions." And then Anticlea came.

Lie quiet Divus. I mean, that is Andreas Divus,
In officina Wecheli, 1538, out of Homer.
And he sailed, by Sirens and thence outward and away
And unto Circe.

(4–5)

Readers seize what is not the quotation or in subjection to it as being the poem's voice. The authoritative, nonquoted voice that speaks the imperative "Lie quiet Divus" and reveals itself as "I" must be the voice of the poem, the voice that narrates the poem to us. This construction has merit, for one can create a plausible narrative situation here in which the "I" speaks to the creator of the quotation (Andreas Divus).

Similarly, in the concluding eight lines of *The Waste Land,* only one line is not a quotation, and wherever in this dense texture there is not a clear quotation, readers tend to assume (safely or not) that this line presents the voice of the unity-bringing poetic persona:

London Bridge is falling down falling down falling down
*Poi s'ascose nel foco che gli affina*
*Quando fiam uti chelidon*—O swallow swallow
*Le Prince d'Aquitaine à la tour abolie*
These fragments I have shored against my ruins
Why then Ile fit you. Hieronymo's mad againe.
Datta. Dayadhvam. Damyata.
Shantih shantih shantih

(74–75)

The "I" and an apparent reference to both the quotations and the poetic process ("fragments" and "I have shored") back up this assumption: "These fragments I have shored against my ruins." We tend to believe this is the voice of the poem because such a belief constructs a plausible narrative situation and because we cannot easily assign this voice to someone who is clearly *not* the poem's central voice, as we can at the beginning of the poem: "He said, Marie, / Marie, hold on tight. And down we went. / In the mountains, there you feel free" (61). Readers typically unify the end of *The Waste Land* around "these fragments I have shored," but this identification between a statement in the poem and a voice is rarely so easy. Not often does a poet explicitly in one phrase refer to a poem's quotations, its structural technique, and

99

its theme, at one point clinching all these elements together through a single voice that identifies itself as "I."

However, such a reading process still leaves readers with difficulties. For example, such a reading of the ending lines of *The Waste Land* does not define the relation of the quoted parts of the text to the main voice. Further, although readers construct a single voice for sections of *The Cantos,* they are hard pressed to characterize this voice, to show whether the voice is consistent throughout the entire work, and to articulate how the voice unifies theme, imagery, and other poetic elements. That is, readers "recognize" Eliot's and Pound's voices, but is there any way to substantiate this identification? Does it go beyond localized moments? Is this recognition anything more than nostalgia or wish fulfillment in the face of difficult and disunified texts?

One reason that the new poem's voice remains elusive is that the quoted voice's inevitable disruption characterizes how one can read the new poem's poetic voice. The poem's voice does not simply speak the quotation; the quotation radically interrupts the poem's voice. As Theo Hermans points out for Guillaume Apollinaire's poetry, disrupting the discursiveness of a poem causes the poem's persona to diminish in centrality (56). The more disjunction there is, the more difficult it is to find the voice. Since there is such great logical and syntactic fragmentation, finding a voice is more difficult in highly fragmented poems like *The Waste Land* or *The Cantos* than it is in most of Cummings's or Moore's poetry, although the differing textures ensure that even with these latter poets the voice is always muffled.

Signaling the new voice that alien worlds establish in the quoting poem, disjunction provides the key to the quoting poem's unified voice. The presence of the new voice ensures that the reading of the quoting poem will be bumpy, and that the gaps between quotation and new text will be impossible to erase completely in the search for a rhetorical unity. However, the voice now comes through the relations the gaps build into the poem. This unity of voice also will not be first of all directed at how the voice creates a theme for the poem. One expends much more energy discovering *how* the quotations fit and do not fit into a certain structured reading experience of the poem. The unity of the quoting poem comes from the quoting poem's voice, which I will discuss as the pattern of the relations between the voices of the inserted quotations and new text. A relation-structured reading of these poems, then, does not so much assuage the fear of lack of unity as change the discussion's direction away from the traditional focus on unity of theme, imagery, or topic. Although the previous examples show at times a naive response to voice, such readings are correct in sensing that creating some kind of poetic unity in the quoting poem comes from a dramatizing of the interaction between voices. Poetic unity—the voice—comes from the reading process, the types of relations (or metaphoric structures) that readers construct.

## Lyric Versus Dramatic Voice

A distinction between dramatic and lyric voices, based upon how many voices the poem presents to the reader, begins to uncover the types of relations that create the quoting voice. Critics such as George Wright and Sharon Cameron argue that the lyric voice is single while the dramatic voice is multiple (Cameron, 22–23; Wright, 110). These two voices are the boundaries of the quoting poem's voice. Basing the voice of the quoting poem primarily on number does much to explain these poems' characteristics, for the voice of the quoting poem is created primarily by encouraging or suppressing multiple voices. The lyric quoting voice almost totally controls the new inserted voices and attempts to erase them. In contrast, the dramatic voice allows a number of different voices to exist and to flaunt their original textures; indeed, the dramatic voice can be found only in these different voices. The more disruption the quotation brings, the more dramatic the voice is; the less disruption, the more the poem approximates the lyric. In the quoting poem, the lyric voice meets many conservative poetic strategies, such as the establishing of authority; the dramatic voice encourages the experimental, such as the free play of signifiers.

But these distinctions are somewhat artificial, for no quoting poem is either purely lyric or purely dramatic. As quotation and allusion are points along a continuum, so are lyric and dramatic voices. In *Lyric Time* Cameron recognizes the pull towards multiple points of view in the lyric; Wright similarly complicates his paradigm, arguing that in "lyrical" dramas one character thoroughly dominates the others; the other characters are present merely to show the contours of the main character. "Dramatic" lyrics show struggles between opposing points of view, including an opposition between the poet and her persona (Cameron, 88, 207–10; Wright, 110). The lyric poem cannot escape some contamination of the dramatic voice; as the quoting poem appropriates the dramatic voice, lyric elements intrude. The quoting poem is always a hybrid, establishing its distinctive voice by emphasizing or suppressing one of the two voices, by establishing either of those voices that Bakhtin calls monologic or dialogic.

If there indeed is such a thing, the most natural voice in the quoting poem is the dramatic voice, for that voice most clearly acknowledges the alienness of the quotation. (Indeed, allusions, while able to reach a much purer lyric voice than can quotations, cannot reach the limits of the dramatic voice in the way that quotations can.) Poets approximate a dramatic voice through the fiction of a lack of control over the quotations. Poets employ a variety of techniques to establish this seeming lack of control: they increase the number of quotations and tinker with their length; they strategically place the quotation; they deemphasize symbolism; they increase disjunction.

*The Cantos* most nearly approach a pure dramatic voice. In a poem like *The Cantos,* the dramatic voice establishes itself through syntactic and visual disjunctions, which allow for a more free functioning of disruptive voices:

> Sound slender, quasi tinnula,
> Ligur' aoide: Si no'us vei, Domna don plus mi cal,
> Negus vezer mon bel pensar no val."
> Between the two almond trees flowering,
> The viel held close to his side;
> And another: s'adora"
> "Possum ego naturae
> non meminisse tuae!" Qui son Properzio ed Ovidio.
>
> (20.89)

Radically differing voices interrupt each other, seize control, and abruptly fade away. The quotation's syntactic and visual disruptions feed off each other; accentuating one usually involves accentuating the other. The quotations begin or end at the beginning or ending of lines, and our usual reading habits create a slight pause at each point. The introductory colons stiffly announce more disjunction than does the smooth integration of Moore's poetry. In addition, the complete visual and syntactic independence separating "s'adora'" from "Possum ego naturae" has no choice but to create a gap between these two units. In an aggressively dramatic poem such as this, the disruptions between quotations stymie any controlling theme, and thus the poem's surface tends to present a series of voices, no one voice clearly establishing control or point of view. The disjointed syntax allows voices to interrupt each other. At its clearest, then, the dramatic quoting voice is an ambiguously presented voice. Control occurs only through a seeming lack of control.

As Pound's *Cantos* also shows, the poet creates a dramatic voice by introducing a great number of quotations. As the number of quotations increases, the possible interrelationships increase exponentially. Given the individual texture of each quotation, it becomes difficult to have anything but the vaguest voice control all these voices. Pound often couples this great number of quotations with an insistence on presenting the many quotations as unadorned as possible, a move that allows as much room as possible for the integrity of the quoted voices. Any plausible central voice here reduces to a whisper:

> These fragments you have shelved (shored).
> "Slut!" "Bitch!" Truth and Calliope
> Slanging each other sous les lauriers:
> *That* Alessandro was negroid. And Malatesta
> Sigismund:
> > *Frater tamquam*
> *Et compater carissime: tergo*
> > . . . *hanni de*
> > . . *dicis*
> > . . . *entia*
> Equivalent to:
> > Giohanni of the Medici,
> > Florence.
> Letter received, and in the matter of our Messire Gianozio,
> One from him also, sent on in form and with all due dispatch,
> Having added your wishes and memoranda.
>
> > > (8.28)

There are plenty of traces of control here, but none that seem to imply a single authority or strategy. The obsessive purity with which Pound quotes the letter from Malatesta (mirroring the partially obscured seal of the original manuscript) contrasts with his cavalier misquotation of Eliot.

The results for voice? Misquoting Eliot highlights the discursive self-consciousness of *The Cantos*' voice. When Pound explicitly misquotes Eliot, we hear Pound's voice (because we know the misquotation to be deliberate) and wonder at his motivations. We try to find clues for the narrator's voice within the quotation. By contrast, the Malatesta quotation is self-conscious in its accuracy. Paradoxically, Pound's self-conscious recording both attracts attention to the form of *The Cantos* as a work and ensures that the quotation's original voice is not written over. Pound takes pains to keep his slang out of the translation of the letter in order to present the original voice as unencumbered as possible. He presents his voice as a recording voice. The change between the Malatesta and Eliot voices allows for "slut" and "bitch" to react coyly with the written-over borrowing from Eliot (by their juxtaposition referring to Eliot). Curiously, the only words in quotation marks in this passage are not quotations from a specific source—but Pound wants readers to read them as quotations because the quotation marks remove responsibility from the poem's recording voice.

Such dramatic effects are not limited to Pound. In any longer poem with many different quotations from different sources (and different *types* of sources), such as Moore's "Marriage," it is difficult to find the central voice and its strategies:

> "Married people often look that way"—
> "seldom and cold, up and down,
> mixed and malarial
> with a good day and a bad."
> "When do we feed?"
> We occidentals are so unemotional,
> we quarrel as we feed;
> self lost, the irony preserved
> in "the Ahasuerus *tête-à-tête* banquet"
> with its small orchids like snakes' tongues,
> with its "good monster, lead the way,"
> with little laughter
> and munificence of humour
> in that quixotic atmosphere of frankness
> in which, "four o'clock does not exist,
> but at five o'clock

the ladies in their imperious humility
are ready to receive you";

(89)

This series of voices, all on the same topic, but all pulling in slightly differing directions, demonstrates why Moore's longer quoting poems are so difficult, presenting the greatest challenge to the reader who wants to find out what they "mean." In "Marriage," the fractured voices point to Moore's lack of commitment to any single position in this "anthology"; the form and number of the voices may more profoundly suggest Moore's ambivalence and lack of allegiance to the topic. By contrast, "New York"'s clinching quotation, "accessibility to experience," seems much tamer. Although the greater syntactic disjunction in *The Waste Land* and *The Cantos* more spectacularly highlights how the quotations are working at different purposes, in both of those poems and in "Marriage" the frequency of quotations similarly impinge on voice, for the large number of quotations in each poem stymies attempts to find a lyric voice. Rather than being controlled by a single strategy, the quotations seem to talk to each other.

Lengthy quotations also help create a dramatic quoting voice. The more extensive the quotation becomes, the more readers look for the poetic voice in the quotation itself, and less in the relation of the quotation to the rest of the poem. The quoted voice stays long enough to acquire complexity and establish several characteristics within itself, and so its texture can neither be easily written over by a single strategy, nor subordinated to another voice. Thus, in many of Pound's cantos in which Pound uses lengthy quotations (such as in the Malatesta cantos), many readers discover that they cannot find "Pound" in a particular quotation; they can find Pound only in the thematic relation of this quotation to the rest of the poem. By naming certain cantos after their dominant quotations (e.g., the Adams or Malatesta cantos), readers implicitly recognize this function of lengthy quotations. The voice of the quoted sources dominates the new poem.

By foregrounding the quotation's voice one establishes a dramatic rather than a lyric strategy. At the same time, the original theme of the quotation, constructed in the quotation's original world, achieves more prominence. The result? A poem such as *The Cantos* that uses lengthy quotations (especially from argumentative or "nonaesthetic" texts) can become didactic. Despite its free play, the lengthy quotation can take on its original rhetorical functions as it establishes the characteristics of its original world.

In contrast, the less extensive the quotation is, the more readers look for the poet's voice in the relation between quotation and the rest of the text. It is easier for the *relations* between many quotations and the rest of the text to have a similar texture than it is for the voices of the quotations themselves all to have the same sound. (Relations, after all, are abstract concepts, quite able to overrun extraneous detail.) The short quotation plays a part in determining the poetic voice, but it does not within itself contain the voice, for in such a small space the quotation's voice cannot establish a presence that controls the entire poem. The shorter quotation tends to have just one significant characteristic for which the poet uses it. As such, this one characteristic is often easily incorporated into the strategy of the poem, as happens when Cummings's poetry uses advertising. As Moore's poetry demonstrates, incorporation intensifies as the syntactic connection between quotation and new text becomes smoother:

> O
> Bird, whose tents were "awnings of Egyptian
> Yarn," shall Justice' faint zigzag inscription—
>     Leaning like a dancer—
>         Show
> The pulse of its once vivid sovereignty?
>
> ("To Statecraft Embalmed," 51)

This use of short quotations more easily allows for the creation of a lyric voice; Moore barely allows a dramatic relationship to establish itself here.

A further method by which poets establish a dramatic voice is in the placement of the quotation. Although the quotation that ends the poem often seems to sum up everything, its presence is duplicitous. Instead of affirming the lyric voice, the ending quotation introduces dramatic instability and conflict, even in as lyric a poet as Marianne Moore:

the white volcano with no weather side;
the lightning flashing at its base,
rain falling in the valleys, and snow falling on the peak—
the glassy octopus symmetrically pointed,
its claw cut by the avalanche
"with a sound like the crack of a rifle,
in a curtain of powdered snow launched like a waterfall."

("An Octopus," 103)

To be sure, the quotation—almost as an authority—neatly clinches the logic and succession of images of this poem. But the voice of W. D. Wilcox's *The Rockies of Canada* adds an intrusive bump to the smooth texture of this ending. Instead of validating the voice of the poem that has gone on before, the ending quotation destabilizes it. The poem's controlling voice does not return after the presence of this quotation. Partly because of its obscure origins, the ending quotation introduces a radical separation from the rest of the text, and redefines the text that has gone before. By giving this quotation the last word, whatever voice that has up to this point controlled "An Octopus" gives up some control to the quotation, especially since this quotation climaxes what has been a finale of very energetic description. In addition, given the linear structure of this particular poem, it is impossible for this quotation's voice to control the entire poem. In "No Swan So Fine" the beginning quotation ("No water so still as the / dead fountains of Versailles") can by virtue of its position set the direction for the poetic voice that follows. In "An Octopus," however, linearity prevents the quotation from reaching back to the beginning of the poem. Neither can the voice of the poem subsume the ending quotation. The poem's voice must enter some dramatic dialogue with the quotation, in a way that it doesn't when the poet's voice herself firmly ends the poem:

If external action is effete
    and rhyme is outmoded,
        I shall revert to you,
    Habakkuk, as on a recent occasion I was goaded
        into doing by XY, who was speaking of unrhymed verse.
This man said—I think that I repeat
    his identical words:
        "Hebrew poetry is

prose with a sort of heightened consciousness." Ecstasy affords
the occasion and expediency determines the form.

("The Past Is the Present," 117)

Here, the ending voice is the voice of the poem. This final voice has a
heavy authority, as it does in "An Octopus." Unlike the quoted ending
of "An Octopus," however, the final voice does not introduce dramatic
instability but closes it off. Almost inevitably, the last presence of the
speaker's voice here sounds epigrammatic.

Accompanying any poet's decision to accentuate or muffle the dra-
matic voice is that poet's relation to the use of the symbolic in poetry.
In much the same way that an ending quotation destabilizes the poem,
the Modernist distrust of the symbol leads to dramatic confrontations
in quoting poetry. A central poetic strategy clearly dominates the sym-
bol, and as such a quotation used as a symbol can also surrender its
function and voice to this central domination, as repeatedly occurs in
Cummings's poetry. The quotations in Cummings's lines "say can you
see by the dawn's early my / country 'tis of centuries come and go" are
used symbolically, to refer to a recognizable public attitude; almost any
lines from any patriotic song could do. But if a poem's quotations do
*not* have a symbolic function, the voice of the quoting poem seems
more dramatic because there is less control over the quotations' voice
and function.

Pound, and to a lesser extent Eliot and Moore, did not frequently
use clear symbols in his poetry. In *The Poetics of Indeterminacy* Marjorie
Perloff discusses the anti-Symbolist strain in Pound's writing. Accord-
ing to Perloff, this strain gives *The Cantos* its peculiar texture, celebrat-
ing idiosyncratic textures rather than mashing these textures together
to form a smooth, symbolic paste (159–66). If the quotation is not so
much symbolic as it is celebrated for its idiosyncratic texture (as it often
is in the poetry of Moore, Eliot, and Pound), its own peculiar voice
will dominate and will assert itself against other voices in the poem.

Since the quotation's opposition to the new text is inherent to quot-
ing poetry, all quoting poetry has at least a partially dramatic voice.
The lack of a center of control in this dramatic voice hides traditional
poetic unity. In the quoting poem the dramatic voice can create tradi-
tional types of poetic unity only awkwardly, since it is hard to find a
single clear voice in the poem, and only a single voice can establish
poetic unity. The control comes more from the relations of the voices

of the quotations among themselves than in relation to a central poetic voice.

But the purely dramatic poem bounds only one extreme of the quoting voice, and like most extremes it is never realized. No poems achieve a pure dramatic voice; the quoting poem inevitably has something of a metavoice that is missing from drama, a voice that interacts dialogically with the quotations (Bakhtin, "Discourse," 266). Always dominated by a more primary voice that fills in where the quotation is absent and that differs from authorial presence, the quotation itself rarely achieves first-person presence. In the dramatic quoting poem there is not so much a clear sense of the pure drama's conflict between equal characters as of a single voice guiding the other voices. The voice in the dramatic quoting poem differs from the voice in a real drama because at times the quoting poem presents a pure central voice (not an implied authorial presence, as in drama). We do hear a voice in Pound's *Cantos* that is separate from the quotations and that has some primacy over them, if not with the efficiency and neatness that Bedient suggests for the voice of *The Waste Land*.

As the dramatic elements of the quoting voice imply a lack of control, the lyric elements imply control. The form of the quoting poem, all that shows the shaping intelligence of the poet, becomes part of the central, lyric voice. What Guillaume Apollinaire argued for Picasso and his collages is just as true for the quoting poem:

> Picasso has sometimes dispensed with ordinary paints and made reliefs from cardboard and pictures from pieces of paper pasted together: when he does so he obeys a plastic inspiration, and these strange, uncouth and ill-matching materials become noble because the artist confers on them his own strong and sensitive personality. (qtd. in Fry, 113)[1]

The poet cannot avoid having a shaping intelligence show through. No quoting poem can therefore totally escape the lyric. With Pound the poetic voice gives the *appearance* of a drama, but it does not want to give up completely the prerogatives of the lyric. Pound is too egocentric, more so than Moore, whose poetry looks more lyric than Pound's, but often acts more dramatic. Pound wants readers, especially readers of the middle and later cantos, to assent to some specific assertions about the world, assertions that can be made clear only if the poet's attitude to the quotations is clear. Other voices are subservient to the main voice. But the quoting poem most closely approximates the lyric voice when a single intelligence, present in all aspects of the poem, clearly governs how readers appropriate the poem's structures.

Sometimes assertions of a lyric voice can be spectacular. Eliot's "these fragments I have shored" at the end of *The Waste Land* is so striking because it controls so much of the poem—the discourse, theme, and the other quotations of the poem. But along with our recognizing that this phrase controls so much of the poem comes the implication that the controlling elements of this phrase must be anticipated by previous elements of the poem, including the quoted voices. The lyric voice signaled by "these fragments I have shored" also must be heard vaguely throughout the poem. Since the voice is only partially heard in the lyric "I," one can discuss the characteristics of this presence only by discussing the other elements of the poem. Thus, the voice is heard less spectacularly, but in some ways more insistently, in all elements of the poem that show a shaping intelligence—in short, in all the poem.

The lyric quoting voice is self-assured, authoritarian, in control. Whether naive or ironic (as in this sonnet by Cummings), the poetic stance is clear:

O It's Nice To Get Up In,the slipshod mucous kiss
of her riant belly's fooling bore
—When The Sun Begins To(with a phrasing crease
of hot subliminal lips,as if a score
of youngest angels suddenly should stretch neat necks
just to see how always squirms
the skilful mystery of Hell)me suddenly

grips in chuckles of supreme sex.

In The Good Old Summer Time.
My gorgeous bullet in tickling intuitive flight
aches,just,simply,into,her.     Thirsty
stirring.     (Must be summer.     Hush.     Worms.)
But It's Nicer To Lie In Bed
                    —eh? I'm
not.     Again.     Hush.     God.     Please hold.     Tight
                                                        (203)

By surrounding a syntactically incomplete section of the quotation, Cummings ensures that the voice of his own poem controls the quotation since this voice completes it. Cummings accentuates the control by radically enjambing some of the quotations into the new text. The mixing increases because the new poem's capitalization writes the voice of the new poem over the voice of the quotation, calling attention to the shaping voice of the poem. In the same manner, the sonnet form constricts free play or previous forms of the quotation. The lyric voice attempts to swallow the quotation.

As this selection from Cummings shows, the quoting poet establishes a lyric voice through several means, including the poem's rhetoric, its cultural judgments, lineation and stanzaic arrangement, quotation marks, syntax, and diction. Although it usually is a diminished unity, unity created mainly through a poem's rhetoric can encourage a lyric voice. Thus, in Moore's poetry the quotations are less aggressively enjambed than are the quotations of Cummings's poetry, and they therefore create for themselves a more free voice in the poem. But they do not assert their individual texture so aggressively that they remove themselves from the rhetorical strategies of the poem's dominant voice:

"No water so still as the
    dead fountains of Versailles." No swan,
with swart blind look askance
and gondoliering legs, so fine
    as the chintz china one with fawn-
brown eyes and toothed gold
collar on to show whose bird it was.

Lodged in the Louis Fifteenth
    candelabrum-tree of cockscomb-
tinted buttons, dahlias,
sea-urchins, and everlastings,
    it perches on the branching foam
of polished sculptured
flowers—at ease and tall. The king is dead.

("No Swan So Fine," 31)

Here, and in much of Moore's poetry, readers strive to fit the discrepant quoting voice into the poem's rhetorical strategy as it is revealed by the poem's nonquoted voice. The lyricality of the poem's voice comes primarily through rhetoric, rather than through a nonparaphrasable attitude, as it does with Cummings, or through a series of recurring relations, as it does with Pound. But formal control is not so obvious here as it is in Cummings's poem. Most noticeably, Moore does not obviously deform the quotation to fit into her stanzaic form. As John Slatin points out, Moore always quotes prose to avoid the struggle between the borrowing and the borrowed text's forms (88–91). Moore's rhetorical form is more traditional than are Cummings's exploded sonnets, but Moore works more thoroughly at exploiting a polyphonic voice. Consequently, Moore looks more traditional at first glance, but she also has more to offer Postmodern sensibilities than does Cummings.

In "No Swan So Fine," the lyric voice is achieved primarily through the poem's rhetorical coherence, which unifies both quotation and new text. In face of the textual disjunction that the quotation brings, readers posit a central frame of reference that provides a logical structure. An alert reader notices the parallel syntactic structures in the first stanza and assumes some sort of equation is being made between the quotation and the rest of the stanza. Unity of purpose dominates here, even if later in the poem the values of this unity may be undercut. The feature-article quotation brings in a set of popularly accepted values concerning the pathos of elegance lost through revolution (Willis). These values, along with much of the rest of the poem's text, are rhetorically unified, and respond univocally to the support and undercutting of the poem's last sentence: "The king is dead." All of these elements ultimately fit the rhetorical strategy of the poem's central voice, a strategy that results in an ironic commentary on the death of elegance.

The less the poetry uses syntactic fragmentation, and the fewer quotations there are, the easier it is to discover Moore's rhetorical voice. What cannot initially be rhetorically unified forms part of the poem's difficulty and the slight dramatic character of the voice: the second, unknown presence and its trailing characteristics, such as the quotation marks and the quotation's unknown original function. The poem's voice here vacillates much more strongly than does Cummings's poetry between freedom and restriction, between lyric and dramatic tendencies.

Cultural judgments in quoting poetry strengthen the lyric voice because they establish the authority of the poetic persona. Gerard

Genette's narrative theory argues that we count as the writer's voice anything that betokens a cultural judgment or establishing of values as opposed to pure reporting. Genette's critical practice shows that to varying degrees all writing is caught up in these judgments; in fact, these judgments are the most "natural" form of language, and can swallow up all other forms (139–43). In all poetry, including quoting poetry, readers put these cultural judgments together to construct a poetic voice. All parenthetical comments, all contemporary or personal allusions that differ from the world of the quotation, and all value judgments contribute to the voice of the poetry. The more of these judgments there are, the more lyric the voice is.

Cummings's poetry presents many cultural judgments because his satire demands tight control of a single voice, but even Pound, the most dramatic of quoting poets, shows these cultural judgments. For instance, in Pound's poetry readers listen for the American slang, and for forms of nonpoetic diction. Eventually, with Pound, even Greek script and Chinese ideograms become part of his cultural judgments, for the poetry shows that these writings have value for Western culture—as Williams repeatedly grumbled, the quotation takes on authority. Certain repetitions in Pound's poetry, such as the American slang comments on European culture, also become part of the voice. The quotations one chooses also result from value judgments, and can lead to widely differing voices—Eliot's high art quotations give him a voice that in its cultural discriminations differs from the voice Moore acquires through her feature articles and advertisements.

Perhaps most immediately, the look of the poem, especially such elements as its lineation and stanzaic arrangement, shapes the voice. The more the quotation has been visually changed from its appearance in its original context, the more the poet adopts a lyric strategy. In using lineation to help create a voice the poet can end-stop the quotation, separating the quotation from the rest of the text, and usually retaining the quotation's original lineation. Such a strategy encourages the original properties of the quotation and the dramatic voice to assert themselves. More usually, the poet will in some way enjamb the quotation by running it into the new text, consequently enhancing the lyric voice. Thus, in "unnoticed woman" Cummings relineates "A Visit from St. Nicholas" to fit in with his rhyme scheme and so puts his stamp on the quotation:

also,tomorrow the daily papers will feature
Peace And Good Will,and Mary with one lung
extended to the pumping Child,and "'Twas

the night before Christmas when all through the house not a
    creature
was stirring,not even a mouse. The stockings were hung
by the chimney with care in hopes that Saint Nicholas"

(129)

Instead of the quotation's rhyme interacting within itself, the relineation points the quotation to the quoting text. "Creature" and "hung" are now the rhyme words, which, by pointing to "feature" and "lung," demonstrate their new function by their integration into the new text. The quotation's original rhythm and rhyme scheme tug against such an imposition, but such unsuccessful tugging merely highlights Cummings's control. In addition, the regular forms one finds in much of Cummings's writing (however disguised, as in the sonnet partially quoted above) enhance the unified qualities of the poetic voice. The poet's control is clear in his acknowledgment of poetic tradition, an acknowledgment that governs the entire reading of the poem. The poet's controlling lyric voice gains primacy over the original or free functioning of the quotation.

Few Modernist poets use traditional forms to shape an entire poem, however. Most visual cues for the poet's voice are less obtrusive. For example, by capitalizing the beginning letter of the first words of a line (as the line appears transcribed *in the new poem*), the poet puts more of his own mark on the quotation; with the original capitalization intact there is more disruption and less of the poet's voice within the quotation. Again, the controlling force of the poet bumps the quotation into line with the rest of the poem.

Even the decision to use or not to use quotation marks has implications for poetic voice. Quotation marks show the voice of a persona who wishes his reader to know a quotation is taking place, a reader who should know (but may not actually know) how the poem is self-consciously put together. At the same time quotation marks highlight the shaping voice of the poet, for quotation marks are a sign of controlling ownership while the rest of the poem acknowledges its distance.

Quotation marks distance the quotation from the rest of the poem, frequently ironically.

Overriding the quotation's prosody also brings in the lyric voice. Of the poets discussed in this study, Moore and Cummings don't as obviously use prosody to call attention to the separate dramatic existence of their quotations. The prosody often remains homogeneous throughout a particular poem, even if this usually means sacrificing the original prosody—and thus some of the disruptive voice—of the quotation. For these poets, the main prompt to set off the quotation *as* quotation is our cultural knowledge or visual awareness that it is a quotation (through footnotes, quotation marks, etc.). This unobtrusive pointing out of the quotation fits in well with their poetic projects—Moore's and Cummings's poems take on many of the qualities of the lyric voice, but at the same time their quotations cause readers to be very much aware of the poem's discourse.

Of possible stylistic decisions, decisions about syntax most typically affect voice, and can simultaneously express and suppress the lyric voice. Among the four poets discussed here, Moore especially attempts both to establish free play for the quotation (a dramatic strategy) and to keep a lyric control over it. For example, in several of her poems Moore uses an *it is, it is not* structure to introduce her quotations. This use of forms of *to be* accentuates quotations as independent units, separate items not as easily part of any persona. The catalog structure often seen in her poetry easily allows quotations to be introduced as objects on a par with the other elements of a catalog:

> It is not the dime-novel exterior,
> Niagara Falls, the calico horses and the war-canoe;
> it is not that "if the fur is not finer than such as one sees others wear,
> one would rather be without it"—
> that estimated in raw meat and berries, we could feed the universe;
> it is not the atmosphere of ingenuity,
> the otter, the beaver, the puma skins
> without shooting-irons or dogs;
> it is not the plunder,
> but "accessibility to experience."
>
>                    ("New York," 77)

In using this structure Moore doesn't swallow up the voice of her quotations as much as does Cummings with his quotations. She presents them as independent units in the poem, even though controlled by the poem's syntax. They thus relate ambiguously to the rest of the poem—not so much in their meaning, but in how readers assimilate this voice into the rest of the poem. In other words, the form of *to be* makes it difficult to discover exactly how much irony the quotation carries. The denotation of "it is" is clear, but unlike many other verbs, "it is" does not have many poetically expressive connotations, with the exception of some overtones of passivity and objectivity. The function of these overtones is made more cryptic through the use of the distancing quotation marks. As does juxtaposition in some of the more spectacular quoting poems, here "it is" gives readers significantly incomplete instructions on how to use the quotation.

Yet although the "it is" allows the quoted voice to exist independently, at the same time "it is" controls the quoted voice. This control shows up in the strong logical connection between quotation and new poem: the quotation is clearly subordinated to the voice saying "it is." In these definitions in the poem, the "it is" has much authority. "It is" does not imply any doubt; it asserts an identity between the quotation and the surrounding text. With the quotation dominated in this way, a single voice results. The slight disjunction this technique gives supports Moore's coolly ironic voice and the exploratory, nondogmatic nature of her poetry. Since this type of relation between text and quotation occurs regularly, the disjunction readers encounter in the poem is of one sort, filling a single poetic project and voice.

Readers can also find the voice of the quoting poem in syntactic structures that are not immediately contiguous to the quotation. In all cases, syntactically stated logical relations that are not part of the quotation show the presence of a shaping intelligence. These relations are the quoting poem's voice. For example, the repetitive use of "ands" in the early cantos are always the voice of Pound, the arranger. Only the central voice of the poem could be responsible for them:

> I sat on the Dogana's steps
> For the gondolas cost too much, that year,
> And there were not "those girls," there was one face,
> And the Buccentoro twenty yards off, howling "Stretti,"

And the lit cross-beams, that year, in the Morosini,
And peacocks in Koré's house, or there may have been.

(3.11)

The poetic relations that these "ands" introduce are of one kind: they introduce something like a list, and keep the voice of the poet distant, allowing for the free play that is part of Pound's poetic strategy. There is no clear causal connection between the items in the list. The "ands" introduce events that, like Moore with her quotations, caught Pound's fancy. The strongest relation that the "ands" introduce is a series of historical parallels that have a tone of wry reminiscence. The clearer and more active the logical connection (for example, the less a poet uses *be* verbs), the more lyric the voice. Cummings, therefore, has a much more lyric voice than does Pound.

How diction establishes the quoting poem's voice raises issues similar to those just discussed. It is easy to see how in a nonquoting poem a poet's idiosyncratic lexicon can create a voice. The quoting poem complicates this process since some of the phrases are not original with the poet. At times with quoting poetry, the poet attempts to circumvent even this most basic problem. Poets such as Moore and Pound silently emend the quotation better to fit the new poem's voice (consequently removing it from being a pure quotation, although readers usually cannot take this change into account in their reading experience). Thus, the first lines of Moore's poem "No Swan So Fine" quote a caption that appeared above a photograph in the *New York Times Magazine,* 10 May 1931 (8). But Moore, as she often does in her poetry, transforms the original. The original caption, itself marked as a quotation, read "There is No Water So Still as in the Dead Fountains of Versailles." In her poem Moore silently replaces the words with the slightly different version she used in her poetry: "No water so still as the / dead fountains of Versailles." By removing the weak form of *to be* and the prepositional phrase, the change makes the opening of the poem much more aphoristic and gives it a slightly fusty nineties sound to go with the image of the swan. Such changes allow the quotation to work more univocally with the next few phrases:

"No water so still as the
    dead fountains of Versailles." No swan,

with swart blind look askance
and gondoliering legs, so fine
    as the chintz china one with fawn-
brown eyes and toothed gold
collar on to show whose bird it was.

                                                      (31)

A single, lyric voice can more clearly result from this epigrammatic quality and syntactic parallelism.

Pound's typical strategy is to introduce changes in diction that are not clearly his alone but that intertextually refer to other stylistic worlds and so push the quotation beyond its denotations, and beyond the voice of the poem. The change is in keeping with the less lyric voice of *The Cantos*. In his first canto, for example, Pound translates Andreas Divus's translation of Homer:

And then went down to the ship,
Set keel to breakers, forth on the godly sea, and
We set up mast and sail on that swart ship,
Bore sheep aboard her, and our bodies also
Heavy with weeping,

                                                      (1.3)

But strictly speaking, although it typically functions as a quotation, a translation is not a pure quotation, for the changed phrasing allows a new voice to show through. Pound applies this principle with a vengeance, making sure another voice is heard in the Anglo-Saxon rhythms. We hear Pound muffled in the translation, as we do in many of the later cantos when Pound adds an American yawp to his translation of Renaissance documents. With these changes, literal denotations acquire new connotations.

These sorts of additions abound in *The Cantos*, helping to create Pound's voice, a voice that vacillates between the lyric and the dramatic, depending on how much authoritative control Pound exerts at a particular point in the poem. Moreover, the effects of diction on the voice of the quoting poem go beyond the techniques analyzed so far. *Any* slang or stylistic changes that seem inconsistent with a quotation (i.e., any stylistic elements that are not part of a quotation's world) form the poetic voice.

What, then, does *The Cantos* reveal about its voice through its diction? It often is a voice in which intellectualism and irreverence for poetic materials simultaneously dominate, a voice in which a strong central presence brings in other strong voices and both overpowers them and gives them freedom to establish their own rhetorical and stylistic functions:

> Et omniformis," Psellos, "omnis
> "Intellectus est." God's fire. Gemisto:
> "Never with this religion
> "Will you make men of the greeks.
> "But build wall across Peloponesus
> "And organize, and . . .
>> damn these Eyetalian barbarians."
> And Novvy's ship went down in the tempest
> Or at least they chucked the books overboard.
>
> How dissolve Irol in sugar . . . Houille blanche,
> Auto-chenille, destroy all bacteria in the kidney,
> Invention-d'entités-plus-ou-moins-abstraits-
> en-nombre-égal-aux-choses-à-expliquer . . .
>
> (23.107)

The force of the poet is seen whenever the quoting poem's nonquoting text exerts syntactic control over the quotation. Pound establishes this force by literally tearing the quotations from their old texts, leaving behind crucial syntactic completions.[2] Thus, in the selection just quoted, Pound does not control his quotations by inserting into the syntax clear logical connections. The syntax between these jaggedly torn quotations is missing, creating disjunction. The sudden shifting of topics that results from this syntactic disruption is also part of Pound's voice, regardless of whether or not we find a clear reason throughout *The Cantos* for this type of shifting. Pound's quoting "Omnis intellectus est omniformis" ("Every intellect is capable of assuming every shape") states what the poet is capable of doing, but it only implicitly gives a disarming reason as to why the poet might appropriate a quotation: because it's there.

As the preceding quotation from Marsilio Ficino might suggest, the structure of this voice is not completely consistent throughout as lengthy a work as *The Cantos*. The voice changes between the first three cantos and number 4. In canto 4 the voice becomes less archaic (less bound by the character of the lengthy individual quotations) and becomes much more Pound's typically jumpy voice. As logical connectors in the syntax disappear and readers begin to create for themselves this syntax as they read, the increasing use of juxtaposition changes the voice. This sudden shifting makes Pound's voice seem authoritarian, capricious, and intimidating—for example, we cannot unequivocally find Pound's reasons in canto 23 for juxtaposing Psellos with Malatesta with Madame Curie.[3]

In the quoting poem, the strong lyric voice implies either of two relationships with the quotations. The poet can either accept or repudiate the quotations, for ambivalence or attempts at pure objectivity introduce dramatic qualities. Acceptance, creating a single stance between author and poetic voice, ideally has no dramatic overtones. But unequivocal acceptance does not occur in Modernist poetry, probably because to the postromantic poet such a stance seems naive. When Pound accepts his quotations the most unequivocally, the cantos begin fading to the status of treatises (e.g., the Adams cantos).

With acceptance not often seen as a valid mode of constructing quoting poetry, the strongest lyric voice is the satiric voice found in Cummings's poetry. Cummings's poetry uses cultural judgments, syntax, diction, and disjunction in order to create a persona whose voice goes beyond the equivocation of irony and reaches to satire. Cummings's use of American idiom, for example, sets up a stronger lyric voice than does Pound's idiom, which is much more tongue-in-cheek, and allows both positive and negative attitudes to the idiom to exist side by side. Pound allows his American idiom to exist both outside of and within the quotation, creating a complex dialogue of values both towards the quotation and the idiom. The attitude to American idiom is single throughout individual poems by Cummings, who uses American idiom to characterize and therefore subvert the values of his quotations:

> "next to of course god america i
> love you land of the pilgrims' and so forth oh
> say can you see by the dawn's early my
> country 'tis of centuries come and go
> and are no more what of it we should worry
> in every language even deafanddumb

thy sons acclaim your glorious name by gorry
by jingo by gee by gosh by gum

(267)

The contrast between idiom and quotation allows the quotation's language to be infected by the implicit values of the quoting poem's dialect. The univocal satire directed at the quotation's values is less than subtle.

Cummings also frequently capitalizes quotations in order to introduce irony through inappropriately inflating the quotations' importance. Such capitalization also indicates the quotation has become part of public speech: "land above all of Just Add Hot Water And Serve" (228). Further, although Cummings like Pound tears the syntactic edges off his quotations, Cummings uses the surrounding syntax (either through clear rhetorical integration or violent but unannounced enjambment) to indicate clearly how the reader is to use the quotation. In Cummings's poetry, the syntactic introduction will usually subvert the original power of the quotation, but not through syntactic disjunction. Cummings uses syntactic disjunction not to introduce a new direction created by a second voice, but to show how the poem's voice has stopped thinking, and is now nothing but reflexes: "say can you see by the dawn's early my / country 'tis of centuries come and go / and are no more what of it we should worry." To use disjunction in the way that Pound and Eliot do would require both a more sophisticated, fragmented voice in the poem and more meaning to be completed by readers. Since the voice in Cummings's poetry is frequently the object of satire, a dispersing fragmentation would subvert the unidirectional poetry.

The end result of all this manipulation is clear. Cummings, more than anyone else, takes a quotation and does something to its original function that the reader immediately notices. Cummings usually uses well-known quotations in order that his readers can unequivocally see his creative power over these quotations. The reader's sense of the quotation in a distorted context, distorted by the acting of a persona's single voice, is central to the experience of reading Cummings's poetry:

take it from me kiddo
believe me
my country, 'tis of

121

you,land of the Cluett
Shirt Boston Garter and Spearmint
Girl With The Wrigley Eyes(of you
land of the Arrow Ide
and Earl &
Wilson
Collars)of you i
sing: land of Abraham Lincoln and Lydia E. Pinkham,
land above all of Just Add Hot Water And Serve—
from every B.V.D.

let freedom ring
                    ("POEM, OR BEAUTY HURTS MR. VINAL," 228)

Unlike quotations in *The Cantos,* the quotations here have a highly
symbolic function. The symbolism that results from readers' awareness
of the quotation's texture does not so much dwell upon the quotations'
individual qualities as upon the type of worlds these quotations repre-
sent. The recurring relation between the American patriotic quotation
and American capitalism (here, a mixture of quoted advertising slogans
and name brands) gives this poem its energy, its unity, and its voice.
The recurring relation is between two types of quotations in counter-
point (one a more strict quotation than the other), controlled by a
single voice. These two quotations create a strictly consistent relation.
The recurring relation results in a rushing, breathless voice, a voice that
speeds over and enjambs quotations without keeping any distance from
the quotations or the process, the voice of the Boobus Americanus.
The consistency and the lack of distance allow this voice to dominate
as a lyric voice.

To be sure, readers base the poem's single-mindedness upon a differ-
ence within the text. Cummings wants to present the original quoted
voice, but he wants the voice to sound ugly, to acquire a function
opposing its typical uses. This opposing function creates the slight
dramatic confrontation between author and voice which satire as a
mode implies. Although satire introduces a strong distinction between
the poet and his persona, Cummings's satiric voice is also the strongest
lyric voice because in Modernism only satiric quoting gives an easily
identifiable persona and a stable, consistently overriding relation with
the quotations. Through its unity, the quoting lyric/satiric voice also

presents a poetry that is "easier" to read than dramatic quoting poetry. The reason for this ease is that the text's overriding of the quotation makes quite clear the solutions to the problematic disjunction introduced by the quotation. Therefore, despite the conflict, and all the poem's recognizing of different worlds, in Cummings's poetry the voice is lyric. The conflict is within a single point of view (that of the persona) rather than among separate characters (Cameron, 23). Paradoxically, satire, which leads to readers' opposite perceptions of what the poem seems to say, leads to unity of voice.

Eliot and Pound hide the lyric voice most aggressively, the plethora of voices and the disjunction conspiring to fragment a voice. Yet as we have seen in Pound's poetry, although this more complex use of quotations makes this process of finding a lyric voice more difficult, finding elements of such a voice is not impossible. Eliot's poetry similarly has lyric elements, but, unlike Pound, Eliot constructs his voice more through rhetoric and symbolizing. In *The Waste Land,* finding the central voice involves first discovering the poem's rhetorical strategies. Allow me to return once more to the problematic ending of *The Waste Land.* In an attempt to achieve some rhetorical unity, many readings jury-rig the diverse quotations into similar worlds having similar values. The text can be divided into the images of ruin, the transition ("Why then Ile fit you"), and the ambiguous benediction:

London Bridge is falling down falling down falling down
*Poi s'ascose nel foco che gli affina*
*Quando fiam uti chelidon*—O swallow swallow
*Le Prince d'Aquitaine à la tour abolie*
These fragments I have shored against my ruins
Why then Ile fit you. Hieronymo's mad againe.
Datta. Dayadhvam. Damyata.
        Shantih shantih shantih

                                         (74–75)

The main poetic voice must coherently interact with the rhetorical strategies that one can achieve by simplifying the quotations' worlds. The unity of the poem comes through readers deciding, through some self-constructed notions of proximity, what the simplified worlds in a particular poem may be. For this section of *The Waste Land,* the most basic similarity that can unite all these disparate worlds seems to be ruin. Thus, in order to unify the voice at the end of *The Waste Land* one may posit that "*Le Prince d'Aquitaine à la tour abolie*" fits into the more general world of the ruined values of Western civilization. Within each unit of the poem there may be more synthesizing that readers do—in this section of the poem readers decide what type of ruin each quotation depicts.

This unifying employs a consistent strategy. Rather than highlighting the aggressively individual texture of each quotation's world, lyric readings allow simplicity—and a certain amount of ambiguous symbolizing—to dominate. Several reasons account for this tendency. First, the textures of the worlds here fit together closely enough to make some overriding of their differences defensible. The quotations also fit more neatly into a central rhetorical strategy than do most of the quoted worlds in *The Cantos,* and they consequently encourage some symbolizing. In this poem (with its short quotations and rhetorical strategies) the more disjunction one finds, the more one categorizes the quotations into types and functions. To remove disjunction from the poem by rewriting it—for example, to rewrite "London Bridge is falling down falling down falling down" to "As I sit fishing I notice that London Bridge is falling down falling down falling down"—is to show how the lack of verbal syntax connecting the quotations to the main text turns these quotations much more into a static, personality-less world, a world that fits into the nonnarrative stasis and simplicity of a symbolic structure. The simplicity allows for the lyric voice to assert itself.

Where is the voice of *The Waste Land,* then? As mentioned near the beginning of this chapter, at discursive moments the central voice seems to announce itself boldly: "These fragments I have shored against my ruins." As it does in this poem, discourse always announces the presence of the voice. In addition, we take this phrase as the poem's voice because we cannot assign this voice clearly to some other persona, as we tentatively can do with the beginning of *The Waste Land.* The use of "and" as a connective between two phrases contributes to the slightly breathless and nonevaluative quality of "he took me out on a sled, / And I was frightened" (61). These lines do not connect with very much of the sound of the rest of the poem. The voice here sounds too innocent to be the voice of *The Waste Land,* unless it is the voice at an early point in its psychological history.

But at other points in the poem the voice shows through as univo-
cally as it does at the end. For example, the poem's second paragraph
seems to speak with the central voice of the poem:

> What are the roots that clutch, what branches grow
> Out of this stony rubbish? Son of man,
> You cannot say, or guess, for you know only
> A heap of broken images, where the sun beats,
> And the dead tree gives no shelter, the cricket no relief,
> And the dry stone no sound of water.
>
> (61)

We have heard this voice, with its emphasis on dryness and alienation,
in other of Eliot's poems. In addition, alienation and dryness recur as
elements of other worlds throughout this poem, but here they are
presented in what on the surface does not appear to be a quotation, to
be a second voice and another world. In this section an authoritative
voice comes through, either in the speaker or behind it.

But even though at times in *The Waste Land* it seems that readers
can construct a lyric voice, inevitably a quotation or a series of quota-
tions comes along to overwhelm and hide this voice, allowing the voice
to present itself only in elements that ambiguously reappear in different
contexts. Such burying doesn't just happen at the end of the poem.
Thus, the bewildering series of exclamations at the end of The Burial
of the Dead displaces and causes to disappear the voice readers have
constructed up to that point:

> "That corpse you planted last year in your garden,
> "Has it begun to sprout? Will it bloom this year?
> "Or has the sudden frost disturbed its bed?
> "O keep the Dog far hence, that's friend to men,
> "Or with his nails he'll dig it up again!
> "You! hypocrite lecteur!—mon semblable, mon frère!"
>
> (63)

Given their symbolic functioning, however, these subversive quotations
do not assert alternative voices as much as do the quotations in *The
Cantos*. Because one can easily simplify into the preoccupations of the

lyric voice those elements that overwhelm the lyric voice, the central voice of *The Waste Land* is not so much replaced as it is muffled. This finding and losing is the voice of *The Waste Land*.

Eliot's work shows most clearly how in the quoting poem attempting the lyric voice is often an attempt to create what Lyotard terms a "grand narrative." The lyric-leaning quoting poem evokes a grand narrative not simply through employing a unifying strategy, but by employing a unifying strategy that points beyond a single person, to a larger cultural unity. The text attempts to explain some big picture. The idea of the grand narrative and how it might be evoked in the quoting poem may be able to explain some of the contradictory urges in Pound's poetry, and suggests reasons for the attraction he has had for contemporary poets. At the end of his life Pound claims: "it coheres all right / even if my notes do not cohere" (116.797). The reason the notes that are *The Cantos* don't cohere, don't provide a narrative, is that Pound in *The Cantos* opts for a dramatic voice and consequently tries to achieve a grand narrative with materials and a method that work against this urge. In emulating Pound, Postmodern writers use his dramatic voice but avoid using that voice to construct a grand narrative.

In poems that emphasize the lyric voice, readers unify differing worlds under one simplified world, creating a new world under control of a central voice, the voice of the new poem. This voice is rarely as clearly governed by the author's "own words" in the way the end of *The Waste Land* is ("These fragments I have shored against my ruins"); more typically, it is governed by the author's own words and the quoted words in tension. The unity of the quoting poem, then, is not neat, packageable; and the tension in it, always in the background of even the strongest lyric poem, shows that dramatic and lyric elements constantly battle for control.

## Impersonal Poetry

"Mature poets steal": when studying borrowed objects one finally has to turn to the person who is doing the borrowing. The quoting poem's voice, whether lyric or dramatic, has an ambiguous relation to the poet who creates it, for quoting muffles personal expression. It does so because at the center of the quotation, the quoting poet has all but disappeared. As Maud Ellmann argues for *The Waste Land*, "Caught in an infinite quotation, the 'I' is exposed as a grammatical position, rather than the proof of the presence of the author" (15). And so, many Modernists use the borrowed words of quotation as a distancing device. The use is remarkably successful. Almost all the techniques I have presented in this book point to or complicate issues of objectivity and impersonality. While the coolly distanced, ironic or objective voices one finds in Eliot and Moore typify the quoting poem, Pound's frenetic techniques similarly distance his writing. And even with Cummings, the use of a poetic persona who speaks borrowed words ensures that one cannot immediately attach to the quoting voice characteristics which are *personal,* immediate.

Impersonality and distance define and are defined by quoting poetry; indeed, this double relationship applies to all of quoting Modernism. For example, Cubism, valuing the importance of intellect over emotion in experiencing and creating art, stressed a conceptual approach to art. As if to underscore this impersonality, Picasso, Braque, and Gris often signed their collages on the back (Kahnweiler, 86), thus muting the idea of authorship. During the least representational moments in Cubism, Picasso and Braque's works were often confused with each other. Quoting poetry shows the same impersonality. Pound seemed to speak for poetry as machine when in 1910 (a year or two before the first collages became public) he argued that "poetry is a sort of inspired mathematics, which gives us equations, not for abstract figures, triangles, spheres, and the like, but equations for the human emotions" (*Spirit,* 14). In 1919, Eliot's authoritative "Tradition and the Individual Talent," which presents art as "a continual extinction of personality" and "an escape from emotion" (40–43), apparently culminated a move to end personal expression in art.

But Modernism's supposed impersonality has been discussed so often that it has, until the last few years, become one of the clichés of Modernist poetry.[4] Much analysis of Modernist impersonality has been simplistic, as if the Modernists, a monolithic, univocal group, had identical ideas on what personal expression and emotion in art were and had succeeded in expurgating these elements from their poetry. These clichés about emotionless Modernist art *are* clichés. Modernist critical theory shows much more sophistication, ambiguity, and contradiction than these pronouncements can cover. Thus, in "Hamlet" Eliot argues that to understand why Shakespeare attempted to write the play we need to know elements of his biography (49). Modernism has a strong romantic residue; personal expression never disappears from Modernist art—although it may be muted. The truth therefore lies between two extremes, for it is equally undeniable that many Modernist poets tried to create a somewhat impersonal poetry in order to remove a perceived sloppy emotional immediacy from poetry.

The distance of quoting is more noticeable than its capacity for personal expression, however. Moreover, quoting is a startling manifestation of the Modernist concern for objectivity, for it shows both why quoting may have attracted "objective" Modernist writers, and how poets physically build distance into their poems. The basic models for the quoting poem's objectivity are constructed from several versions of what Eliot called the objective correlative. Given the influence that the Symbolist idea of art as self-contained object (rather than as expression of the poet's personality) had achieved by the first decade of this century, and the simultaneous residue of romanticism with its emphasis on a transformative creativity, the many versions of the objective correlative which can be found in Modernism seem almost inevitable. Eliot's version, of course, is most famous:

> The only way of expressing emotion in the form of art is by finding an "objective correlative"; in other words, a set of objects, a situation, a chain of events which shall be the formula of the *particular* emotion; such that when the external facts, which must terminate in sensory experience, are given, the emotion is immediately invoked. ("Hamlet," 48)

Eliot here closely allies emotion with personal expression. Personal distancing and an objectifying of the poem result when one presents the formula for an emotion rather than the emotion itself.

These ideas and their implications for reading are not limited to Eliot's opaque formulation. Eliot's Hamlet essay was published in 1919, but many years earlier Mallarmé had argued that the artist is "to paint not the thing itself, but the effect it produces," a theory later appropriated by the Cubists (qtd. in Gray, 16). Edmund Husserl first used the term "objective correlative" in his *Logical Investigations* (1900), and Eliot was aware of this use (Schwartz, 9). Henri Bergson's influential *Introduction to Metaphysics* was published in 1903 and translated into English by 1913. It also presents an indirect method for expression:

No image can replace the intuition of duration, but many diverse images, borrowed from very different orders of things, may, by the convergence of their action, direct consciousness to the precise point where there is a certain intuition to be seized. By choosing images as dissimilar as possible, we shall prevent any one of them from usurping the place of the intuition it is intended to call up. (14)

These ideas for art were not expressed only by this self-contained group of aestheticians, to filter down later to artists. In 1913 Ford Madox Ford (Hueffer) argued that juxtaposition was valuable "not because any particular 'lesson' may be learned, but because such juxtapositions suggest emotions" (185). This emphasis on juxtaposed art as presenting equations for emotions quite early translated into arts other than poetry. In *Gaudier-Brzeska* Pound quotes Henri Gaudier-Brzeska, who in a letter from France some time before 1915 wrote: "I SHALL DERIVE MY EMOTIONS SOLELY FROM THE ARRANGEMENT OF SURFACES, I shall present my emotions by the ARRANGEMENT OF SURFACES, THE PLANES AND LINES BY WHICH THEY ARE DEFINED" (28). The photographer Alfred Steiglitz, in discussing his series *Equivalents,* posited that "all art is but a picture of certain basic relationships; an equivalent of the artist's most profound experience of life" (qtd. in Thomas, 9).

Almost all statements of the objective correlative mention the distancing of equations and imply some escape from highly personal expression, but at the same time they argue that art presents equations for *emotions*. Yet, as Eliot points out in "Tradition and the Individual Talent," these emotion-equations that the poet makes are not in any sense ordinary, experiential emotions—in a sense they are not emotions at all (43). The process of making emotions is a distancing, a remove. Art doesn't just present emotion, it presents *equations* that represent it. This distancing inevitably removes some of the immediacy of the original emotion and personal expression. The scientific metaphors used in many of the Modernist discussions is no accident; the distancing is intended.

Read in this way, quoting poems and much other Modernist poetry can be seen as an attempt at (not an achieving of) an objective presentation of the personal. This attitude perhaps helps to explain Eliot's argument in "Tradition and the Individual Talent" for a separation between "the man who suffers and the mind which creates" (41), an argument that earlier found philosophical expression in his dissertation on Bradley, where Eliot argues that "we know that those highly-organized beings who are able to objectify their passions, and as passive spectators to contemplate their joys and torments, are also those who suffer and enjoy the most keenly" (*Knowledge*, 23). Several years later, Ezra Pound similarly correlated objectivity and emotion. With his high sense of the poet's calling, Pound argued in 1915 that "intense emotion causes pattern to arise in the mind—if the mind is strong enough" ("Affirmations," 374). In Pound's poetry, emotions become objectified in the perceived object that calls up the emotion (Schwartz, 67).[5]

As Don Geiger points out, Eliot in his poem does not so much (like the Romantics) express emotion as he *makes* an emotion (93–94). The emphasis on *transformation* of the personal into art is what most Modernist writers mean by the impersonality of art. Totally "impersonal" art just doesn't ring true with Modernist poetry. For example, now that more of Eliot's biography is known, one cannot in any usual sense refer to *The Waste Land* as an impersonal work of art. Rather than removing emotion, the poem distances, objectifies, and dramatizes it.

If we understand the objective correlative as a distancing agent for personal expression, it becomes clear how quotations not only fit in with, they encourage the sorts of concerns just mentioned, and create the objective-sounding voices of the quoting poem, voices that we have become accustomed to think of as typical for Modernist poetry. The encouragement occurs on several levels. First, the juxtaposed disjunction inherent in quoting poetry muffles personal expression. In his review of *Ulysses*, Pound argues that hetereogeneity creates equations that present the poet's mind: "this varigation of dialects [in *Ulysses*] allows Joyce to present his matter, his tones of mind, very rapidly" ("Paris Letter," 625). At times in the quoting poem there is more of the poet's method than of the poet's direct emotion present. The gaps in quoting poetry, especially its highly disjunctive poetry, obscure personality because they contain the personality of the poet implicitly (through readers' inferences) rather than explicitly. The relation, and the personal values that relation may contain, is implied rather than directly stated. The implicitness distances the voice.

Second, Modernist quoting poems have a formalist bias that distances the poet. As Marjorie Perloff points out, this juxtaposition removes psychological intensity by highlighting the "linguistic play of surfaces" over psychological expression (*Indeterminacy*, 62, 63). Quotations, because they emphasize a self-enclosed intellectual relation among worlds, deemphasize the direct emotional expression of poetry—compare what seems to be the purely cerebral angst of Eliot's *Waste Land* with the ostensibly visceral *Howl* of Allen Ginsberg.

Third, quoting poetry distances the poet because it treats language and experience as an object.[6] By using other people's words, poets present other writers' texts as equations for the emotion rather than the emotion itself, a double remove that objectifies the poetry. The quoted text, as a consequence of its having achieved validity in another context, removes direct emotion and "proves" the validity of the emotions being expressed through the quotation. Creating in the midst of intense personal pain, Eliot has no need to present himself as directly as Robert Lowell did *himself*. After all, the Cumaean Sibyl provided a resonant context that Tom Eliot couldn't hope to duplicate, and it gave the added bonus of objectively placing the poem's speaker in a proven tradition of endless suffering. The Sibyl's "I want to die" is authentic, but as a quotation it becomes a shared, mythic experience.

Finally, not only do quotations make the poem less highly personal, they distance personal expression so that it remains present but just out of reach, a shimmering mirage. Robert Pinsky, in analyzing Robert Lowell's lines in "For the Union Dead" ("William James could almost hear the bronze Negroes breathe") posits that this semiquotation allows Lowell to use phrases that he would rather not put in his own voice. Lowell evokes an ideal for contrast and admires it without claiming it as his own (16). Modernist quotations, poised between assimilation and nonassimilation, similarly allow poets to say and not to say things, to attempt to remove the presence of their own voices. As already noted, Pound dramatizes and complicates this half-ownership at the beginning of canto 8, where he obviously misquotes Eliot: "These fragments you have shelved (shored)," and follows this up by putting in quotation marks and assigning a previous context to words he would prefer not to own completely: "'Slut!' 'Bitch!' Truth and Calliope / Slanging each other sous les lauriers" (28). By saying and not saying, quotations are the perfect mode for the ironic generation that the Modernists are. Quotations ensure that readers cannot identify the voice of the poem with the subjective poet herself. Because they are such a public medium, quotations become a way of cloaking the personal.[7]

Eliot, Pound, Cummings, and Moore exploit these distancing uses of the quotation to varying degrees. Marianne Moore in many ways presents the most simple case. Charles Molesworth's biography shows how intensely private many of Moore's poems are, with their references that, at the time of these poems' first publication, could have been known only to very close friends and members of the immediate family. Quotations complement this privacy. Moore's voice is private partially because the typical, informed reader does not know her sources and therefore is unsure both of their original personal content and of the poetic voice's attachment to them. This reticence encourages readers to accept the poem as an objective presentation of data and closes off rather than encourages readers' access to the personal aspects of the poetry. The greatest emotional involvement by the voice in Moore's poetry is an ironic one, a mode that establishes distance. With her syntactic connections and her use of quotations in a rhetorically coherent scheme, strategies that could be useful in creating a personal voice, Moore at times goes to great lengths to keep the personal voice out of her poetry. Often the privatizing extends to the way she introduces her quotations into the poetry: although the syntax is coherent, the personal voice is muffled. Consider her "When I Buy Pictures." Counting the title, the 1935 version of the poem introduces four instances of the lyric "I" in the opening three lines:

> or what is closer to the truth,
> when I look at that of which I may regard myself as the imaginary
>     possessor,
> I fix upon what would give me pleasure in my average moments:
>
> (70)

As a highly personal voice this is already a bit weak; the self seems posed and objectively analyzed. The poem suggests a situation as possible and generic more than it lives the situation as a present reality. Further, after these instances the "I" disappears, even when readers would most expect it to assert itself, most notably in the last line of the following section, as the poem moves back to a human reaction to pictures:

the satire upon curiosity in which no more is discernible
than the intensity of the mood;
or quite the opposite—the old thing, the mediaeval decorated hat-
box,
in which there are hounds with waists diminishing like the waist of
the hour-glass,
and deer and birds and seated people;
it may be no more than a square of parquetry; the literal biography
perhaps,
in letters standing well apart upon a parchment-like expanse;
an artichoke in six varieties of blue; the snipe-legged hieroglyphic
in three parts;
the silver fence protecting Adam's grave, or Michael taking Adam
by the wrist.
Too stern an intellectual emphasis upon this quality or that detracts
from one's enjoyment.

(70)

The objectifying tendency of the opening lines is realized here as the personal pronoun shifts to "one," to a hypothetical, generic person.

The eight drafts of this poem in the Rosenbach Library show that Moore vacillated with the poem's conclusion. As in many of her poems, a quotation is put in a position of rhetorical strength near or at the end of the poem. In most early drafts of the ending of this poem Moore reasserts the opening lyric "I": "I see that it is 'lit with piercing glances into the life of things.' / And I take it in hand as a savage would take a looking-glass." The decision apparently was not a comfortable one, for the drafts show many reconsiderations, with her decision in the poem's first published version (the July 1921 issue of *The Dial*) being a removal of personal actions and the personal "I" from the quotation's introduction and from several other phrases. In 1935 and in her *Complete Poems,* Moore removes the personal even further by omitting the last line of the poem: "then I 'take it in hand as a savage would take a looking-glass.'" The final version of the poem's ending thus reads:

Too stern an intellectual emphasis upon this quality or that detracts
from one's enjoyment.

It must not wish to disarm anything; nor may the approved triumph
   easily be honoured—
that which is great because something else is small.
It comes to this: of whatever sort it is,
it must be "lit with piercing glances into the life of things";
it must acknowledge the spiritual forces which have made it.

(70)

With the 1921 version's last line removed, there is no personal pronoun
at the end of the poem: no "I," and no objectified "one." The attention
is not on the purchaser of the picture but on the artwork itself. The
passive construction in the new penultimate line further hides a per-
sonal agent, and gives an appearance of objectivity. (Pushing Moore's
voice even further into the background, the final quotation contains
an unacknowledged semiquotation from "Tintern Abbey" within it-
self.)

At times Moore goes to even greater lengths. A quotation in "New
York" reads: "it is not that 'if the fur is not finer than such as one sees
others wear, / one would rather be without it'" (77). As Moore ac-
knowledges in her notes to *Selected Poems* (and even here she misquotes
slightly), the original quotation had a clearly personal voice: "If it is
only as good as that which I see other people wear, I had rather be
without it" (131). Moore adds a measure of impersonality to the quota-
tion's noncommital introduction. Moore's change fits her poetic strat-
egy, and the strategy of many Modernist poets. The quotations, which
by definition are removed from the voice and emotion of the poet, are
here removed even further. In her poem "Silence," which concludes
her 1935 *Selected Poems,* Moore employs a tricky bit of self-referential
distancing as she approvingly quotes the father of a Miss A. M. Ho-
mans (*Selected Poems,* 139–40; Slatin, 151): "the deepest feeling always
shows itself in silence; / not in silence, but in restraint" (121). In this
poem, and in much of her poetry, Moore lives out the implications of
the quotation by quoting, a practice that distances her.

Pound uses a more recognizable canon than does Moore, but al-
though the system of relations may at times be consistent (Pound's
recurring use of "ands," for example), his rhetorical purposes are often
obscure, and, unlike Eliot, he avoids symbolism. These tendencies pri-
vatize his poetry without *necessarily* making it objective or unemotional.
But like all quoting poets, Pound quotes to hide the personal, and in

doing so he creates the appearance of a more objective and more private poetry. At times this hiding is very complex, as it is in the opening canto:

> "But thou, O King, I bid remember me, unwept, unburied,
> "Heap up mine arms, be tomb by sea-bord, and inscribed:
> "*A man of no fortune, and with a name to come.*
> "And set my oar up, that I swung mid fellows."
>
> (1.4)

This quotation becomes symptomatic for the whole work. Given the nature of this work that Pound is writing and Pound's personal history at the time, it may be natural to hear Pound's voice in the *"man of no fortune, and with a name to come."* But the quotation can not confidently be ascribed to Pound's personal voice in *The Cantos*. Using the voice of Old English alliterative verse, Pound is translating a translation of Homer. As Philip Furia points out, Pound was aware that Homer himself was retelling this oldest section of the *Odyssey* (4). Further, the voice at this point of the poem is quoting Odysseus who is quoting Elpenor who quotes his own epitaph. At a level of seven removes, readers cannot easily find the personal voice.

Although Pound removes himself, he more casually uses personal pronouns than does Moore. A typical example is the opening of canto 3, which seems unequivocally to place Pound the poet in his own personal historical context:

> I sat on the Dogana's steps
> For the gondolas cost too much, that year,
> And there were not "those girls," there was one face,
> And the Buccentoro twenty yards off, howling "Stretti,"
> And the lit cross-beams, that year, in the Morosini,
>
> (3.11)

From Pound's biography we can know the year, the location, and even the song being howled. Yet this use of personal pronouns and history does not present Ezra Pound as Ezra Pound, the personal speaker of this poem. Discussing the modern American emphasis on the individual voice, Linda Wagner argues that human experience can be perceived as image: the personal voice becomes "convention, an expected means of conveying authentic emotional reality that may or may not be authentic autobiographical reality" (110). Thus, although some of Pound's allusions are intensely personal, they are placed next to such quoted texts as those by Homer or Sigismund Malatesta and so achieve a mythic and public quality. The five lines just quoted are followed by lines that put Pound in a much larger context:

> And peacocks in Korés house, or there may have been.
> > Gods float in the azure air.
> Bright Gods and Tuscan, back before dew was shed.
> Light: and the first light, before ever dew was fallen.
> Panisks, and from the oak, dryas,
> And from the apple, maelid,
> Through all the wood, and the leaves are full of voices,
> A-whisper, and the clouds bowe over the lake,
> And there are gods upon them,
> And in the water, the almond-white swimmers,
> The silvery water glazes the upturned nipple,
> > As Poggio has remarked.
>
> > > > (3.11)

In the quoting poem personal elements are soon viewed as mythic, as part of a larger, public history.

In Eliot's opinion, good art results from this mythmaking; life becomes a "simplification . . . into something rich and strange" ("London Letter," August 1921, 214). Part of this simplification is the removing of the poet's directly personal voice while creating an "impersonal" art. Only by removing many of the textual quotations and by situating the composing of the poem in a very obvious present context, as Pound does in the Pisan cantos, does Pound's personal history begin to poke through the mythic.

As does Pound in *The Cantos,* Cummings and Eliot also attempt to remove the personal by attempting to create a public voice. Yet although Cummings's quotations are most in the public domain and his meanings are readily accessible, he does quote rather than use his own words. A double remove is set up because Cummings always uses satire when he quotes, and the satire distances him. His voice becomes idiosyncratically private.

Eliot establishes the most public voice, a voice that simultaneously achieves an intense privacy that cloaks, critics are beginning to suspect, a highly personal and emotional poem. Eliot's canon of quotations is more recognizable than is Pound's, and he reaches for the symbolic more often; art *simplifies* life into "something rich and strange." Further, through his use of public symbols by which he creates a myth and places contemporary life into that myth, Eliot attempts the appearance of objectivity most often. His poetry has meanings which are accessible, universal, "assumable"—and so seem less personal. The public poet is rarely the personal poet.

But attempts to remove the poet's person can never completely succeed. Even Eliot, that man so private that the best biography of him has many silences, that man who can almost obscure himself behind his public voice, cannot completely create an impersonal voice. Eliot and all Modernist quoting poets obsessively return to certain sources, and have consistent interactions with them in their poems. These poets get known by the company they keep, and how they behave when they are in that company. Further, if we see the poetic voice as the element that controls *how* the quotations are used, every poem has a distinctive voice, be it lyric or dramatic. This voice can never be completely impersonal or objective. Although the quoting poem may attempt to cloak personal expression, the equations for emotions are still personally determined. The relations between quotation and the rest of the poem are still the working of the individual poet's mind, and thus are inescapably personal.

Perhaps the most telling moment is when Eliot tries to distance himself from himself. In *The Waste Land* Eliot does not present his personal history. He *quotes* it, and in so doing tries to turn it into an object:

> "My nerves are bad to-night. Yes, bad. Stay with me.
> Speak to me. Why do you never speak. Speak.
> What are you thinking of? What thinking? What?
> I never know what you are thinking. Think."
>
> I think we are in rats' alley
> Where the dead men lost their bones.
>
> (65)

Readers do not allow perfect success to this fantastic sleight of hand; Eliot can not totally obscure himself in *The Waste Land*. Edmund

Wilson, one of the first perceptive critics of *The Waste Land,* argues that the poem is "charged with a strange poignancy which seems to bring us into the heart of the singer" (144). In this passage, because we know something of Eliot's biography, we (barbarically, perhaps) assign part of A Game of Chess to his voice and his life with Vivien Eliot. Even within this most public quoting poem it is impossible to create an impersonal voice.

This step back from the surface of the quoting poem to a consideration of whose voice is speaking in the quoting poem has underscored a discovery of earlier chapters: the quoting poem is the field on which strategies essential to the larger Modernist project tug in opposing directions. The quoting poem is both profoundly repetitive *and* original; it is neither purely lyric nor dramatic, neither univocally personal nor impersonal. As my conclusion will argue, this sense of opposing strategies allows quotation to be a usable tool for contemporary culture.

# Conclusion: Beyond Modernism

——My dear William: At what date did you join the ranks of the old ladies? Among the male portion of the community one constantly uses fragments of letters, fragments of conversation.

——Ezra Pound to William Carlos Williams

To hell with youse. I ain't tryin' to be an international figure.

——William Carlos Williams to Ezra Pound

## Williams and the Transformation to Contemporary Quoting

Quoting directs reading practices in many different ways: it can create disjunction, a perceived impersonality, a dramatic voice, satire, symbolism, nonlinearity, and many other effects useful to various Modernist poetics. In creating these different effects, quoting foregrounds and complicates effects found in other, nonquoting Modernist texts. The diverse, self-conscious effects that quoting produces, effects that can tug in opposing directions, show why quotation has not left our aesthetic vocabulary, or diminished to a curious footnote to literary history. Quoting is useful, as Raymond Carver asserts in "Woolworth's 1954":

> "Linger a little, for thou art fair."
> I know who said that. It fits,
> and I'll use it.

(4)

As does much contemporary quoting, Carver's text continues discussions begun in Modernism's quoting poems. "I know who said that" both acknowledges the multiple voices of the quoting poem and the power that such cultural knowledge brings, while "It fits, and I'll use it" disingenuously addresses the function of the quotation in the new text. It does so in a way we've seen before. The reason for quotation given here is casual, opaque ("It fits")—the poet as *bricoleur* (or, as Carver would probably prefer, a handyman). Often as self-consciously as does Carver here, many contemporary writers have found quotations to fit into their poems. Poets requiring as differing reading activities as Louis Zukofsky, Robert Penn Warren, Robert Lowell, Charles Olson, Adrienne Rich, Richard Wilbur, John Cage, John Ashbery, and the $L=A=N=G=U=A=G=E$ writers hold on to the Modernist practice of quoting; indeed, especially in arts other than literature quoting is often seen as *the* Postmodern aesthetic.

Some forms of quotation enhance some typically Postmodern techniques, techniques that can take in dominant poets as diverse as Rich and Ashbery, and even address the extreme play of writing in $L=A=N=G=U=A=G=E$ poets. The selective appropriation and transformation of "Modernist" quoting begins most tellingly with an argument and a poet who has been grumbling at the edges of this study: William Carlos Williams. In his denunciation of *The Waste Land* as a catastrophe and his celebration of the physical world and the individual's creative personality, Williams may seem the least likely poet to quote. And he did not quote during the years of high Modernism. Yet in 1946, twenty-four years after *The Waste Land* and at the beginning of what is now being seen as the Postmodern era, Williams published the first book of *Paterson,* a work that quotes newspapers, historical treatises, and personal letters. (The later books of *Paterson* continue and diversify this quotation, extending the quoting to interviews and to the poetry of such canonical writers as Thomas Gray, Dante, and Chaucer.) *Paterson* book 1 is not the last gasp of Modernism. More than twenty years have gone by since the appearance of the first quoting poems, and Williams achieves some new effects as he fully develops some techniques begun in Modernism, techniques that Postmodern writers also find useful. Further, as the compulsive arguing with Pound might suggest (no one other than Williams managed the peculiar mixture of patience and obsession that allowed him to have a single, forty-year argument with Pound), Postmodernism finds a method in the participants of that long argument. Both Williams and Pound work out ways of quoting that Postmodernism finds useful.

Williams's search for a usable poetic form heated up in the thirties, after the publication of his *Collected Poems, 1921–1931* and even more so after the 1938 *Complete Collected Poems*. Williams, looking back to what most critics saw as an Imagist career, chose the William Carlos Williams issue of the *Briarcliff Quarterly* to formulate his turn in direction in the following way, beginning with familiar concepts, and with a familiar antagonist:

> We [Williams and Pound] parted years ago, he to move among his intellectual equals in Europe, I to remain at home and struggle to discover here the impetus to my achievements, if I found myself able to write anything at all. . . . He left the States under the assumption that it was mind that fertilizes mind, that the mere environment is just putty and that—assuming one's self great the thing to do in this world is, or was then, to go to Europe, which he did." ("Australian," 205)

Men like Pound "have divorced themselves from the primary source of their fertility and so remain without new sources, playing with the past" ("Australian," 208). New poetry needed something different from this, Williams argued, and he posited a literary source that develops "from the present, from the hurley-burley of political encounters which determine or may determine it, direct. This is definitely not the academic approach to literature. It is diametrically opposed to the mind to mind fertilization of the classical concept" ("Australian," 207).[1]

The first book of *Paterson* was self-consciously Williams's response both to Pound and to the need for a new form. In 1943 Williams wrote to Robert McAlmon: "I'm in process of writing a book, the book I have contemplated doing for many years—prose and verse mixed: 'Paterson'—an account, a psychologic-social panorama of a city treated as if it were a man, the man Paterson" (*Letters,* 216). Two things stand out here: the idea that prose and verse would be mixed, and second, but a contributory cause of the first, a sense of *Paterson* as a sociological document. The tension between the desires for a sociology and an individual psychology will be unresolved throughout *Paterson,* most tellingly in its quotations and Williams's control over them. While to McAlmon Williams presents *Paterson* as conjoined psychology and sociology, he much more often dwells on the poem's sociologic aspects. In doing so Williams perhaps overstates the sociology of the poem, an overstatement due perhaps to the alienness of such a concept to the dominating lyric tradition. Yet sociology is a concept that does fit the epic tradition that the longer quoting poems attempt to modulate into twentieth-century forms. Consequently, in defining his place in Modernism, Williams was to write in his *Autobiography* that "I took the city as my 'case' to work up, really to work it up" (392). Thus, when Williams writes "I will make a big, serious portrait of my time" ("Notes in Diary Form," 62), "big" suggests that this is a composite portrait, a portrait of a time—sociology.

That portrait would be objective:

> The truth is that news offers the precise incentive to epic poetry, the poetry of events; and now is precisely the time for it since never by any chance is the character of a single fact ever truthfully represented today. If ever we are to have any understanding of what is going on about us we shall need some other means for discovering it.
>
> The epic poem would be our "newspaper," Pound's cantos are the algebraic equivalent but too perversely individual to achieve the universal understanding required. The epic if you please is what we're after, but not the lyric-epic sing-song. It must be a concise sharpshooting epic style. Machine gun style. Facts, facts, facts, tearing into us to blast away our stinking flesh of news. Bullets. (qtd. in Weaver, 120)

Again, later in his *Autobiography* he was to write: "That is why I started to write *Paterson:* a man is indeed a city, and for the poet there are no ideas but in things" (390). In *Paterson* book 1, that objective nature of "things" gets made as clear as possible through Williams's semiquoted gloss: "No ideas but in things" gets translated as "No ideas but in the facts" (28). A different form of objectivity than that voiced by Eliot, Williams's facts find their source in a sociological collection of data rather than the expression of an individual's mind. Williams's lengthy prose quotations attempt to record and establish a communal rather than an individual voice. In *Paterson,* facts are extremely useful for Williams: they allow him to use a sort of folk quotation in which individual quotations mute the individual author in order to suggest a larger social origin (the letters from Gladys and the particularized yet generic "Cress" letters), they allow him to edit quotations, and they allow him to begin the Postmodern move to the genre quotation: the quotation chosen for its texture (and behind that texture *perhaps* the quotation's argument), not its author.

All of these considerations are played out in the first lines of *Paterson*. After an opening self-quotation, Williams begins the poetry of the poem with:

To make a start,
out of particulars
and make them general, rolling
up the sum, by defective means—
Sniffing the trees,
just another dog
among a lot of dogs. What
else is there? And to do?
The rest have run out—
after the rabbits.
Only the lame stands—on
three legs. Scratch front and back.
Deceive and eat. Dig
a musty bone

(3)

*Paterson* is a beginning, an insouciant start that attempts to find the general in the particular. The goal of this finding, however, has a mathematical objectivity about it—there is a "sum." But in arriving at this sum the poet must use "defective means." The defective means are, I think, the way in which he gathers facts for this project. As facts, the quotations are gathered haphazardly, the way a dog indiscriminately sniffs trees. (With his "It fits and I'll use it," Carver would like that image.) But it is a lonely project, with all the other dogs having gone off (to Europe, presumably) to chase rabbits. Only one dog is left, and he is lame, and occasionally sits to scratch. This self-deprecating tone never leaves *Paterson:* after all, what do dogs sniff for, and what do they do when they find the right-smelling tree? This deprecation, directed both at himself and at his facts, creates a text that coolly manages its quotations, a coolness that Postmodernism picks up and exploits much more thoroughly.

In Williams's view, America provided the necessary facts—a simple enough counterproposal, but one loaded with complications, since according to Williams an authentic American tradition had yet to be founded. In writing to Henry Wells that *Paterson* was a "social instrument" that "embraces everything we are" (*Letters,* 286), Williams presents *Paterson* book 1 as his attempt to provide these facts that document a usable American tradition, and to do so in a more ambitious, documentary way than did his earlier writing. Quotations that illustrate this voice come from an American canon rooted in a specific place and in specific things, for example, from local newspapers such as the *Paterson Advertiser.* By their selection as part of the American voice, these quotations acquire value, although this value implies neither a single-minded acceptance nor an ironic rejection of the quotations. As is usual in this poem, Williams gives little interpretive direction to readers on how to appropriate particular quotations, although he clearly states general principles. Williams shows more clearly *how* this voice is established than *what* are its characteristics. This lack of directions toward particular instances is slightly disconcerting since there is clearly an onus upon the reader to get the American idiom "right."

Presenting facts in the American idiom demands terms that are new, a newness which itself creates problems. Writing of Poe, Williams stated: "Invent that which is new, even if it be made from pine from your own yard, and there's none to know what you have done. It is because there's no *name.* . . . It is only that which is under your nose which seems inexplicable" (*American Grain,* 226). Williams applied this directly to his own life: "Already I have been informed that *Paterson* will not be accepted because of its formlessness, because I have not organized it into some neo-classic *recognizable* context" (*Letters,* 239). The recognizable context against which these terms would apply were partially expressed prosodically: "I am trying in *Paterson* to work out the problems of a new prosody—but I am doing it by writing poetry rather than 'logic' which might castrate me, since I have no ability in that medium (of logic)" (*Letters,* 257–58). As many critics have discovered, Williams did not explain his prosody very clearly, and Williams himself (in retrospect) thought he did not completely reach his American line in *Paterson.* Yet although the prosody seems impossible to measure, it does appear to have two components: rhythmic (aural) and intellectual. The emphasis on the movement of the mind is a concern that Williams carries from his first Modern poems, and it ties him to the other quoting Moderns. But "sound" is Williams's idiosyncratic addition to the other concept. These components are at times discussed together, as a single unit, as a search for a usable measure. Williams ends his letter to Kay Boyle in this way:

> Quantitative, qualitative, these things have lost all clear meaning for us. Then just there is the place for invention. The metronome beat of doggerel makes us restless, lowers us to nonsense. The forced timing of verse after antique patters wearies us even more and seduces thought even more disastrously—as in Eliot's work. But a new time that catches thought as it lags and swings it up into the attention will be read, will be read (by those interested) with that breathlessness which is an indication that they are not dragging a gunny sack flavored with anise around for us to follow but that there is meat at the end of the hunt for us—and we are hungry. (136)

A time "that catches thought" has an allegiance to the movement of the mind as much as it does to sound, if the two can be distinguished. There is a sense in which this movement might best be described in Pound's verse and in what Pound had described in the quoting Moore as logopoeia. Williams argued for Pound's work: "The measure is an inevitability, an unavoidable accessory after the fact. If one move, if one run, if one seize up a material—it cannot avoid having a measure, it cannot avoid a movement which clings to it—as the movement of a horse becomes a part of the rider also—[.] That is the way Pound's verse impresses me and why he can include pieces of prose and have them still part of a *poem*. It is incorporated in a movement of the intelligence which is special, beyond usual thought and action" ("Excerpts," 108).[2]

With this emphasis on the movement of the mind, the sound of the poem will also inevitably change, resulting in Williams turning for his understanding of this sound to his conception of the American language, not to traditional literary forms.[3] As the emphasis on movement shows in the following quotation from Williams's review of Pound, this logopoeia is also a sound: "We seek a language which will not be at least a deformation of speech as we know it—but will embody all the advantageous jumps, swiftnesses, colors, movements of the day— — that will, at least, not exclude language as spoken—all language (present) as spoken" ("Excerpts," 109). Williams argues to Kay Boyle that prose is the originator of this double meaning: "Prose can be a laboratory for metrics. It is lower in the literary scale. But it throws up jewels which may be cleaned and grouped. I don't think any poetry ever originated in any other way" (*Letters*, 130). That is why Williams insisted on the continuity between prose and verse, as he did in several letters, here to Parker Tyler:

> All the prose, including the tail which would have liked to have wagged the dog, has primarily the purpose of giving a metrical meaning to or of emphasizing a metrical continuity between all word use. It is *not* an antipoetic device, the repeating of which piece of miscalculation makes me want to puke. It *is* that prose and verse are both *writing*, both a matter of the words and an interrelation between words for the purpose of exposition, or other better defined purpose of *the art*. Please do not stress other "meanings." I want to say that prose and verse are to me the same thing, that verse (as in Chaucer's tales) belongs *with* prose, as the poet belongs with "Mine host," who says in so many words to Chaucer, "Namoor, all that rhyming is not worth a toord." Poetry does not *have* to be kept away from prose as Mr. Eliot might insist, it goes *along* with prose and, companionably, by itself, without aid or excuse or need for separation or bolstering, shows itself by *itself* for what it is. It *belongs* there, in the gutter. Not anywhere else or wherever it is, it is the same: the poem. (263)

Prose is capable of revealing the actual; *Paterson*

> called for a poetry such as I did not know, it was my duty to discover or make such a context on the "thought." To *make* a poem, fulfilling the requirements of the art, and yet new, in the sense that in the very lay of the syllables Paterson as Paterson would be discovered, perfect, perfect in the special sense of the poem, to have it—if it rose to flutter into life awhile—it would be as itself, locally, and so like every other place in the world. For it is in that, that it be particular to its own idiom, that it lives. (*Autobiography*, 392)

To Ralph Nash, the first critic who looked closely at Williams's use of prose, Williams wrote an effusive letter: "A man must, without relinquishing any of the reasons for the poetry with which he surrounds himself and with which the great of this world, at their most powerful, surround him, fight his way to a world which breaks through to the actual. This has always been my most pressing concern. . . . It has always stood between me and Ezra Pound for instance" (323–24). Despite his disclaimer, Williams is actually close to Pound's form of quoting here, for Williams partially bases his quoting on a principle similar to Pound's dislike of the abstractions in "mediocre verse." Pound argues that a phrase such as "'dim lands of peace' dulls the image. It mixes an abstraction with the concrete. It comes from the writer's not realizing that the natural object is always the *adequate* symbol" ("Few Don'ts," 201). For Williams, *Paterson*'s quotations function as natural objects inextricably linked to the American landscape.

Allowing for the creation of effects similar to those found in Pound's use of lengthy quotations, Williams's lengthy prose quotations allow readers to notice the qualities of an American voice most strongly. Quotation is important, for Williams cannot create this voice out of nothing. This voice at times must be a quoted voice—the poem fails if Williams can find an American voice only in his own ruminations on America. The American voice must also be part of the "real" world, and *Paterson*'s quotations prove that it is. Williams exhibits this real world, this evidence of an American voice, by delineating these quotations very clearly from his own writing (the line of dots in the prose indicates I have omitted a lengthy portion of quoted document):

They turn their backs
and grow faint—but recover!
            Life is sweet
they say: the language!
            —the language
is divorced from their minds,
the language .   . the language!

If there was not beauty, there was a strangeness and a bold association of wild and cultured life grew up together in the Ramapos: two phases.

In the hills, where the brown trout slithered among the shallow stones, Ringwood—where the old Ryerson farm had been—among its velvet lawns, was ringed with forest trees, the butternut, and the elm, the white oak, the chestnut and the beech, the birches, the tupelo, the sweet-gum, the wild cherry and the hackleberry with its red tumbling fruit.

.   .   .   .   .   .   .   .   .   .   .   .   .   .   .   .   .   .   .   .   .   .   .   .   .   .

Cromwell, in the middle of the seventeenth century, shipped some thousands of Irish women and children to the Barbadoes to be sold as slaves. Forced by their owners to mate with the others these unfortunates were succeeded by a few generations of Irish-speaking negroes and mulattoes. And it is commonly asserted to this day the natives of Barbadoes speak with an Irish brogue.

I remember
a *Geographic* picture, the 9 women
of some African chief semi-naked
astraddle a log, an official log to
be presumed, heads left:

(12–13)

Although in most of Williams's prose passages the quotation is close to exact, that is not the case here. Williams is using a genre quotation, culling the passage from his notes from various sources (Sankey, 40, 41n). To most readers that Williams could envision reading the poem (careful readers, but readers who would choose not to avail themselves of either his sources or his manuscripts), this passage appears to be a quotation, and functions as such. The passage "works" as a quotation because of Williams's (in this area, at least) close relation to Pound's Modernism—despite the very different consequences that his emphasis on the local and the new measure would have for his choice of subject matter. Delineation here occurs in the same ways that delineation occurs in much dramatic Modernist quoting. The syntactically unannounced changing textures of language clearly signal that another world has been entered. In addition, the use of different type size delineates the quotation from the rest of the text. That should suggest, by the way, that, although it may not promote a hierarchy of values, *Paterson* does not just have an unproblematic continuity between poetry and prose—Williams instructed the publisher to use different typefaces for the poetry and prose sections of *Paterson* (Mariani, 503). Further, since Williams does not impose a new lineation on the quotation, the quotation asserts its original texture quite strongly. As in *The Cantos,* the quotation here also is not aestheticized; printing the document *as a document* gives readers a set of instructions differing from the nonquoted text.[4]

Yet for someone who presents such an urgently stated program which itself has an antiacademic claim, this is an opaque passage. The opacity comes from a struggle between thematics and texture, the quintessential struggle of the quoting poem, and a resolution of it that uses the dramatic techniques of Pound. In *Paterson* Williams wants a specific type of news and facts, news and facts which indicate a valuable texture, a mode of thought, an idiom. But the thematics of the poem seem to pull in the opposing direction from what readers might expect—for all of Williams's celebrating of the locally American, so much of his poem is about divorce, a failure, a lack of contact.

Quotations and their management situate themselves at the crux of this problem. While the passage introducing these descriptions of people seems to address itself to language, the quotations and examples all have to do with people, and silent, voiceless people at that, people whose actions are unexplained or enigmatic. In the passage I quoted above the movement is from an assertion, to an exhibit of the language that seems to indicate grotesque social injustice (slavery), to the voiceless yet eloquent African wives, who are silent, but apparently translated into the terms of the American landscape (for Williams, this is a translation, *not* a quotation). The formal devices Williams uses to manage these quotations, when directed at the thematic concerns of this poem, do not resolve the opacity. There is no safe way to gloss an individual quotation's function and relation to the theme of divorce; readers typically come up with something general, as Nash did, who argued that they all tended to illustrate some form of failure (23–24). But if this is so, one cannot clearly discover what kind of failure, and whose failure. The "their" of "the language / is divorced from their minds" could refer to the writers of the passage (a textural issue). But then why quote a narrative about people and refer to these people in the nonquoting parts of the poem? More likely, the "their" could refer to the people in the passage (a thematic issue). But then why quote? A third possiblity is that the prose passages are analogies of contemporary society, and the "them" is twentieth-century America. But parables function awkwardly in dramatic quoting poems like this one, and the assertion that this is a contemporary reference still does not clarify why it might be useful and necessary to create the appearance of a lengthy prose quotation to achieve this reference.

A more overt, nonquoted statement of the theme, a statement that in addition has a clearer relation to the quotations, does not settle the problem. For example, one of the poem's clearest strategies is to develop an American tradition by distinguishing between false and true language. In one of the rare nonquoting prose passages of book 1, which he sandwiches between two prose quotations, Williams presents the conflict between false and true language:

> A false language. A true. A false language pouring—a language (misunderstood) pouring (misinterpreted) without dignity, without minister, crashing upon a stone ear. At least it settled it for her. Patch too, as a matter of fact. He became a national hero in '28, '29 and toured the country diving from cliffs and masts, rocks and bridges—to prove his thesis: Some things can be done as well as others. (15)

The deaths by water of Mrs. Cumming and Sam Patch with which Williams surrounds this passage, and to which Williams refers here, apparently bear on the relationship between a false and a true language. The effects of a false language are clear: false language, misunderstood and misinterpreted, crashes "upon a stone ear." The passage implies that false language is a problem of both reader and writer: for the writer, it is "without dignity"; for the reader, it is "misunderstood" as it "crashes upon a stone ear." Williams further complicates the effects of false language by having, in his nonquoting passages of the poem, the falls themselves be a symbol of language. The language, crashing upon the stone, kills them both.

> Patch leaped but Mrs. Cumming shrieked
> and fell—unseen (though
> she had been standing there beside her husband half
> an hour or more twenty feet from the edge).
>
> : a body found next spring
> frozen in an ice-cake; or a body
> fished next day from the muddy swirl—
> both silent, uncommunicative
>
> (20–21)

Thus, the materials on Sam Patch and Mrs. Cumming, like the quotation about the Barbados slaves, most probably illustrate in the events they narrate (rather than in the texture of the language itself) some failure of language, although such reference is far from clear.

Williams inserts the unclarity between action and language (and be-
tween language and meaning) into the quoted prose passage about Sam
Patch by editing the prose in the manner of Marianne Moore (an easy
proposition when one is working with texts that one's audience has not
read). According to Mike Weaver (204), in the following passage Wil-
liams introduces the comments about failed speech:

> On the day the crowds were gathered on all sides. He appeared and
> made a short speech as he was wont to do. A speech! What could
> he say that he must leap so desperately to complete it? And plunged
> toward the stream below. But instead of descending with a plum-
> met-like fall his body wavered in the air—Speech had failed him.
> He was confused. The word had been drained of its meaning.
> There's no mistake in Sam Patch. He struck the water on his side
> and disappeared. (17)

Action and language in a joint failure: given the close connection
between the quotations and failure, where does one find the American
terms that Williams had been searching for? One finds the terms in the
management of the quotation. The quotations prevent Williams's own
divorce from the language, as Nash suggests (23). Williams's managing
of all these disparate details is the American idiom at its best. Readers
are to watch Williams's mind work, to watch the dog sniffing and
marking the trees. *Paterson* book 1 leaves us with an illustration of a
struggle, a struggle Williams refers to at the beginning of section 2,
which follows the flurry of quotations I have just examined:

> There is no direction. Whither? I
> cannot say. I cannot say
> more than how. The how (the howl) only
> is at my disposal (proposal) : watching—
> colder than stone .
>
> (18)

Not only does the poem assert a new, Postmodern aesthetic ("There is
no direction"), the poet can only refer to the process, not to the mean-
ing: "I cannot say more than how." In doing so, the poet plays with
the accidents of language: the "how (the howl)" is Whitman's barbaric

yawp translated into the twentieth century; the poet's "proposal" is the new terms that he creates for American poetry in *Paterson*.

The resulting open form establishes several effects. It allows Williams to insert into the poem a host of heterogeneous material aimed at establishing a historical and sociological witness for Paterson the city. *All* the qualities of America must be developed in order to create an American voice. Second, texture is emphasized. Throughout the poem Williams asserts that there are "no ideas but in things," and in this poem he emphasizes the status of quotations as things. Their physical presentation on the page as alien objects emphasizes this status. Finally, the use of quotations that both establish and hinder an American voice gives the poem a sense of process, of developing, of testing and rejecting options. In Williams's—probably fair—version of Modernism, Pound is much more sure (though mistaken in his certainty) than is Williams that he has found an authentic voice. In *Paterson* Williams has himself accused by Pound that "Your interest is in the bloody loam but what / I'm after is the finished product" (37).

Despite Williams's assertions of difference, it is Pound with whom Williams (and behind Williams, many Postmodern poets) has the closest ties. Both poets structure their major works as the struggle to find a voice. Both poets, distinguishing between false and true language, attempt to discover a community of textual values based in part upon prose documents. Both *The Cantos* and *Paterson* are poems about texts in a way that the poems of the other quoting Modernists are not. Both poets are concerned with the social effects of their poetry, effects which are referred to discursively in their texts. Both poets give readers a dramatic poetic voice ("open form"), one which does not give many instructions on how readers should appropriate the quotations. As Paul Christensen argues, in the use of such aesthetic principles as *"profusion, inclusion,* the *ill-assorted,"* Williams in the late 1930s began a move to Postmodernism (145). Pound, with his use of dramatic voice, is his nearest kin. As a corollary to this interest, both *The Cantos* and *Paterson* are rooted in things, a rootedness that removes emphasis on symbolism. At the same time, both texts have a very dogmatic posture. Thus, while Pound and Williams come to different conclusions, both poets start with similar aesthetic presuppositions, and they structure their writing in similar ways.[5]

## Adrienne Rich

Among contemporary poets, Williams's desire for a consciously American poetry has diminished along with America's literary inferiority complex, and the politics that Pound's quoting espouses has found no inheritors. But many contemporary writers do quote, following neither Cummings nor Moore nor Eliot, but employing partially the poetics of Williams and Pound. Adrienne Rich, for example, returns to the authority and political involvement that is seen in Pound. With the same zeal, and with much more clarity and tolerance, Rich also attempts to remove the blackout of history. And like both Pound and Williams, she attempts to establish the voice of this hidden community.

In this context, Rich's documenting her quoting poems gains importance. As Rich's note to her poem "Paula Becker to Clara Westhoff" shows, the poem is part of a larger process that attempts to make a past accessible:

> Some phrases in this poem are quoted from actual diaries and letters of Paula Modersohn-Becker, which were shown me in unpublished translations by Liselotte Glozer. Since then, an annotated translation of the manuscripts has been published by Diane Radycki: *The Letters and Journals of Paula Modersohn-Becker* (Metuchen, N.J.: Scarecrow Press, 1980). (331)

Unlike readers of Moore's poetry, Rich's readers are not supposed to take the notes as a way to discover her "probity"; these notes have a different function than showing that the quotations do indeed have a source. Both the context and content of the source are important. In contrast to the notes to *The Waste Land,* this note does not outline an aesthetic plan for the text; rather, it presents the names of those who participate in removing this text from the blackout of history, and gives publishing data for those who might like to buy it. This information in the notes establishes what the poetry has already made clear: Rich tries to create a historical record, to establish evidence. In so doing, Rich, like Williams, attempts to create a language out of what has been suppressed.

This political concern infuses her poetry, with a less formalist bent than it has in most Modernist quoting. Rich tries to recover people rather than texts, and people are less easily aestheticized:

Planetarium

> *Thinking of Caroline Herschel (1750–1848)*
> astronomer, sister of William; and others.

A woman in the shape of a monster
a monster in the shape of a woman
the skies are full of them

a woman "in the snow
among the Clocks and instruments
or measuring the ground with poles"

in her 98 years to discover
8 comets

(114–15)

Rich directs at persons her attempts at recovery and her reactions to the quotations. Rich attempts to remove the textual disembodiment that accompanies much Modernist quoting; here, she adds facts: Herschel's dates, names, relations, occupation, and discoveries. In "Culture and Anarchy" Rich quotes biographical texts and addresses the writers of these texts: "the sudden torrent of your typing // Rough drafts we share" (276). As "Culture and Anarchy" also shows, Rich's recovery of the personal involves a biblical belief in the power of naming names:

> light welling, searching the shadows
>
> Matilda Joslyn Gage; Harriet Tubman;
> Ida B. Wells-Barnett; Maria Mitchell;
> Anna Howard Shaw; Sojourner Truth;
> Elizabeth Cady Stanton; Harriet Hosmer;
> Clara Barton; Harriet Beecher Stowe;
> Ida Husted Harper; Ernestine Rose
>
> and all those without names
> *because of their short and ill-environed lives*

(278)

The metaphor introducing this litany is clear. Names call up personal histories. When Rich in this way removes quotation's textual disembodiment, she adds to the quoting poem the possibility for a much clearer *political* agenda. In these lines and throughout her poetry Rich recovers records and traces of formerly lost people.

The process of recovery is essential, and it always is a struggle. At times the struggle appears to be won, as in poems like "For a Russian Poet" and "Phantasia for Elvira Shatayev," in which Rich blurs the distinction between quotations and her own language in an attempt to fuse an identity, a common language and experience. The poem struggles to remove the doubleness that the quotations introduce. The ambiguity of this struggle comes out in "Snapshots of a Daughter-in-Law," in which the poetic voice simultaneously closes and accentuates distance: "The argument *ad feminam*, all the old knives / that have rusted in my back, I drive in yours, / *ma semblable, ma soeur!*" (36). Rich wrenches this quoted voice from its past use in Baudelaire and especially its quotation in *The Waste Land* to a new function that redefines a tradition and creates a new one. As Williams's new tradition was for himself in *Paterson*, Rich's new tradition is hardly a noncompetitive, nurturant, and peaceable gathering.

Perhaps this struggle within the community accounts for how at other times, such as in "Culture and Anarchy," the quotations stand out in bold relief, their different texture and the idiosyncracy of their biographical detail establishing an irrevocable distance:

leaping the torrent all that water
already smelling of earth

> Elizabeth Barrett to Anna Jameson:
> *... and is it possible you think*
> *a woman has no business with questions*
> *like the question of slavery?*

(277)

Whether or not Rich manages to close the distance between herself and her sources, a question remains: Is Rich's attempted recovery of people possible, given the thinglike, textural properties of quotations, and the oppositions these quotations present? The question can be answered only by examining how these quotations refer to worlds outside of the text. Especially when placed in the context of Rich's poetry, the textural properties of the quotation sharpen its referential function: the quotations typically include evidence of biographical persons, with clear psychological traits, an inclusion strengthened by the context with which Rich surrounds these quotations. The textural properties of the quotation discompose readers, but discomposes them to an awareness of persons who survive primarily in texts, to a new political awareness.

The boundary between quotation and new text at times stymies the recovery of persons. These persons survive, but survive in texts, texts which are distinct from the new, appropriating text. Blurring the distinction between quoting and quoted voice removes some of this distance, but it does not always serve Rich's purposes. To be politically and poetically effective, these quoted voices have to sound distant, for living in this world has created problems which one cannot remove. The business of poetry is to discover how to use those problems most effectively.

## John Ashbery

Pound and Williams's Postmodern appropriators are a varied group. John Ashbery, for example, presents concerns radically removed from those of Rich, and works much more with Modernist discoveries of the dramatic voice, of open form.[6] As do many contemporary poets in their writing, Ashbery in "Self-Portrait in a Convex Mirror" opts for a coolly ironic, distanced poetry that appropriates quotations (quotations of texts, not of people) but never accepts them. In the present context, Pound and Williams's (to say nothing of Eliot and Cummings's) attempts to create a community of voices often seem naive. More so even than does the structure of *Paterson,* the dramatic structure of "Self-Portrait in a Convex Mirror" relies for much of its energy on keeping its quotations at a distance. In addition, Ashbery examines the working of an individual, not a communal, mind—a move that, when granted popular contemporary assumptions about how the mind works, necessitates a more ruminative method, a greater lack of closure.

The poem's title first signals these differences. The title indicates several removes from reality: this is a poem (a reflection) about a reflection of a reflection, which itself is once distanced from reality. In *The Cantos* Pound uses a similar structure. As mentioned earlier in this book, Pound adds an Anglo-Saxon rhythm to a translation of a translation in canto I. But Pound is intent upon recovering texts and is much less concerned with making the *subject* of the poem his personal reaction to this removal.

Ashbery builds this highly personal removing into the structure of his poem from the beginning. The poem's opening lines begin with similes which remove directness:

> As Parmigianino did it, the right hand
> Bigger than the head, thrust at the viewer
> And swerving easily away, as though to protect
> What it advertises.
>
> (68)

The simile removes, distances the writing. The simile establishes an identity while at the same time admitting difference more strongly than does metaphor, for the difference is made explicit ("As," "as though"). The identity-difference is paralleled by the description of the hand, which seems "to protect / What it advertises."

This revealing and hiding is precisely the function that quotations take on in this poem. They seem to promise presence (they attempt to represent a representation of the portrait), and at the same time they admit difference (they are a double removal from the work itself):

> It is what is
> Sequestered. Vasari says, "Francesco one day set himself
> To take his own portrait, looking at himself for that purpose
> In a convex mirror, such as is used by barbers . . .
> He accordingly caused a ball of wood to be made
> By a turner, and having divided it in half and
> Brought it to the size of the mirror, he set himself
> With great art to copy all that he saw in the glass,"
> Chiefly his reflection, of which the portrait
> Is the reflection once removed.
>
> (68)

Ashbery's quoting it is not an attempt to get as close to the artwork itself as possible—it illustrates difference, distance, a voice and a work always distanced from the poem's voice.

As it does in Modernist quoting in general and in Williams, quoting in this poem ensures distance, creates a remove. But Ashbery's removal takes on overtones different from much Modernist quoting, for the removal that his quotations accentuate in the reading process is not primarily a removal of a personal voice and personal responsibility. His relation to the quotations is made relatively clear through precise syntactical relations between quoting and quoted text.

Rather than hiding the presence of the poet, the removal is critically directed at Parmigianino's attempt in his "Self-Portrait" to create an artwork entirely self-contained and complete. The quoting thus has a decidedly anachronistic character. As Richard Stamelman points out, Parmigianino's self-portrait and Ashbery's poem are at odds with each other: the portrait is self-contained (Parmigianino attempts "to copy all that he saw in the glass"), but the poem is open-ended. By the end of the poem it is clear that an "accurate" self-portrait, such as Parmigianino attempts, is impossible. The original world of the quotations, with their presenting of Parmigianino's aesthetic, is used to arrive at very different ends, primarily addressing itself to the poem's discourse. The quotations embody the impossibility of Parmigianino's attempt to create a completely self-contained, perfectly mimetic work. Given the emphasis on removal in this poetry, the *idea* of quoting rather than the *context* of the quotation is important.

Ashbery's anachronism is a means to what is often seen as a purely aesthetic end—an internalized exploration of the Modern dramatic voice. But unlike Williams's exploration of a culture's sociology, which ensures a centrifugal force to the quoting poem, Ashbery's dramatic voice is more centripetal and turns toward the free play of the poet's mind. The concept of free play is useful because the interaction is in Ashbery's mind rather than (as it is in Pound) between the quotations. The force of the poem is on Ashbery's reaction to the quotation rather than on the quotation itself. The quotation has little independent integrity.

Ashbery establishes the primacy of the quoting voice through devious means. At least on a surface level, the poem establishes clear relations between quotations and nonquoting text. But the smooth, authoritative introduction of the quotation belies its actual functioning in this poem. In the section just quoted and throughout the poem, Ashbery uses a very old-fashioned, academic way of acknowledging quotations and ensures that the quotations are syntactically integrated into the poem—ostensibly a move to establish referential control. However, like Ashbery's project in general, the integration of the quotation creates smooth syntax in a poem in which referentiality is unclear (Perloff, *Indeterminacy,* 10). Especially as the poem progresses, lengthy sentences and many pronouns combine to cloud the surface of the poem. The assurance of the language contrasts with the indeterminacy of reference, allowing Ashbery to use very different means to create a poetry as cool and distanced as that of Moore.

This difference begins to explain the difference in removal between Ashbery's poem and much of Modernist poetry. The personal voice is much more involved in Ashbery's poetry and in interacting with the quotations, a difference that extends to the way in which free play functions in this poem. Readers sit back and watch the mind of the poem engaged in free play, and participate in this play only upon direction from instructions explicitly given in the text, instructions that ostensibly represent the mind of the poet.

Despite these significant differences, however, some similar aesthetic concerns bring Ashbery closer to Pound and Williams than to other quoting Modernists. All three poets use some notion of free play to remove referential stability and symbolizing from their poetry. All three poets write a highly discursive poetry that concerns itself with the process of writing while creating texts about texts. Described in this way, the quoting poetry of these three writers is part of a single tradition, separate from traditions to which Eliot, Moore, or Cummings may belong.

## L = A = N = G = U = A = G = E Writing

Ashbery's explorations of the free play of the mind are advanced and challenged by those contemporary writers known as the L = A = N = G = U = A = G = E poets. These poets create a poetry that is recognizably in Ashbery's tradition, yet in some ways antagonistic to it, a poetry that both attacks quotation and explores its possibilities. As does the poetry of Ashbery, L = A = N = G = U = A = G = E writing removes itself from "standard" propositional discourse, while at the same time it plays with and highlights the conventions of such discourse. To get at these conventions, these writers will occasionally quote propositional discourse, at times even playing with that text most confident of the stable meanings and traceable histories of words, the dictionary:

to
clean
over: T
formal.
whip. b.
or surpass
completion or
etc.: They need
into shape. 6. 1
19) 7. lick the d
stroke of the tongue
by taken up by one str
cream cone. 10. See salt
b. a brief, brisk burst of ac
pace or clip; speed. 12. Jazz.
in swing music. 13. lick and a
perfunctory manner of doing some
time to clean thoroughly, but gave
promise. (ME lick(e), OE liccian; c.
akin toGoth (bi) laigon, L lingere, GK
(up) – licker, n.
Lick (lik), n. a ring formation in the
the face of the moon: about 21 miles in
lick er-in (lik er in), n. a roller on
chine, esp. the roller that opens the st
the card and transfers the fibers to the
Also called taker-in. (n. use of v. phra
licking (lik ing), n. 1. Informal. a.a p
thrashing. b. a reversal or disappointm
2. the act of  one who or that which lic
licorice (lik e |                          | ish, lik rish

viewing
point

("ludicrous stick")

Tina Darragh is here concerned with the exact quotation of the 1966 edition of the *Random House Dictionary of the English Language,* but surely not so much to preserve a record of that text as to examine how one can use a text for new, divergent purposes. But one of the divergent purposes here is not the play of the author's mind: the quoting of the text is too mechanical for that. And to talk about voice here is surely beside the point. Rather, the presence of the author's mind in interacting with this quotation is more directed at linguistic than at psychological interests; it attempts to get readers to reexamine how words mean, how contexts shape words. The wry title, phallic shape of the poem, the outline, and its being presented as a *poem* all create a new context that challenges the "normal," objective functioning of the dictionary.

As Darragh's text begins to show, one of the chief assumptions $L = A = N = G = U = A = G = E$ writing wishes to challenge is the idea that language is an objective machine for creating meaning. $L = A = N = G = U = A = G = E$ writers disagree that

> knowledge has an "object" outside of the language of which it is a part—that words refer to "transcendental signifieds" rather than being part of a language which itself produces meaning in terms of its grammar, its conventions, its "agreements in judgment." Learning a language is not learning the names of things outside language, as if it were simply a matter of matching up "signifiers with signifieds," as if signifieds already existed and we were just learning new names for them. . . . Rather, we are initiated by language into a (the) world, and we see and understand the world through the terms and meanings that come into play in this acculturation. . . . In this sense, our conventions (grammar, codes, territorialities, myths, rules, standards, criteria) are our nature. (Bernstein, "Objects," 60)

In short, these writers are concerned with language *as language*. But this tired phrase has energy in this poetry, for it redefines both communication and quotation. In $L = A = N = G = U = A = G = E$ poetry, writes Charles Bernstein, one finds "an insistence to communicate. Not, perhaps, where communication is schematized as a two-way wire with the message shuttling back and forth in blissful ignorance of the (its) transom (read: ideology)" ("Introduction," 75). That is, writing is not just pure propositional communication.

Bernstein goes on to argue that such writing "takes as its medium, or domain of intention, every articulable aspect of language" ("Introduction," 75). Two implications follow from this: first, these writers use every genre of literature, and often mix genres. According to Bernstein, $L = A = N = G = U = A = G = E$ writing "does not privilege any single mode, including the expository logic and speech-derived syntax that dominate contemporary writing practice. Distinctions between essays and lyrics, prose and poetry are not often observed." Texts use many different modes, a move that "counts more on a recognition of the plastic qualities of traditional genres and styles than on their banishment," and that "increases the capacity of writing for expression" ("Introduction," 76, 78). In such a system, *genre* is too constricting a term, a term that assumes one can compartmentalize writing.

The use of many genres without privileging any one has a second implication. Bernstein envisions as a "constructive" writing practice "a multi-discourse text, a work that would involve many different types and styles and modes of language in the same 'hyperspace.' Such a textual practice would have a dialogic or polylogic rather than monologic method" ("Writing," 591). The lack of privilege and the polylogic character of such writing naturally lead to quotation. When one emphasizes the modes of language, and how language is composed of structural codes, the idea of a text as *individual* expression disappears. Quotation is not a large additional step, for quoting is the same as using any other mode of language. Consider this three-tiered writing from Steve Benson:

<pre>
First and foremost      I was trying to realize
formulated by cat hairs  an ideal form but I was
all over the clothes     stopped at an intersection
of the massive butcher   presumably at any rate        The crisis passed
with a pained smile      the cop told me it was         we all released from
breaking tradition over   having forced me to pull over  our congested stained
the hull of a remodeled My head was bandaged with  chests a relieved groan
tanker. He sought the words thoughts of this ideal form  The sun figuratively
</pre>

(192)

As it was for Darragh, the quoting of three differing voices here is not an attempted recovery of persons (as in Rich's poetry) or texts (as it is for Pound), but, in a move perhaps most indebted to Williams, a genre quotation of "different types and styles and modes of language."

This emphasis on modes of language points out the affinities this writing practice has with Marxist criticism, and how these affinities shape quotation. Another L = A = N = G = U = A = G = E poet, Barrett Watten, argues that these writers do not attempt to aestheticize language; in this writing "style has an ethical rather than aesthetic basis, and the act of writing is set up on a different axis as a result" ("for CHANGE," 485–86). More important, language (and the people who use it) are socially determined. As Charles Bernstein writes, "There are no terminal points (me-you) in a sounding of language from the inside, in which the dwelling is already/always given" ("Introduction," 75).

Further, because language is shaped by cultural forces, the self is totally immersed in language and is unable to get above, to acquire an "objective" view. As a consequence one does not worry about the disintegration of the lyric voice. Any "self" that one may find in L=A=N=G=U=A=G=E poetry is not the self of lyric poetry; one does not find that aggressive projection of an identifiable "person." One quotes the voice of social constructs. Thus, to discuss the voice of a L=A=N=G=U=A=G=E poem is beside the mark: there are no persons in the poem; there is just *writing*.[7] The L=A=N=-G=U=A=G=E quoting poem is not Ashbery's poem of individual mental process. Barrett Watten notes that in such a "polylogic" construct "the differentiation of meanings produced calls into question the person at the center"; in such writing "the mediating persona has been abandoned" ("Method," 600–602). The abandonment of a mediating persona is not just a move to a dramatic voice; Watten points out the difference between the Surrealist André Breton and L=A=N=-G=U=A=G=E writer Carla Herryman: Breton's writing, although composed of disparate images, has a single persona behind it. In Harryman's writing there is "much more distance to the 'you'" ("Method," 609–10).

Coupled with the emphasis upon modes rather than upon specific instances of language, such a dissolution of personality does not require acknowledging the quotation. L=A=N=G=U=A=G=E writers move beyond quoting: all uses of language are personality-less, all uses are quotation (what a deconstructionist might call citation). These writers sometimes directly quote, sometimes use genre quotations. Nonquotations have the same "different texture" function as do quotations. Ron Silliman's "Blue" begins with a quotation of Valéry that can be tied conceptually to the sentences following it:

The Marchioness went out at five o'clock. The sky was blue yet tinged with pink over the white spires which broke up the east horizon. The smell of the afternoon's brief shower was still evident and small pools of clear water collected in the tilt of the gutters, leaves and tiny curling scraps of paper drifting in the miniature tides which nonetheless caught and reflected the swollen sun, giving the boulevard its jeweled expression. (84)

But readers don't need to know this is Valéry. As Bernstein points out, Valéry is satirizing the conventions of the novel ("Introduction," 77), and so he appropriates its sound in parodying it, as does Silliman appropriate it here, smoothing it into the first paragraph, which is a quotation of a mode of language: the calm evocation of mood and setting in the nineteenth-century novel, which depends upon the assumption that completeness is possible, that one can reconstruct a context.

Later in this work, the contrasting textures of language point to several very different modes of language:

> Mother simply likes to have books. Like a serenade, only earlier. He lets the clay on his hands begin to dry. Fuchsia blossoms stain the walk, the doorknob strangled by rubber bands. Another thing, pepper is not a corn. (85)

This puzzling use of language is not surreal, for it is not dominated by a single personality. This writing is *writing:* modes of language in conflict. The modes here move from quoting personal, domestic communication ("Mother simply"); to a musical metaphor that is closed off by a non sequitur, temporal closing ("Like a serenade, only earlier"); to another discussion of an art, but this time with a narrative element ("He lets"); to domestic advice ("Fuschia blossoms") oddly connected with other household affairs of uncertain status ("doorknobs strangled"); to a more authoritarian advice, a setting the record straight that is peremptorily connected to an unstated, earlier context ("Another thing"). These moves are made more abrupt through the juxtaposition of two modes in language in one sentence, through insisting on a logical connection where there is none.

How do we appropriate these modes of language? "Blue" gives a wry answer, ending the work with a return to the "narrative" and the subject (a person) of the beginning, supposedly giving closure:

> At the arched door of the restaurant she checks her watch, a delicate gold bracelet dangling from her wrist. Bands of a deep orange streak a near purple sky, the brisk air shuddering in the small trees, slender branches bending back. Children begin to gather up their toys; lights on, their homes begin to glow. The host, recognizing the Marchioness, invites her in. (85)

This seems to end a story. At the beginning the Marchioness leaves, and here she has arrived. But there is no closure; the text has wandered far afield both texturally and conceptually. The neatness of the ending is a wry comment that the quest for unity is futile. The tie to the Marchioness is arbitrary, even in this seemingly single-textured conclusion. As with the two modes of language juxtaposed in one sentence, here too the poem insists on readers making connections while the text subverts these attempts.

In texts like "ludicrous stick" and "Blue" $L=A=N=-G=U=A=G=E$ writers emphasize, as did Pound seventy years earlier in a letter to Williams, how "utter originality is of course out of the question" (6). Following up the implications of this phrase much more strictly than Pound ever could have imagined, these writers argue that all language is a borrowed collection of different voices. The difference between quotation and other uses of language is one of degree and cultural conditioning. In quotation, the fact that the "dwelling" has already been given is just more obvious than it is in other, more "normal" uses of language. Because of this simple change in presuppositions, readers are left with writing radically different from Modernist writing.

The writing is not only radically different, much of Modernist and $L=A=N=G=U=A=G=E$ quoting are based on mutually exclusive principles. Who is right about quotation? It depends on how you keep score. If $L=A=N=G=U=A=G=E$ writing calls the shots, it wins the political argument, being much more aware of the ideological basis of forms of language. On the other hand, if Modernist quoters call the shots, Modernism provides a more widely expressive aesthetic, for the ability to distinguish among various degrees and forms of appropriation gives these poets a technical range and sensitivity that is not accessible to $L=A=N=G=U=A=G=E$ writers. Between these two groups of writers looms an essential distinction: Modernist quoters believe that quotations come from people; $L=A=N=-G=U=A=G=E$ writers do not. For Modernist writing this distinction has two corollaries. First, because they see texts as the property and expression of persons, Modern quoting poems are able to distinguish quotations from allusion. Some modes of language are less quotation than others, and you can exploit this difference. (Even Bernstein begins to acknowledge this in his analysis of "Blue," where he draws attention to Silliman's quoting *both* Valéry and the conventions of the nineteenth-century novel.) Second, this belief in persons, coupled with a distinction between quotation and allusion, implies that some parts of the quoting poem are original with the poet. When Eliot writes "April is the cruellest month," his writing has a sonorous objectivity that readers have heard before in poetry. However, the Modernist quoting poem underscores that that peculiar combination of words in that peculiar place is original. By claiming that all uses of language are in some way quotation, $L=A=N=G=U=A=G=E$ writing both affirms and denies an essential discovery of Modernism: the exactly quoted texture of a text has amazing aesthetic possibilities that are not open to allusions.

But $L=A=N=G=U=A=G=E$ writing and Modernism are not in total conflict; $L=A=N=G=U=A=G=E$ writing is in some senses an inheritor of the Modernist quoting poem. The changes that Modernism—and especially Williams and Pound—have made to make $L=A=N=G=U=A=G=E$ writing and Rich's and Ashbery's poetry a viable option include an exploitation of the struggle with quotations because of their inevitable doubleness (not first of all an attempt to *resolve* that struggle). The changes thus include a sense of the richness of quoting's ability simultaneously to reach after contradictory effects, to destroy the unifying urge in poetry. Stealing does not just lead to invention; the stealing that goes on in the quoting poem is also an invitation to anarchy.

# Notes

## Chapter 1

1. Unless noted otherwise, all quotations of poetry in this study come from these four books:

Cummings, E. E. *Complete Poems 1904–1962*. Ed. George J. Firmage. New York: Liveright, 1991.

Eliot, Thomas Stearns. *The Complete Poems and Plays of T. S. Eliot*. London: Faber and Faber, 1969.

Moore, Marianne. *Selected Poems*. London: Faber and Faber, 1935.

Pound, Ezra. *The Cantos of Ezra Pound*. New York: New Directions, 1970.

2. My definition of *reader* is admittedly general and fluid, but it prevents cumbersome argument each time I use the term. It is primarily a heuristic device that allows me an empirical basis for examining how quoting influences comprehension and reading practices. By reader I will usually mean "competent Western reader," with the cultural knowledge and reading skills one could commonly attribute to such a construction. My reader is not a "superreader," one who theoretically could know everything to be known about a text, for sometimes poets (especially Marianne Moore) depend upon readers' ignorance of sources. In this study the use of a *reader* is context based, determined by the sorts of claims the text at hand makes. Since I present texture as dominating the distinction between quotation and allusion, my reader usually has a formalist interest. I will point out when my definition of *reader* moves away from these formal activities.

3. As mentioned in the body of this text, critical writing about quotation has pointed in a limiting direction. The deconstructionist critique of context should make us aware of the limited usefulness of source studies, for source studies are never done; they lead to an infinite regress. My analysis of the texturally based interaction between source and new text avoids that methodological problem.

Many more works than I could possible cite here raise tantalizing speculations on the functions of quotation in poetry, but these speculations do not develop into arguments. The preface to Marjorie Perloff's *The Futurist Moment* begins to discuss the texture of a borrowing and to make comments similar to those I raise in chapter 2, but the book's focus on Futurism does not allow for a detailed look at the formal implications of quotation for poetry, especially American poetry. Most typical of work dealing with quotation is Gertrude Patterson's *T. S. Eliot: Poems in the Making,* a book that does not distinguish Eliot's use of images from his use of quotations. Hugh Kenner in *A Homemade World* gives a brief yet insightful analysis of the use of quotations in Moore's poetry but does not discuss the possibility of quotations as a more general poetic practice (102). Philip Furia's *Pound's Cantos Declassified* discusses the use of documents in *The Cantos,* but does not give primary attention to the aesthetic properties of these documents.

The finest work on quotation in an individual poet's work occurs in several books on Marianne Moore. In *Marianne Moore: Imaginary Possessions* Bonnie Costello goes further than most critics in acknowledging that quotations are the most distinguishing feature of Moore's work, but she spends only one paragraph in discussing their features as a recurring technique (163). John Slatin is more thorough in discussing quotation as a recurring feature of Moore's poetry. Among other points he makes, Slatin argues well for the sense in which quotations interrupt and yet are a part of the main text of Moore's poems. For Moore's manipulation of her quotations, see Taffy Martin's *Marianne Moore: Subversive Modernist,* particularly pages 92–112.

Because most critics see quoting as an idiosyncratic technique decided on individually for an individual poem, quotation as a genre has been discussed systematically by only four contemporary literary critics: Herman Meyer in *The Poetics of Quotation in the European Novel,* Laurent Jenny in "The Strategy of Form," Michael Wheeler in *The Art of Allusion in Victorian Fiction,* and Elizabeth Gregory in "Quotation and Modern American Poetry." As it includes allusions and excludes poetry, Meyer's definition of quotation does not fit the purposes of this study. Jenny's article is more complete, but directs itself at fiction and does not adequately consider how technique may structure the effects of quoting. Wheeler's work also deals solely with fiction. Further, because Wheeler's text defines quotation as an "identifiable word, phrase or passage taken from an adopted text" and defines allusion as "the generic term for quotations and references," quotation becomes a very general term denoting "shared stylistic similarities," a term that includes both what I call quotation and allusion (2, 3). Elizabeth Gregory's extremely useful dissertation, by examining different questions, leads to quite different conclusions. Because Gregory has chapters on individual poets (Williams, Moore, and Eliot) she cannot be systematic, especially about formal matters. Gregory also sets up her argument as initially one about originality and often does not allow for a rigorous working out of the difference between quotation and allusions. The most complete bibliography of quotation has been prepared by Udo Hebel: *Intertextuality, Allusion, and Quotation.*

4. My use of *world* is indebted to Paul Ricoeur, who in *Interpretation Theory* describes the world of a text as the "ensemble of references" that texts open up (36). In another context, Ricoeur argues that the "world" is not what the text says, but the thing about which the text speaks (*Essays on Biblical Interpretation,* 100). World has implications beyond this sense of subject matter. The world of a text is not just its implied theme; textural aspects also support values—Shakespeare's dislike of euphuism was not just stylistic. I am avoiding using Bakhtin's similar idea of the "language" of a text since the term language does not easily refer to things other than texts, and since, in the context of quotations, the usual denotative specificity of "language" may be confusing.

5. Since this arrangement of textual practices occurs along a continuum, it is important to keep in mind the Modernist predisposition to reach for effects possible with the pure quotation rather than the allusion end of the spectrum. Genre quotations occupy a tentative middle ground between allusions and pure quotations. With a genre quotation the reader is aware that the writer is referring to a particular type of work, but the reader cannot ascertain either whether the verbal patterns *exactly* replicate a particular text or whether the particular text even exists. This type of quoting depends on a limited amount of ignorance in the reader and works primarily for certain recognizable genres of texts, for instance, Pound's quoting legal documents or Moore's quoting feature articles. The characteristic voice of the genre being quoted is important.

6. By the same token, a lack of visual signifiers can hide quotations. If there are no visual clues and the reader's cultural repertoire is not sufficient to read a quotation knowingly, the poetic effect is the same as if the poet had not quoted. The practical consequences of this visual pragmatism are such that in Pound's poetry, the different languages function as quotations even though in many cases they are not actually quotations, while unacknowledged quotations often are read as part of the "straight" text, or as part of Pound's parodying voice. *The Cantos* and many of Moore's quoting poems use all of these methods to hide and reveal false and real quotations, playing with and manipulating the less-than-ideal readers that we all are.

A question surfaces from this discussion: Is it the primary function of criticism so to increase our cultural repertoire that the visual cues are never needed? For example, how useful is it in Moore's poem "An Octopus" to identify the place of the quotations in the National Parks brochure from which they are taken? For poems like *The Waste Land* and *The Cantos,* it may be useful to increase readers' cultural repertoire so that the visual recognition of the quotation becomes secondary, as does recognition of the quotation's textural properties. But such criticism can create hermetic artifacts accessible only to members of a highly educated club and creates a reading that differs in kind (not in degree) from earlier, visually oriented and less "sophisticated" readings of the poem. Discovering that a passage of *The Cantos* is "actually" a quotation does not answer the more important question, the question of how the poetry works. Critical attention is usefully redirected from the intertext to questions of intertextuality. Specifically, readings of *The Cantos* and other quoting poems must take into account the use of visual cues and how author's notes initially direct reading.

7. I am indebted for this idea to Rosalind Krauss, who argues that a visual work of art shifts from representation to formalism when it borrows from other works (92).

8. In the last chapter I will discuss how the emphasis on writing can in some poetry lead to the dissolution of a speaking voice. For now, however, I will assume the framework within which most quoting poetry works: the duplication of another text's writing also calls up a voice of that quoted text.

## Chapter 2

1. The idea of these two worlds in tension says much about the structure of both quoting poetry and Modernist poetry in general. First, it reinforces what became a critical truism—the artwork attempts to become autonomous, relating just to itself, independent of the physical world outside of itself. The cliché has some life in it yet. To some degree these worlds of the quotation are self-contained units. They refer to external reality, but competing against this mimesis is the energy the quoting work emits as it struggles to control the quotation. The dynamism of this internal struggle, based upon self-referential rules, at times obscures and so seems prior to references to the external world. The emphasis on autonomy discussed here also prepares the way for an aesthetic of quoting. As Harriet Janis and Rudi Blesh point out in their study of collage, one can use objects from the real world in an artwork only when the artwork has achieved an autonomous existence from the real world—when it is an object itself (13).

2. There are many differences and developments in Pound's writing that I do not address here. In *The Genesis of Ezra Pound's Cantos* Ronald Bush demonstrates how Pound's theory about *The Cantos* changes over time, how the concept of the ideogram addresses only certain aspects of the poem's development (3–20). This book does not quarrel with that assessment, but it concentrates on a unifying aspect in Pound's critical writing. In all Pound's writing there is some emphasis on non-linear movement, on relation.

3. In his dissertation on the philosopher F. H. Bradley, Eliot gives some reasons for the dominance of relations over the objects they relate. Eliot argues that one cannot directly know either objects or one's own personality, but only some relation between them. In fact, consciousness comes only through relation: "Consciousness, we shall find, is reducible to relations between objects, and objects we shall find to be reducible to relations between different states of consciousness; and neither point of view is more nearly ultimate than the other" (*Knowledge,* 30).

As a result of this emphasis on relation, Eliot does not distinguish between the types of activity undertaken by a poet and a good reader of that poetry, and his criticism can be viewed as a primer on how to read poetry. The critical reader notices and duplicates the poet's creative process:

> If you compare several representative passages of the greatest poetry you see how great is the variety of types of combination, and also how completely any semi-ethical criterion of "sublimity" misses the mark. For it is not the "greatness," the intensity, of the emotions, the components, but the intensity of the artistic process, the pressure, so to speak, under which the fusion takes place, that counts. ("Tradition," 41)

The activities of reading and creating are similar, as they are for all quoters. In a typical use of sources, in her review of *The Sacred Wood,* Moore approvingly quotes Eliot: "it is to be expected that the critic and the creative artist should frequently be the same person" (52–53).

4. The Cubist struggle with representation limits the scope of this analogy. But as Clement Greenberg points out, on a more structural level the energy derived from relations still asserts itself. The various elements of the collage "change places in depth with one another, and a process is set up in which every part of the picture takes its turn at occupying every plane, whether real or imagined, in it.... The flatness of the surface permeates the illusion, and the illusion itself re-asserts the flatness. The effect is to fuse the illusion with the picture plane without the derogation of either—in principle" (48).

5. At one point Frank agrees that reading is inevitably temporal, but he argues that this temporality has not stopped writers from using specific techniques in attempting to achieve the impossible, to achieve a spatial form (60n). Such a formulation still overstates the case and does not take into account much of the Modernist theory that I have cited. A more accurate description of instantaneity in Modern writing is given by G. Giovannini, who has argued that the "whole work of art" one eventually experiences has been arrived at through a temporal sequence. Poems like *The Waste Land* do not so much imitate the three-dimensional arts as they compress regular techniques and juxtapose elements without using transitions (191). Since it is *reading,* reading Modernist poetry necessarily is a temporal activity.

More general discussion of the relation between space and time in art has been very complex. Expanding upon Frank's theory, W. J. T. Mitchell argues that spatiality does not imply stasis (274). Mitchell's theory, while apparently expanding on Frank's discussions, actually undercuts the intent of much traditional "spatial form" criticism. Roman Jakobson argues that the difference between literature and visual art is that the synthesis of a visual work of art occurs while the work as a whole is still accessible to the senses; in literature the work has vanished (344). Rudolf Arnheim shows how sequential perception is also integral to the visual arts (8–9).

Chapter 3

1. Emerson's position has complexities and modifications that I will not go into in detail here, choosing to use the epigrammatic logic in his writing that more clearly set the terms for an American discussion than do his qualifications of these epigrams. His qualifications to the outright dismissal of quotation might be best signaled by his essay "Self-Reliance," which begins with three epigraphs and contains several authoritative quotations within it. In his late essay "Quotation and Originality," Emerson further argues that "all minds quote. Old and new make the warp and woof of every moment. There is no thread that is not a twist of these two strands" (158). Emerson does reconcile his demand that people tell him what they know to this later demand. Basically, Emerson wants American writers to say the old authentically, true to their new situation:

> We cannot overstate our debt to the Past, but the moment has the supreme claim. The Past is for us; but the sole terms on which it can become ours are its subordination to the Present. Only an inventor knows how to borrow, and every man is or should be an inventor. ("Quotations" 180—81)

Although the terms have modulated, in Postmodern criticism this initial discussion about originality, translated through Modernism, has become central. The quoting poem continues to be its most problematic site. For example, the question of iterability is a question about originality.

2. Unless stated otherwise, all quotations from Williams's letters are taken from *The Selected Letters of William Carlos Williams,* ed. John C. Thirlwall (New York: McDowell, Obolensky, 1957). For the letter to Boyle, rather than using the date of 1932 given by John Thirlwall in the *Selected Letters,* I am working with the corrected date given by Paul Mariani in his biography of Williams (806).

3. Despite these formalist premises that dominated early Modernism, Williams was right in seeing that quotations have political connotations. Williams smelled mustiness in Eliot's poetry because he thought the quoted past necessarily attempted to impose authority. However, the quoting poem's political connotations come from a much more active poetic relationship, and so are *able* to take on a wider range of activity than Williams claimed.

The quoting poet blows the dust off aesthetically unused artifacts and in so doing has what, in the case of Pound, Christine Froula calls a "commitment to lived history" (4). But blowing the dust off artifacts means that this "commitment to lived history" is seen not so much at the center of the quotation (its original values) as in how the quotation in relation to the rest of the poem creates new thought. Schwartz argues that any text that presents through its form "alternative and perhaps more productive forms of thinking, feeling, and acting" (112) commits itself to interacting with the world. By appropriating and transforming a public voice (once quoted, any voice is a public voice), the quoting poet is inevitably a socially concerned poet.

4. In a letter to Margaret Anderson in 1917, Pound argues that "the strength of Picasso is largely in his having chewed through and chewed up a great mass of classicism; which, for example, the lesser cubists, and the flabby cubists have not" (113). *Real* artists chew on the classics. Poets should aggressively handle the past and put it to everyday use.

5. An emphasis on the universal and deemphasis on the local begins also to affect one's attitude to the quotations one uses, for it can lead to denigrating the local—or at least, not putting primary value on it.

6. This re-presenting in a new context, governed by the rules of a new aesthetic, does much to explain why some Modernist poets were interested in quoting. In "Tradition and the Individual Talent" Eliot notes both how the artist is evaluated by comparison with dead poets and how the artist redefines the dead (38). Quotations cause the reader to work out on a small scale (and with some of the same implications for canon formation) the issues of "Tradition and the Individual Talent."

7. It's hard to imagine a more fortuitous confluence than that of photography and quoting establishing themselves as fine arts in this century. Early critics of photography charged that the camera was an exact recorder of life and thus extinguished the creative personality of the artist. The charge was defended in the same way that the use of quotations can be: photography is art because the artist selects what she chooses to represent, she frames it, she uses juxtaposition, she calls attention to objects that were not earlier considered to be worthy of artistic representation, and she highlights the purely formal aspects of the represented object instead of what the object represents. As it is in the quoting poem, mimesis is a foundational yet small part of photography as art. The exact imitation is always put in a new context, and thus achieves some new function.

8. These characteristics also shape the form self-expression takes in her poetry. Moore at times changed the syntax or wording of quotations to fit what she wanted the poem to do—a move that pushes these quotations to allusion. However, without a look at the sources upon which these quotations are based, for most readers such knowledge of Moore's originality remains out of reach, and Moore's quotation marks force allusions to function as quotations.

9. In *The Matrix of Modernism* Sanford Schwartz argues that Modernism is suffused with metaphoric techniques, given that *metaphor* implies some comparison. Schwartz demonstrates how the comparison aspect of metaphor extends beyond metaphor to include all of Modernist technique, such as "the abrupt juxtaposition of seemingly unrelated particulars; ambiguity, which establishes surprising relations between the various meanings of a single expression; paradox, which unifies apparent opposites; and irony, which reveals underlying differences between things superficially similar" (74).

10. The quotation's exactness also separates it from its *original* setting, delineating the portion of the quoted text from the entire text of which it originally formed

a part. The resulting difference from allusions is that allusions can easily bring in the thematic issues of their entire source text because the disjunction of allusions are not so precise in their reference to the text from which the poet removes them. A three-word allusion may sum up an entire scene from *Hamlet*. But the aggressively duplicated texture of the quotation limits the quotation's reference primarily to the lines quoted. The reproduced texture of the quotation ensures that a reader's attention is most drawn to the idiosyncracies of that quotation, not to nonpresent elements of the source text. The world of the rest of the quoted text is brought in only in relation to the more specific world of the quotation. Reference to the rest of the quoted text is much less exact, much more allusive.

11. For example, think of *Finnegans Wake,* which shows a much more heavy concentration on the sensuous aspects of words than on their meanings. To a friend who couldn't understand *The Waste Land,* "Joyce retorted with the question that Eliot might himself have asked, 'Do you have to understand it?' He objected to the notes to the poem for the same reason" (Richard Ellmann, 495).

12. These contradictions ensure that the crude artwork discomposes and challenges presuppositions. Wolfgang Iser argues that one must find a way to incorporate the inherent difficulties of modern literary works into the reading experience, for the difficulties, by hindering comprehension, show readers the inadequacy of the usual ways in which they structure their thinking (18).

## Chapter 4

1. Part of the answer to how at times readers hear a single, lyric voice in *The Cantos* may come from Richard Chase's analysis of multiple points of view in narrative. While discussing Faulkner's work, Chase argues that if a multiple point of view has enough voices, it takes on the voice of an omniscient point of view (207). In its approximating the lyric voice the quoting poem also takes on the narrative's omniscient point of view and its implications for voice.

2. For many readers, in the case of Pound "force" may be too appropriate a word. In her review of *The Cantos* Moore approvingly quotes William Carlos Williams when she asks if every moment of *The Cantos* is masterful: "The 'words affect modernity,' says William Carlos Williams, 'with too much violence (at times)—a straining after slang effects. . . . You cannot *easily* switch from Orteum to Peoria without violence (to the language). These images too greatly infest the Cantos'" ("Cantos," 272). The ellipses indicate Moore's reading of this reading of the quotations is as idiosyncratic and as fraught with personal allegiances as is her quoting in her poetry. Williams's essay originally reads:

1) His words affect modernity with too much violence (at times)—a straining after slang effects, engendered by their effort to escape that which is their instinctive quality, a taking character from classic similes and modes. You cannot *easily* switch from Orteum to Peoria without violence (to the language). These images

too greatly infest the *Cantos,* the words *cannot* escape being colored by them: 2) so too the form of the phrase—it affects a modern turn but is really bent to a classical beauty of image, so that in effect it often (though not always) mars the normal accent of speech. ("Excerpts," 107)

In her trimming this quotation Moore chooses to emphasize the unseemly quality of heterogeneous quoting; Williams's original, arguing about how words take "character from classic similes and modes," emphasizes the political consequences: "words *cannot* escape being colored" by their original sources, a point made more clear in his second objection.

3. When Pound rewrites what are known as the ur-cantos, first published in *Poetry* in 1917, he more often exploits a dramatic voice, in which quotations are not clearly spoken by a single, controlling voice.

4. Among the critics who have helped sensitize readers beyond the clichés of the nonpersonal voice are J. Hillis Miller (*Poets of Reality*) and Theo Hermans (*The Structure of Modernist Poetry*). In *The Poetics of Impersonality* Maud Ellmann argues that the desire for impersonality has a simultaneous pull in the opposing direction, and that *impersonality* can imply any or all of the following concepts: reticence, extinction of the self, and universal vision. Ellmann also indicates how quotations might be bound up in the problem of impersonality.

5. The emotion-equation is achieved not through a poet's direct expression, but through what happens in interaction with the object. The resulting objectification makes it proper that the emphasis in discussing personality in the Modernist poem should be on the *process* of creating emotions, a process duplicated by readers of the poetry. J. Hillis Miller argues that for Eliot poetry is the expression of emotion; by using emotive images the poet causes the reader to experience exactly the same emotion that caused the poet to create the image. These images, by their expression in rhythm and words, can articulate emotions buried in the psyche of the poet (150–54).

6. Several critics have pointed out how quotations often mark the poet's "reticence" (Costello, 185). Eliot uses his found images "as a way to avoid rhetoric" (Bush, *Eliot,* 118), while Pound "retreats behind the network of meanings engendered by the disjointed textual surface of the poem" (Hermans, 116). And Moore's quotations show "the separateness of the empirical object from the poet's imaginary structures" (Costello, 96).

7. If an author decides to use those methods and quotations that lead to a private system (for example, Moore's use of her family's pet names and letters, or Williams's use of private letters in *Paterson*), there still is a difference between these quotations and an author's use of esoteric but nontextual personal references. The difference comes about because we still recognize a second voice. The obscurity of personal reference is a different type of obscurity.

## Conclusion

1. This rejection of the "mind to mind" concept may explain why of the writers in this group, Williams most thoroughly and practically believed in the notion of an artistic *community*. That may be why his work, much more thoroughly than that of T. S. Eliot (who "modernized himself *on his own*") emphasizes the present and the local.

2. Paul Mariani argues that Williams found this form in the work of Byron Vazakas: "the wedding of a long prose line to a sharply defined jagged-edged stanza, each independent, yet each complementing the other. That nuclear fracturing of line and meaning would have enormous consequences for *Paterson*" (492).

3. As Weaver points out, in the late twenties Williams's analogies for literature came from physics, not from linguistics (65). Although as early as 1913 he was writing about the aural, Williams's interest in poetry seems to shift in the twenties and thirties from the visual to the aural and to meter. When he moves to a longer line Williams seems to be more interested in the sound of language; further, only at this point is the quotation of *Paterson* possible.

4. This communal project of *Paterson* is also not without assertions of dominance; Williams's voice in the poem is not the voice of a self-effacing member of a literary commune, gently supporting the ideals of the whole. As Weaver points out (201), Williams begins the poem by quoting himself ("Rigor of beauty is the quest"). Williams does not quote poetry (except his own); with a few exceptions in *Paterson* books 2 through 5, he quotes exclusively from prose, selections that in addition have no literary history. By allowing his to be the only poetic voice, Williams does not give up his individual prerogatives as creator. Further, Williams uses lengthy quotations more exclusively than does Pound because he wants his own (nonquoted) voice to be more clear in the poetry outside of the quotations. His voice can at times sharply correct the quoted voices. An American tradition, creating effects as varied as the quoted voices composing it, is prodded into our consciousness through the steering, nonquoted voice in *Paterson*. As it is in Pound, the American voice is a quarrelsome one.

5. If there is a clear relation from Pound to Williams to contemporary quoting poetry, and if quoting poetry is central to Modernism and Postmodernism, *Modernism* takes on a definition to which some may object. For one, Wallace Stevens has no longer as commanding a presence. Harold Bloom and others observe the strong romanticism in Stevens, a romanticism that insists on a lyric "I." The lyric conventions that Stevens uses, especially the strong central voice that disallows dissent from outside of itself, does not admit quotations. The genius of Williams is that he negotiates a space between Pound and Stevens: the voice outside of the quotations is quite clear, and the quotations assert themselves in a strong way.

6. In the world of Rich's poetry, Ashbery's discursive, ironic distance is a politically banal act. Ashbery's attention to the free play of the mind is a political

act only if one can push to the margins the problem of the individual's immediate relation to society. Rich, of course, uses quotations precisely to highlight that problem.

7. This tendency to see writing as a functioning of codes is partially anticipated by the dramatic tendencies of Modernist quoting. The impersonal nature of much dramatic poetry allows writing to function as code. The multiple voices Pound uses in *The Cantos* do not mean that the quoting poem has multiple characters engaging in action. As Eliot writes, "Character is created and made real only in an action, a communication between imaginary people" ("Three Voices," 104). The conflict between the quoting and quoted voices is not a conflict of action, and rarely a conflict of psychology. Other than for isolated moments in *The Cantos,* the quoted voices in the poem are disembodied; there is rarely a character who speaks the quotation.

# Works Cited

Apollinaire, Guillaume. *The Cubist Painters: Aesthetic Meditations 1913*. Trans. Lionel Abel. 1913. Reprint. Documents of Modern Art, no. 1. New York: Wittenborn, 1949.

Arnheim, Rudolf. "The Unity of the Arts: Time, Space, and Distance." *Yearbook of Comparative and General Literature* 25 (1976): 7–13.

Ashbery, John. *Self-Portrait in a Convex Mirror*. New York: Viking, 1975.

Bakhtin, Mikhail M. "Discourse in the Novel." In *The Dialogic Imagination,* trans. Caryl Emerson and Michael Holquist; ed. Michael Holquist, 259–422. Austin: University of Texas Press, 1981.

———. "From the Prehistory of Novelistic Discourse." In *The Dialogic Imagination,* trans. Caryl Emerson and Michael Holquist; ed. Michael Holquist, 41–83. Austin: University of Texas Press, 1981.

———. "The Problem of Speech Genres." In *Speech Genres and Other Late Essays,* trans. Vern W. McGee; ed. Caryl Emerson and Michael Holquist, 60–102. Austin: University of Texas Press, 1986.

Barr, Alfred H. *Picasso: Fifty Years of His Art*. New York: Simon and Schuster, 1946.

Bedient, Calvin. *He Do the Police in Different Voices:* The Waste Land *and Its Protagonist*. Chicago: University of Chicago Press, 1986.

Benson, Steve. "From THE BUSSES." In *In the American Tree,* ed. Ron Silliman, 192. Orono, Maine: University of Maine Press, 1986.

Bergson, Henri. *An Introduction to Metaphysics*. Trans. T. E. Hulme. London: Macmillan, 1913.

Bernstein, Charles. "Introduction." *Paris Review* 86 (Winter 1982): 75–78.

———. "The Objects of Meaning." In *The L = A = N = G = U = A = G = E Book,* ed. Bruce Andrews and Charles Bernstein, 60–62. Carbondale: Southern Illinois University Press, 1984.

———. "Writing and Method." In *In the American Tree,* ed. Ron Silliman, 583–98. Orono, Maine: University of Maine Press, 1986.

Bloom, Harold. *The Anxiety of Influence: a Theory of Poetry.* New York: Oxford University Press, 1973.

Bodenheim, Maxwell. "Isolation of Carved Metal." *The Dial,* January 1922, 87–91.

Borroff, Marie. *Language and the Poet: Verbal Artistry in Frost, Stevens, and Moore.* Chicago: University of Chicago Press, 1979.

Bush, Ronald. *The Genesis of Ezra Pound's Cantos.* Princeton, N.J.: Princeton University Press, 1976.

———. *T. S. Eliot: A Study in Character and Style.* Oxford: Oxford University Press, 1983.

Cameron, Sharon. *Lyric Time: Dickinson and the Limits of Genre.* Baltimore: Johns Hopkins University Press, 1979.

Carver, Raymond. *Where Water Comes Together with Other Water.* New York: Random House, 1985.

Chase, Richard. *The American Novel and Its Tradition.* New York: Doubleday Anchor, 1957.

Christensen, Paul. "William Carlos Williams in the Forties: Prelude to Postmodernism." In *Ezra Pound and William Carlos Williams: The University of Pennsylvania Conference Papers,* ed. Daniel Hoffman, 143–63. Philadelphia: University of Pennsylvania Press, 1983.

Costello, Bonnie. *Marianne Moore: Imaginary Possessions.* Cambridge: Harvard University Press, 1981.

Culler, Jonathan. *On Deconstruction: Theory and Criticism after Structuralism.* Ithaca, N.Y.: Cornell University Press, 1982.

Cummings, E. E. *Complete Poems 1904–1962.* Ed. George J. Firmage. New York: Liveright, 1991.

Daix, Pierre. *Cubists and Cubism.* New York: Rizzoli International, 1982.

———. *Picasso: The Cubist Years 1907–1916.* Trans. Dorothy S. Blair. Boston: New York Graphic Society and Little, Brown, 1979.

Darragh, Tina. "ludicrous stick." *Paris Review* 86 (Winter 1982): 93.

Dasenbrock, Reed Way. *Imitating the Italians: Wyatt, Spenser, Synge, Pound, Joyce.* Baltimore: Johns Hopkins University Press, 1991.

———. *The Literary Vorticism of Ezra Pound and Wyndham Lewis: Towards the Condition of Painting.* Baltimore: Johns Hopkins University Press, 1985.

Davie, Donald. *Ezra Pound: Poet as Sculptor.* New York: Oxford University Press, 1964.

Derrida, Jacques. "Living On." Trans. James Hulbert. In Harold Bloom, Paul de Man, Jacques Derrida, Geoffrey Hartman, J. Hillis Miller, *Deconstruction & Criticism,* 75–176. New York: Continuum, 1984.

———. "Signature Event Context." Trans. Samuel Weber and Jeffrey Mehlman. In *Limited Inc.,* ed. Gerald Graff, 1–23. Evanston, Ill.: Northwestern University Press, 1988.

Eisenstein, Sergei. *The Film Sense.* Trans. and ed. Jay Leyda. New York: Harcourt, Brace, 1947.

Eliot, Thomas Stearns. "Blake." In *The Sacred Wood: Essays on Poetry and Criticism,* 151–58. New York: Knopf, 1930.

———. "The Borderline of Prose." *The New Statesman,* 19 May 1917, 157–59.

———. *The Complete Poems and Plays of T. S. Eliot.* London: Faber and Faber, 1969.

———. "Hamlet." In *Selected Prose of T. S. Eliot,* ed. Frank Kermode, 45–49. New York: Harcourt Brace Jovanovich and Farrar, Straus and Giroux, 1975.

———. *Knowledge and Experience in the Philosophy of F. H. Bradley.* London: Faber and Faber, 1964.

———. "London Letter." *The Dial,* August 1921, 213–17.

———. "London Letter." *The Dial,* October 1921, 452–55.

———. "The Metaphysical Poets." In *Selected Prose of T. S. Eliot,* ed. Frank Kermode, 59–67. New York: Harcourt Brace Jovanovich and Farrar, Straus and Giroux, 1975.

———. "Philip Massinger." In *The Sacred Wood: Essays on Poetry and Criticism,* 123–43. New York: Knopf, 1930.

———. "Reflections on Vers Libre." In *Selected Prose of T. S. Eliot,* ed. Frank Kermode, 31–36. New York: Harcourt Brace Jovanovich and Farrar, Straus and Giroux, 1975.

———. "A Sceptical Patrician." Rev. of *The Education of Henry Adams: An Autobiography,* by Henry Adams. *The Athenaeum,* 23 May 1919, 361–62.

———. "The Three Voices of Poetry." In *On Poetry and Poets.* 2d ed., 96–112. New York: Farrar, Straus and Giroux, 1957.

———. "Tradition and the Individual Talent." In *Selected Prose of T. S. Eliot,* ed. Frank Kermode, 37–44. New York: Harcourt Brace Jovanovich and Farrar, Straus and Giroux, 1975.

———. "Ulysses, Order, and Myth." In *Selected Prose of T. S. Eliot,* ed. Frank Kermode, 175–78. New York: Harcourt Brace Jovanovich and Farrar, Straus and Giroux, 1975.

Ellmann, Maud. *The Poetics of Impersonality: T. S. Eliot and Ezra Pound.* Cambridge: Harvard University Press, 1987.

Ellmann, Richard. *James Joyce.* Rev. ed. New York: Oxford University Press, 1982.

Emerson, Ralph Waldo. *The Journals and Miscellaneous Notebooks of Ralph Waldo Emerson.* Ed. A. W. Plumstead, William H. Gilman, and Ruth H. Bennett. Vol. 11. Cambridge: Belknap-Harvard University Press, 1975.

———. "Quotation and Originality." In *Letters and Social Aims,* 157–79. Boston, 1876.

Fenollosa, Ernest. "An Essay on the Chinese Written Character." Ed. Ezra Pound. In *Instigations.* Ed. Ezra Pound. 1920. Reprint. Freeport, New York: Books for Libraries Press, 1967. 357–88.

Foucault, Michel. *The Order of Things: An Archaeology of the Human Sciences*. Trans. Michel Foucault. London: Tavistock Publications, 1970.

Foye, Edward. "Braque's (real) Art in the 'Still Life with Violin and Pitcher.'" *Artforum,* October 1977, 56–58.

Frank, Joseph. "Spatial Form in Modern Literature." In *The Widening Gyre: Crisis and Mastery in Modern Literature,* 3–62. New Brunswick, N.J.: Rutgers University Press, 1963.

Froula, Christine. *To Write Paradise: Style and Error in Pound's* Cantos. New Haven: Yale University Press, 1984.

Fry, Edward. *Cubism.* New York: McGraw-Hill, [1966].

Furia, Philip. *Pound's Canto's Declassified*. University Park: Pennsylvania State University Press, 1984.

Fussell, Edwin. *Lucifer in Harness: American Meter, Metaphor, and Diction*. Princeton, N.J.: Princeton University Press, 1973.

Gamwell, Lynn. *Cubist Criticism*. Ann Arbor: UMI Research Press, 1980.

Geiger, Don. *The Dramatic Impulse in Modern Poetics*. Baton Rouge: Louisiana State University Press, 1967.

Genette, Gerard. *Figures of Literary Discourse*. Trans. Alan Sheridan. New York: Columbia University Press, 1982.

Gilot, Françoise, and Carlton Lake. *Life with Picasso*. New York: McGraw-Hill, 1964.

Giovannini, G. "Method in the Study of Literature in its Relation to the Other Fine Arts." *The Journal of Aesthetics and Art Criticism.* 8 (1950): 185–95.

Gombrich, E. H. *Art and Illusion: A Study in the Psychology of Pictorial Representation*. Bollingen Series, no. 35. New York: Pantheon Books, 1960.

Gray, Christopher. *Cubist Aesthetic Theories*. Baltimore: Johns Hopkins University Press, 1953.

Greenberg, Clement. "Pasted-paper Revolution." *Art News,* September 1958, 46–49, 60–61.

Gregory, Elizabeth Lee. *Quotation and Modern American Poetry: Eliot, Williams and Moore.* Ph.D. Diss., Yale University, 1989.

Hale, W. G. "Pegasus Impounded." *Poetry* 14, no. 1 (April 1919): 52–55. Reprinted in *Ezra Pound: The Critical Heritage,* ed. Eric Homburger, 155–57. London: Routledge & Kegan Paul, 1972.

Hebel, Udo. *Intertextuality, Allusion, and Quotation: An International Bibliography of Critical Studies*. Bibliographies and Indexes in World Literature, no. 18. New York: Greenwood Press, 1989.

Hermans, Theo. *The Structure of Modernist Poetry*. London: Croom Helm, 1982.

Hill, Geoffrey. "Our Word Is Our Bond." In *The Lords of Limit: Essays on Literature and Ideas,* 138–59. New York: Oxford University Press, 1984.

Hueffer (Ford), Ford Madox. "Impressionism—Some Speculations." *Poetry* 2, no. 5 (August 1913): 177–87.

Iser, Wolfgang. *The Act of Reading: A Theory of Aesthetic Response.* Baltimore: Johns Hopkins University Press, 1978.

Jakobson, Roman. "On the Relation Between Visual and Auditory Signs." In *Selected Writings,* 2:338–41. The Hague: Mouton, 1971.

Janis, Harriet, and Rudi Blesh. *Collage: Personalities Concepts Techniques.* Philadelphia: Chilton, 1967.

Jenny, Laurent. "The Strategy of Form." In *French Literary Theory Today,* trans. R. Carter; ed. Tzvetan Todorov, 34–63. London: Cambridge University Press, 1982.

Kahnweiler, Daniel-Henry. *Juan Gris: His Life and Work.* Trans. Douglas Cooper. London: Lund Humphries, 1947.

Kellett, E. E. *Literary Quotation and Allusion.* 1933. Reprint. Port Washington, N.Y.: Kennikat Press, 1969.

Kenner, Hugh. *A Homemade World: The American Modernist Writers.* New York: William Morrow, 1975.

———. *The Pound Era.* Berkeley and Los Angeles: University of California Press, 1971.

Krauss, Rosalind. "Re-presenting Picasso." *Art in America,* December 1980, 90–96.

Langbaum, Robert. "New Modes of Characterization in *The Waste Land.*" In *Eliot in His Time: Essays on the Occasion of the Fiftieth Anniversary of* The Waste Land, ed. Walton A. Litz, 95–128. Princeton, N.J.: Princeton University Press, 1973.

Laughlin, James. "William Carlos Williams and the Making of *Paterson:* A Memoir." *Yale Review* 71 (Spring 1982): 185–98.

Lewis, R. W. B. *The American Adam.* Chicago: University of Chicago Press, 1955.

Litz, A. Walton. "*The Waste Land* Fifty Years After." In *Eliot in His Time: Essays on the Occasion of the Fiftieth Anniversary of* The Waste Land, ed. Litz, 3–22. Princeton, N.J.: Princeton University Press, 1973.

Lyotard, Jean-François. *The Postmodern Condition: A Report on Knowledge.* Trans. Geoff Bennington and Brian Massumi. Theory and History of Literature, vol. 10. Minneapolis: University of Minnesota Press, 1984.

Mariani, Paul. *William Carlos Williams: A New World Naked.* New York: McGraw-Hill, 1981.

Martin, Taffy. *Marianne Moore: Subversive Modernist.* Austin: University of Texas Press, 1986.

Meyer, Herman. *The Poetics of Quotation in the European Novel.* Trans. Theodore and Yetta Ziolkowski. Princeton, N.J.: Princeton University Press, 1968.

Miller, J. Hillis. *Poets of Reality: Six Twentieth-Century Writers.* Cambridge: Harvard University Press, 1966.

Miller, James E. *The American Quest for a Supreme Fiction: Whitman's Legacy in the Personal Epic.* Chicago: University of Chicago Press, 1979.

Miller, Lewis H., Jr. "Advertising in Poetry: A Reading of E. E. Cummings' 'Poem, or Beauty Hurts Mr Vinal.'" *Word & Image* 2, no. 4 (1986): 349–62.

Mitchell, W. J. T. "Spatial Form in Literature: Toward a General Theory." In *The Language of Images,* ed. W. J. T. Mitchell, 271–99. Chicago: University of Chicago Press, 1974.

Molesworth, Charles. *Marianne Moore: A Literary Life.* New York: Atheneum, 1990.

Monroe, Harriet. "Ezra Pound." *Poetry* 26, no. 2 (May 1925): 90–97. Reprinted in *Ezra Pound: The Critical Heritage,* ed. Eric Homburger, 211–14. London: Routledge & Kegan Paul, 1972.

———. "A Symposium on Marianne Moore." *Poetry* 19, no. 4 (January 1922): 208–16.

Moore, Marianne. "The Cantos." Rev. of *A Draft of XXX Cantos,* by Ezra Pound. In *The Complete Prose of Marianne Moore,* ed. Patricia C. Willis, 268–77. New York: Viking, 1986.

———. *The Complete Poems of Marianne Moore.* New York: Macmillan and Viking, 1981.

———. Foreword to *A Marianne Moore Reader,* xiii–xviii. New York: Viking, 1961.

———. "Idiosyncrasy and Technique." The Ewing Lectures at the University of California, 3 and 5 October, 1956. In *The Complete Prose of Marianne Moore,* ed. Patricia C. Willis, 506–18. New York: Viking, 1986.

———. "Interview with Donald Hall." In *A Marianne Moore Reader,* 253–73. New York: Viking, 1961.

———. Marianne Moore Archive, Philip H. & A. S. W. Rosenbach Foundation Library, Philadelphia.

———. Rev. of *The Sacred Wood,* by T. S. Eliot. In *The Complete Prose of Marianne Moore,* ed. Patricia C. Willis, 52–55. New York: Viking, 1986.

———. *Selected Poems.* London: Faber and Faber, 1935.

———. "Sir Francis Bacon." In *The Complete Prose of Marianne Moore,* ed. Patricia C. Willis, 98–100. New York: Viking, 1986.

Nash, Ralph. "The Use of Prose in 'Paterson.'" *Perspective* 6 (Autumn-Winter 1953): 191–99. Reprinted in *The Merrill Studies in Paterson,* 20–29. Columbus, Ohio: Charles E. Merrill, 1971.

Patterson, Gertrude. *T. S. Eliot: Poems in the Making.* New York: Barnes and Noble, 1971.

Pearlman, Daniel. *The Barb of Time: On the Unity of Ezra Pound's Cantos.* New York: Oxford University Press, 1969.

Perloff, Marjorie. *The Futurist Moment: Avant-Garde, Avant Guerre, and the Language of Rupture.* Chicago: University of Chicago Press, 1986.

———. *The Poetics of Indeterminacy: Rimbaud to Cage.* Princeton, N. J.: Princeton University Press, 1981.

Pinsky, Robert. *The Situation of Poetry: Contemporary Poetry and Its Traditions.* Princeton, N. J.: Princeton University Press, 1976.

Pound, Ezra. *ABC of Reading.* 1934. Reprint. New York: New Directions, 1960.

————. "Affirmations—As for Imagisme." In *Selected Prose 1909–1965*, ed. William Cookson, 374–77. New York: New Directions, 1973.

————. *The Cantos of Ezra Pound*. New York: New Directions, 1970.

————. "Epstein, Belgin and Meaning." *The Criterion*, April 1930, 470–75.

————. "A Few Don'ts by an Imagiste." *Poetry* 1, no. 6 (March 1913): 200–206.

————. *Gaudier-Brzeska: A Memoir*. 1916. Reprint. New York: New Directions, 1960.

————. *Guide to Kulchur*. New York: New Directions, 1952.

————. "How to Read." In *Literary Essays of Ezra Pound*, ed. T. S. Eliot, 15–40. New York: New Directions, 1954.

————. *Instigations*. 1920. Reprint. Freeport, New York: Books for Libraries Press, 1967.

————. "Marianne Moore and Mina Loy." In *Selected Prose 1909–1965*, ed. William Cookson, 424–25. New York: New Directions, 1973.

————. "Paris Letter." *The Dial*, June 1922, 625–29.

————. *Personae*. New York: New Directions, 1926.

————. Rev. of *Poesies* by Jean Cocteau. *The Dial*, January 1921, 110.

————. "A Retrospect." In *Literary Essays of Ezra Pound*, ed. T. S. Eliot, 3–14. New York: New Directions, 1954.

————. *Selected Letters 1907–1941*. Ed. D. D. Paige. New York: New Directions, 1971.

————. *The Spirit of Romance*. 1910. Norfolk, Conn.: New Directions, 1952.

————. "Status Rerum." *Poetry* 1, no. 4 (January 1913): 123–27.

Ransom, John Crowe. "Waste Lands." *New York Evening Post Literary Review*, 14 July 1923, 825–26. Reprinted in *T. S. Eliot: The Critical Heritage*, ed. Michael Grant, 1:172–79. London: Routledge & Kegan Paul, 1982.

Rich, Adrienne. *The Fact of a Doorframe: Poems Selected and New 1950–1984*. New York: W. W. Norton, 1984.

Ricoeur, Paul. *Essays on Biblical Interpretation*. Ed. Lewis S. Mudge. Philadelphia: Fortress Press, 1980.

————. *Interpretation Theory: Discourse and the Surplus of Meaning*. Fort Worth: Texas Christian University Press, 1976.

Ross, James F. *Portraying Analogy*. New York: Cambridge University Press, 1981.

Sankey, Benjamin. *A Companion to William Carlos Williams's Paterson*. Berkeley and Los Angeles: University of California Press, 1971.

Schwartz, Sanford. *The Matrix of Modernism: Pound, Eliot, and Early Twentieth-Century Thought*. Princeton, N.J.: Princeton University Press, 1985.

Searle, John R. "Metaphor." In *Metaphor and Thought*, ed. Andrew Ortony, 92–123. New York: Cambridge University Press, 1979.

Seitz, William C. *The Art of Assemblage*. Garden City, N.Y.: Doubleday, 1961.

Silliman, Ron. "Blue." *Paris Review* 86 (Winter 1982): 84–85.

Slatin, John. *The Savage's Romance: The Poetry of Marianne Moore*. University Park: Pennsylvania State University Press, 1986.

Smith, Grover. *T. S. Eliot's Poetry and Plays: A Study in Sources and Meaning.* Chicago: University of Chicago Press, 1956.

Stamelman, Richard. "Critical Reflections: Poetry and Art Criticism in Ashbery's 'Self-Portrait in a Convex Mirror.'" *New Literary History* 15 (1984): 607–30.

Stein, Gertrude. *The Autobiography of Alice B. Toklas.* In *Selected Writings of Gertrude Stein,* ed. Carl Van Vechten, 1–237. New York: Random House, 1962.

———. *Picasso.* New York: Charles Scribner's Sons, 1946.

Still, Judith, and Michael Worton. Introduction to *Intertextuality: Theories and Practices,* ed. Worton and Still, 1–44. Manchester: Manchester University Press, 1990.

Terrell, Carroll F. *A Companion to the Cantos of Ezra Pound.* 2 vols. Berkeley and Los Angeles: University of California Press, 1980–1984.

Thomas, Richard F. *Literary Admirers of Alfred Stieglitz.* Carbondale: Southern Illinois University Press, 1983.

Tzara, Tristan. *Seven Dada Manifestos and Lampisteries.* Trans. Barbara Wright. London: John Calder, 1977.

Untermeyer, Louis. "Disillusion vs. Dogma." *Freeman* 17, no. 6 (January 1923): 453. Reprinted in *T. S. Eliot: The Critical Heritage,* ed. Michael Grant, 1:151–53. London: Routledge & Kegan Paul, 1982.

Vinal, Harold. *White April.* New Haven: Yale University Press, 1922.

Wagner, Linda W. "Modern American Literature: The Poetics of the Individual Voice." In *American Modern: Essays in Fiction and Poetry,* 95–114. Port Washington, N.Y.: Kennikat Press, 1980.

Watten, Barrett. "for *CHANGE.*" In *In the American Tree,* ed. Ron Silliman, 485–86. Orono, Maine: University of Maine Press, 1986.

———. "Method and $L=A=N=G=U=A=G=E$." In *In the American Tree,* ed. Ron Silliman, 599–612. Orono, Maine: University of Maine Press, 1986.

Weaver, Mike. *William Carlos Williams: The American Background.* Cambridge: Cambridge University Press, 1971.

Wheeler, Michael. *The Art of Allusion in Victorian Fiction.* London: Macmillan, 1979.

Williams, William Carlos. "A 1 Pound Stein." In *Selected Essays,* 162–66. New York: New Directions, 1969.

———. "Author's Introduction." *The Wedge.* In *The Collected Poems of William Carlos Williams,* ed. Christopher MacGowan, 2:53–55. New York: New Directions, 1988.

———. *The Autobiography of William Carlos Williams.* New York: New Directions, 1951.

———. "Excerpts from a Critical Sketch: The XXX Cantos of Ezra Pound," *Symposium* (April 1931): 257–63. Reprinted in *Selected Essays,* 105–12. New York: New Directions, 1969.

———. *In the American Grain.* Norfolk, Conn.: New Directions, 1925. Reprint. New York: New Directions, 1967.

————. *Paterson.* New York: New Directions, 1963.

————. *Kora in Hell: Improvisations.* 1920. Reprinted in *Imaginations,* ed. Webster Schott, 6–28. New York: New Directions, 1970.

————. "Letter to an Australian Editor." *Briarcliff Quarterly* 3, no. 11 (October 1946): 205–8.

————. "Notes in Diary Form." In *Selected Essays,* 62–74. New York: New Directions, 1969.

————. *The Selected Letters of William Carlos Williams.* Ed. and Intro. John C. Thirlwall. New York: McDowell, Obolensky, 1957.

————. "Sermon with a Camera." *New Republic,* 12 October 1938, 282–83.

————. "The Work of Gertrude Stein." In *A Novelette and Other Prose (1921–1931).* Reprinted in *Imaginations,* ed. Webster Schott, 346–53. New York: New Directions, 1970.

Willis, Patricia. "Observations: 'No Swan So Fine.'" *Marianne Moore Newsletter* 2, no. 1 (1978): 2–5.

Wilson, Edmund. "The Poetry of Drouth." *The Dial,* December 1922, 611–16. Reprinted in *T. S. Eliot: The Critical Heritage,* ed. Michael Grant, 1:138–44. London: Routledge & Kegan Paul, 1982.

Wolfram, Eddie. *History of Collage.* New York: Macmillan, 1975.

Wordsworth, William. *Poems, in Two Volumes, and Other Poems.* Ed. Jared Curtis. Ithaca, N.Y.: Cornell University Press, 1983.

Wright, George T. "The Faces of the Poet." In *Perspectives on Poetry,* ed. James L. Calderwood and Harold E. Toliver, 109–18. New York: Oxford University Press, 1968.

# Index